Earth Voices Whispering

'What Gerald Dawe has done so movingly in this book is to bring together without any hint of partisan judgement the poems written on all sides by Irish writers in the five – or more – wars in the thirty years of its coverage. It is an important book, full of despair but also a humanity that might mollify it.'

BERNARD O'DONOGHUE

'This anthology reveals how Irish poets from many traditions have responded to a violent, war-torn half century ... It will be essential reading.'

TERENCE BROWN

'This anthology is a revelation. It fulfils a cultural need. Why has no previous anthology shown us the range and depth of Irish war poetry? Gerald Dawe has done a magnificent job.'

EDNA LONGLEY

Earth Voices Whispering

An Anthology of Irish War Poetry
1914–1945

Edited by Gerald Dawe

for Tom Halpin
with all good wishes

Gerald Dawe
11 — 11 — 08
Collins Barracks
Dublin

BLACKSTAFF
PRESS
———
BELFAST

To the memory of
Robert Greacen

First published in 2008 by
Blackstaff Press
4c Heron Wharf, Sydenham Business Park
Belfast BT3 9LE

Supported by
The National Lottery®
through the Arts Council of Northern Ireland

Published in association with

© Selection and Introduction, Gerald Dawe, 2008
All rights reserved

The acknowledgements on pages 401–7 constitute
an extension of this copyright page

Typeset by CJWT Solutions, St Helens, Merseyside
Designed by Dunbar Design

Printed in England by Cromwell Press

A CIP catalogue record for this book is available
from the British Library

ISBN PAPERBACK 978-0-85640-821-2
ISBN HARDBACK 978-0-85640-822-9

www.blackstaffpress.com

CONTENTS

INTRODUCTION   xix

KATHARINE TYNAN (1861–1931)
Flower of Youth   1

STEPHEN GWYNN (1864–1950)
A Song of Victory   3
Inscription for a Fountain   7

W.B. YEATS (1865–1939)
An Irish Airman Foresees His Death   8
On Being Asked for a War Poem   9
Easter 1916   9
Sixteen Dead Men   11
On a Political Prisoner   12
Reprisals   13
from Meditations in Time of Civil War   14
from Three Songs to the One Burden   16
Politics   17

Æ (1867–1935)
On Behalf of Some Irishmen Not Followers of Tradition   18
Salutation   19
Continuity   21
Chivalry   22
Gods of War   23
Battle Ardour   25
Waste   25
Apocalyptic   26
Tragedy   28
Statesmen   28

EVA GORE-BOOTH (1870–1926)
Easter Week   30
Christmas Eve in Prison   30
To C.M. on Her Prison Birthday   31
Comrades   31

Francis Sheehy-Skeffington 32
Pinehurst 33

LORD DUNSANY (1878–1957)
The Memorial 34
A Dirge of Victory 34
Songs from an Evil Wood 35
To the Fallen Irish Soldiers 38

THOMAS MacDONAGH (1878–1916)
In Absence 39
After a Year 40
The Poet Captain 41
A Dream of Hell 42
Of a Poet Patriot 44
For Victory 45

WILLIAM ORPEN (1878–1931)
The Church, Zillebeke 46

PÁDRAIC H. PEARSE (1879–1916)
The Mother 47
The Fool 48
The Rebel 49
Christmas 1915 51
The Wayfarer 52

MARY DEVENPORT O'NEILL (1879–1967)
Dead in Wars and in Revolutions 53

THOMAS KETTLE (1880–1916)
To my Daughter, Betty, the Gift of God 55

BLANAID SALKELD (1880–1959)
Casualties 56

WINIFRED M. LETTS (1882–1972)
Hallow-e'en, 1914 58
The Call to Arms in our Street 59
Casualty 60

Screens   61
The Deserter   61
Dead   63

ARNOLD BAX (DERMOT O'BYRNE) (1883–1953)
Martial Law in Dublin   64
Shells at Oranmore   64
The Irish Mail   65
A Dublin Ballad – 1916   67

D.L. KELLEHER (1883–1958)
An Upper Room   69

THOMAS CARNDUFF (1886–1956)
Graves of Gallipoli   70
My Land   71
Messines, 17th June, 1917   72
Ypres, September, 1917   72
The Graves of the Unknown   73

JOSEPH MARY PLUNKETT (1887–1916)
When I am Dead   75
The Claim that has the Canker on the Rose   75
New Love   76
Before the Glory of your Love   77
To Grace   77
See the Crocus' Golden Cup   78

FRANCIS LEDWIDGE (1887–1917)
The Call to Ireland   79
In the Mediterranean – Going to the War   80
Thomas MacDonagh   80
After Court Martial   81
War   81
To Mrs Joseph Plunkett   82
A Soldier's Grave   82
The Irish in Gallipoli   83
O'Connell Street   83
Home   84

PATRICK MacGILL (1890–1963)

It's a Far, Far Cry 85
I Oft Go Out at Night-time 86
Before the Charge 87
The London Lads 87
The Dug-out 88
A Soldier's Prayer 89

THOMAS MacGREEVY (1893–1967)

Nocturne 90
De Civitate Hominum 90
The Six Who Were Hanged 92

AUSTIN CLARKE (1896–1974)

The Subjection of Women 95
Six Sentences 98
The Last Republicans 99
from Rightful Rhymes 100
from Mnemosyne Lay in Dust 101
At the House of Commons 104

MONK GIBBON (1896–1987)

Soldiering 105
Lost Hopes 106
Ici 106

C.S. LEWIS (1898–1963)

French Nocturne 109
Victory 110
Apology 111
Death in Battle 112

EILEEN SHANAHAN (1901–1979)

Free State 113
Pastorale, 1946 113

JIMMY KENNEDY (1902–1984)

We're Going to Hang Out the Washing on the
Siegfried Line 114

PATRICK MacDONOGH (1902–1961)
Over the Water   115
War Widow   116

FRANCIS STUART (1902–2000)
Morning in a Town under Bombardment   118
In Time of War   118
Ireland   119
The Trees in the Square   119
Berlin, 1944   120
Out of the Swim   120
Coogan's Wood   121

EWART MILNE (1903–1987)
Speech on Behalf of Inishfail   122
Thinking of Artolas   123
The Wind of Bombers Moon   125
Sierran Vigil   126

GEORGE BUCHANAN (1904–1989)
On Film   128
On the Dead Killed in Two World Wars   128
Kilwaughter   129
Poets of the Next Century   131
War Pilot   131

C. DAY LEWIS (1904–1972)
Bombers   132
Newsreel   133
Watching Post   134
Where are the War Poets?   135
The Dead   136
Will it be so Again?   137
In the Shelter   138
Remembering Con Markievicz   139

PATRICK KAVANAGH (1904–1967)
from The Great Hunger   141
from Lough Derg   142

Beyond the Headlines 143
Epic 144
I Had a Future 144

PÁDRAIC FALLON (1905–1974)
Heroes 1916 146
Dardanelles 1916 147

BRIAN COFFEY (1905–1995)
from Death of Hektor 148

SAMUEL BECKETT (1906–1989)
Saint-Lô 152

SHIELA WINGFIELD (1906–1992)
from Men in War 153

FREDA LAUGHTON (1907– *n.d.*)
The Bombed House 162

LOUIS MacNEICE (1907–1963)
Aubade 163
Carrickfergus 163
from The Closing Album 165
from Entered in the Minutes 166
Convoy 166
Bottleneck 167
Neutrality 168
The Atlantic Tunnel 169

RUDDICK MILLAR (1907–1952)
The Somme 170

GEORGE REAVEY (1907–1976)
The Sinking of the SS *Jutland* 171
The Rape of Europe 176
Hiroshima and After 177

JOHN HEWITT (1907–1987)
Portstewart, July 1914 178
The YCVs and the Ulster Division 179
Brown's Bay, Islandmagee, Spring 1917 179

The Volunteer   180
Nineteen Sixteen, or the Terrible Beauty   180
Encounter Nineteen Twenty   181
To the Memory of James Connolly   181
The Troubles, 1922   182
The Prisoners on the Roof   183
Camaradas y Compañeros   183
August 1939   185
Epitaph for a Conscript, 1940   185
Minor Poet's Dilemma, 1940   185
Second Front: Double Summertime, July 1943   186
Strangers and Neighbours   186
Ulster Winter (1942)   189
To the People of Dresden   190

DENIS DEVLIN (1908–1959)
Annapolis   191
The Tomb of Michael Collins   193
Little Elegy   195
Concentration Camps   197

LIAM MacGABHANN (1908–1979)
The Roads of Kerry   199
Connolly   200

W.R. RODGERS (1909–1969)
War-time   202
Escape   202
The Interned Refugee   203

BRYAN MacMAHON (1909–1998)
Corner Boys   204

SEÁN JENNETT (1910– n.d.)
from Always Adam   206
For Thomas Flanagan   215
The Letter   215
Morning   216
Explosion   217

LESLIE DAIKEN (1912–1964)
Nightfall in Galway 218

DONAGH MacDONAGH (1912–1968)
He is Dead and Gone, Lady … 220
Just an Old Sweet Song 221

CHARLES DONNELLY (1914–1937)
The Flowering Bars 222
The Tolerance of Crows 223
Poem 223
Heroic Heart 224

THOMAS O'BRIEN (1914–1974)
Connolly 226
Beauty We Have Heard Your Voice 227
Always Battling 227
Marching Feet 228
International Brigade Dead 230
Terror 231

GEORGE HETHERINGTON (1916–2001)
Sonnet 232
Las Raices 233

GEORGE M. BRADY (1917– *n.d.*)
The Hosts 234
The Conquerors 235
Have You Walked 236

VALENTIN IREMONGER (1918–1991)
Soldier from the Wars 237

L.J. FENNESSY (1919–1941)
Twenty-Four 239

MAURICE J. CRAIG (b. 1919)
Spring, 1943 241
Kilcarty to Dublin 242

EOGHAN Ó TUAIRISC (1919–1982)
as Aifreann na Marbh   244
from The Mass of the Dead   245

ROBERT GREACEN (1920–2008)
Belfast   254
Spring 1943   254
Poem Written in September   255
Poem to K.D.   256
The Glorious Twelfth   257
Lament for France   258
Sunday in County Monaghan, 1935   260
I.M. Leslie Owen Baxter 1919–1995   261

ROY McFADDEN (1921–1999)
2 September 1939   262
Post-war   262
Armistice Day 1938   264
A Song for Victory Night   264
Dublin to Belfast: Wartime   265
Portrush   266

BRUCE WILLIAMSON (1922–1991)
Homage of War   267

PADRAIC FIACC (b. 1924)
Der Bomben Poet   269
The Other Man's Wound   270
Son of a Gun   270
Soldiers   271
The British Connection   273

PATRICK GALVIN (b. 1927)
My Father Spoke with Swans   275
A Day of Rebellion   277

PEARSE HUTCHINSON (b. 1927)
The Defeated   284
Ostfriesland   285
Judengrasse   288

RICHARD MURPHY (b. 1927)
Oxford Staircase 290
Carlyon Bay Hotel 291
Wellington College 291
Suntrap 292

ANTHONY CRONIN (b. 1928)
War Poem 293
from The End of the Modern World 296
Encounter 300

THOMAS KINSELLA (b. 1928)
The Laundress 301
Downstream 302
38 Phoenix Street 306

JOHN MONTAGUE (b. 1929)
This Neutral Realm 309
A Welcoming Party 311
Waiting 312
A Bomber's Moon 313
A Fertile Balance 314
from Wreaths 317
Speech Lesson 318

JAMES SIMMONS (1933–2001)
In the Desert War 321
Uncle Jack 322
Remembrance Day 323
The Use of History 324
Death of a Poet in Battle-dress 324
A Man's a Soldier 325

BRENDAN KENNELLY (b. 1936)
Old Soldier 326
Wall 327
Bomb 329

MICHAEL LONGLEY (b. 1939)

In Memoriam   332
Wounds   334
Master of Ceremonies   335
Second Sight   335
Ghetto   336
In Memory of Charles Donnelly   339
Ceasefire   340
Buchenwald Museum   341
Partisans   341

SEAMUS HEANEY (b. 1939)

England's Difficulty   342
Trial Runs   343
In Memoriam Francis Ledwidge   343
In the Beech   345
Anahorish 1944   346
The Aerodrome   347

SEAMUS DEANE (b. 1940)

Shelter   349

DEREK MAHON (b. 1941)

from Autobiographies   351
A Kensington Notebook   352
One of these Nights   357
At the Shelbourne   359
During the War   361
Barbara   363

EILÉAN NÍ CHUILLEANÁIN (b. 1942)

from Site of Ambush   365
On Lacking the Killer Instinct   368

EAVAN BOLAND (b. 1944)

Yeats in Civil War   370
The War Horse   371
A Soldier's Son   372
We Were Neutral in the War   373

PAUL DURCAN (b. 1944)
Death Camp   375
The Jewish Bride   376
Fjord   377

ANTHONY GLAVIN (1945–2006)
from Living in Hiroshima   379

VAN MORRISON (b. 1945)
Wild Children   392

POSTSCRIPT
Samuel Beckett: The Capital of the Ruins   394

SUGGESTED READING   398
ACKNOWLEDGEMENTS   401
INDEX OF POETS   408
INDEX OF TITLES   409

INTRODUCTION

It is summer and the eerie beat
Of madness in Europe trembles the
Wings of the butterflies along the canal.

O I had a future.

Patrick Kavanagh, 'I Had a Future'

As I read through numerous anthologies of Irish poetry published in Ireland, Britain and the US since the early 1900s, it struck me how diffuse reaction was to the defining moments of our shared history. While Ireland and Northern Ireland's recent Troubles have occupied considerable political, cultural and poetic space, public and private reaction to the wars of the first half of the twentieth century have not been as widely considered, even though the cost in human and political terms was much greater.

The Irish war poetry of this period has never been anthologised. *Earth Voices Whispering* is the first collection of its kind, bringing together poems that explore, both individually and collectively, the impact of war upon Ireland, its people and its poetics, in the relatively brief thirty-year period between the First and Second World Wars, that includes the Easter Rising, War of Independence, Irish Civil War and Spanish Civil War.

While the views expressed by the poets in this anthology differ dramatically according to individual politics, creed and aesthetics, the poets all share one common bond – the need, the imperative desire, to render their experiences of war into memorable speech and, in so doing, to try to make some sense of what the individual actually lived through. Poetry is both bond and witness.

The experience of the tens of thousands of Irish men who fought in the First World War – including such poets as Thomas Kettle, Stephen Gwynn (both nationalist MPs), Lord Dunsany and Thomas Carnduff – has traditionally been culturally and critically overlooked.

Juxtaposing poems borne out of this experience with the self-sacrificing idealism of Irish nationalists, and the doomed intimacies of the poetry of Pádraic H. Pearse, Thomas MacDonagh and Joseph Mary Plunkett – poems and sentiments traditionally regarded as antithetical – is both radical and illuminating.

Such tensions are played out in the life and poems of Francis Ledwidge. A committed Irish nationalist and a fine pastoral poet, Ledwidge was killed in action during the First World War and remained for subsequent generations a symbol of Ireland's 'other' history – not the history of cultural nationalism and the struggle for Irish independence, but the history of Irish men who, for a multiplicity of reasons, fought and died on foreign fields.

Further contradictions are revealed within the liminal space of this anthology. First and foremost, the work included here conveys the terrible horror and truth of war. Yet it also records a bizarre, perverse beauty in terms of both poetic medium and subject, in the landscape, for instance, of Thomas MacGreevy's Zillebeke in 'A Matisse Ensemble', contrasting sharply with William Orpen's vision of unrelenting mud in 'The Church, Zillebeke'.

Heroism is countered with the sense of loss, grime permeated with glory, the mundane with camaraderie, and exhilaration punctured by relentless reality. The poets included in this anthology lived in full awareness of their own critical times and of their own mortality: in Winifred Letts's poems, a nurse on the front line turns away in pity as a fatally injured soldier dies and a deserter is executed; thoughts of a posthumous life occur to Charles Donnelly as he faces possible death in the olive groves of Spain and imagines how he will be thought of back home in Dublin; Patrick Kavanagh's countrymen follow in their minds' eye the map of the Second World War as it contracts and expands.

The day-to-day struggle to cope with the realities of Emergency Ireland and war-time England is the achievement represented in the poems – and lives – of non-combatants like C. Day Lewis, Roy McFadden and Robert Greacen. Other voices such as Sheila Wingfield, Brian Coffey, Thomas Kinsella and Eavan Boland offer meditations on the historical and archetypal meaning of war.

For the poets born in the 1930s and 40s, such as John Montague, Brendan Kennelly, James Simmons and Seamus Heaney, war is tangential, something overheard or witnessed from afar, etched in the lives and words of family members and neighbours, and found in the childhood landscapes of their poems. Michael Longley's poetry uncovers in his father's service during the Great War a revelation that prompts further reflection on the Holocaust, and on the recent Troubles. Derek Mahon recalls seeing, as a young boy, the triumphant return of the Allied soldiers as they paraded along the Antrim Road in north Belfast, and the Pathe News images of the liberation of the concentration camps. And the toxic nightmare of the atomic bomb in the poetic sequences of Eoghan Ó Tuairisc and Anthony Glavin starkly anatomise the global reverberations of war. History, like war, happens anywhere and everywhere, as the 'local row' turns into fully-fledged atrocities.

Some of the poets included in this anthology are soldiers who paid the ultimate price of war: Francis Ledwidge died in France in 1917; Pádraic Pearse and his fellow revolutionaries were executed for their part in the 1916 Rising. Others, such as Monk Gibbon and Patrick MacGill, suffered physical and mental breakdown.

It is also important to note that other poets such as Leslie Daiken and Ó Tuairisc joined the newly formed Irish Army, and some, like L.J. Fennessy, lost their lives in this service. Many survived their wars and returned to pre-war professions, such as Jimmy Kennedy, George Reavey and Ewart Milne, who, among others, pursued, as best they could, their lives as writers.

Within this anthology, the reader will be able to identify numerous meta-narratives, as the personal and the individual are transformed and given collective commemorative significance through the medium of poetry. The left-wing republican leader James Connolly, executed for his role in the 1916 Rising, is remembered in the poems of Yeats, Thomas O'Brien, John Hewitt and Liam MacGabhann; the pacifist Francis Sheehy-Skeffington, murdered during Easter Week 1916, is a recurrent elegiac presence; and the early death of the young intellectual Charles Donnelly at the Battle of Jarama, 1937, is lamented by several of the poets included here.

Minding the past, however, does not have to be a passive sentiment: in marked contrast to the more traditional laments of, for example, Eva Gore-Booth, W.B. Yeats famously explores what was lost to the future in poems such as 'Easter 1916'. If Yeats produced a new language for the Irish elegy, however, it is also in his poetry that the warring tensions of Irish history are most profoundly articulated at the bloodiest point in the founding of modern Ireland – the War of Independence and the subsequent Civil War.

Observing the events as they happened near his retreat in Thoor Ballylee, County Galway, Yeats depicts in 'Meditations in Time of Civil War' the psychological and social impact of war upon civilians, such as himself, who are both in awe of and shocked by what they see. 'Reprisals', meanwhile, takes us to the ugly, ragged ends of the bloody conflict in the Irish Free State, pointing prophetically to what would become shockingly common occurences, a mere forty years later, in the Northern Ireland Troubles.

There is, too, the sense of remembrance as an end in itself, as in the poetry of Richard Murphy, whereas Francis Stuart and Anthony Cronin locate the sites of conflict at the beginnings of the Second World War in Berlin and London respectively, and the Belfast Blitz of 1941 is Padraic Fiacc's inauguration into the 'twentieth-century / Night-life'.

The way in which memory itself works, the structure of our remembrances, the meaning and experience of heroism and martyrdom, and the language of militarism, are all inscribed in the poems here. And the panorama of history that infuses the poems of Pearse Hutchinson, Eiléan Ní Chuilleanáin and Paul Durcan is conveyed through individual suffering, their voices of personal testimony raised to the level of an intense dramatic monologue.

In Yeats's cautionary unease in writing a 'war' poem, in Austin Clarke's sense of an irretrievably lost idealism, in Dermot O'Byrne's discomfort with the British 'Tommy' en route to Ireland in 1916, the sheer unprogrammatical, unpredictable realities which these poems embody makes for a lasting image of war. The casualties, the hopes lost and retained, the lives lived and forfeited are caught in these poems and in the concluding text of Samuel Beckett's 'The Capital of the Ruins', which was written for Radio Éireann, but never broadcast. It is only right and fitting that the impact of war and the valour of the human spirit should have the last word.

Gerald Dawe
Dún Laoghaire
1 JULY 2008

KATHARINE TYNAN
1861–1931

Tynan was born into a large farming family in Clondalkin,
County Dublin. A prolific poet and prose writer, she is best
remembered for her friendship with W.B. Yeats and Francis
Ledwidge and her involvement in the Celtic Revival. She did
philanthropic work during the First World War and her two
sons served at the Front.

FLOWER OF YOUTH

Lest Heaven be thronged with grey-beards hoary,
 God, who made boys for His delight,
Stoops in a day of grief and glory
 And calls them in, in from the night.
When they come trooping from the war
Our skies have many a new gold star.

Heaven's thronged with gay and careless faces,
 New-waked from dreams of dreadful things,
They walk in green and pleasant places
 And by the crystal water-springs
Who dreamt of dying and the slain,
And the fierce thirst and the strong pain.

Dear boys! They shall be young for ever.
 The Son of God was once a boy.
They run and leap by a clear river
 And of their youth they have great joy.
God who made boys so clean and good
Smiles with the eyes of fatherhood.

Now Heaven is by the young invaded;
    Their laughter's in the House of God.
Stainless and simple as He made it
    God keeps the heart o' the boy unflawed.
The old wise Saints look on and smile,
They are so young and without guile.

Oh, if the sonless mothers weeping,
    And widowed girls could look inside
The glory that hath them in keeping
    Who went to the Great War and died,
They would rise and put their mourning off,
And say: 'Thank God, he has enough!'

STEPHEN GWYNN
1864–1950

Gwynn was born in Dublin and raised in Ramelton, County
Donegal, where his father was parson. A prolific writer and
journalist, Gwynn was one of seven Irish nationalist MPs to
serve in the First World War. His *Battle Songs for the Irish
Brigade* was published in 1915.

A SONG OF VICTORY
1923

Ditches of mud
Where the boot clung till it tore,
Snow-cold water thigh-deep,
Holes in the ground for shelter:
It was not well to be there.

Something glimpsed in the dark:
What did you fire at?
Seldom a form clear-seen,
Never the face of a foeman.
Strange, impersonal war,
No heat, in it, no hate.

But in the heart of night
Sudden crash of the guns:
All the horizon
Pulsed with leaping flashes,
Wide-shooting flashes of anger,
A terrible nation striking.

Then in the gray dank dawn,
Search for one missing.
There in a tangle of wire,

Posts fallen, ruin of sandbags,
What is that darkness?
Wedged in, frost-bound:
Lift him, you, by the head –
– There is no head, sir. –

After a week of that,
Two weeks or three weeks,
Down the trench slowly filing,
Laden creatures, uncouth,
Encumbered, mud-clogged,
Stumble along;
Till at the last, a road,
Open space, deliverance:
And the war-beaten, trench-weary men
Form in a column,
And tramping back to their billets,
Whistle a tune to march to.
Would not your heart be proud of them?

Yonder behind the line,
We met while we rested,
Other men of our country
Who had not counted us friends.
There at ease for a moment,
With the common danger behind us,
About us, before us,
We drank and were pleasant together,
We made comrades.

And from the ditches of mud,
From the pit of destruction,
Word went back to Ireland:
We have met, we have spoken,
Who at home would never have spoken,
Strange to think of it.

And Ireland sitting at home,
Far away from the danger,
Began to think of it,
Even began to feel
A stir in her stiffness.

Suddenly flashed to us there
Word from Ireland:
Ditches of blood in Ireland,
Widening chasms.

We trod our way to the end;
We were part of victory:
And in the face of the world
Ireland disowned us.

Ditches of blood in Ireland.
Hate speeding the bullet
Where man stalked man like a beast,
Aimed, brought down his quarry,
Saw him writhing:
Ditches of blood in Ireland.

So in the end they won,
Won for Ireland.

Grey head of my comrade,
Gallant and comely,
Who in the wider battle
Marched with the young,
With the young men of Ireland,
Ay, and of Ulster,
To a day of high achievement,
And in a moment of victory
Fell:
You, not unforeknowing,

Not without wrench at heartstrings
Yet in a jubilant sacrifice
Offered your life.

Was it for nothing, my comrade?
Is there atonement of healing? Is there reward?
Not yet.

Not for you, who loved Ireland
In a lifetime of service without self-seeking,
Not for you the morose
Sour-visaged enjoyment,
Seeing the men who spurned you
Spurned in their turn.
Rather, O loyal heart,
It may be your time of purgation,
Idle, powerless, apart,
To look upon Ireland.

But when through travail
And purging of evil humours,
This disfigured, self-loathing
And desperate land
From the valley of humiliation
Struggles at last:
When cool air of the mountains,
Sunlight, fresh-running waters,
Wide-sweeping cloud-shadow on meadow
With bird-song at dawn,
Bring back her natural kindness,
Nurse her into serenity,
Renew her peace,
It may be, O comrade, that Ireland
Casting a backward glance on the road she has travelled,
Beyond the descent into victory,
Past the ditches of blood,

Will turn and yearn in her heart for the valour she
    once rejected,
For the wisdom she cast aside;
Will cry in the face of the world, *My faithful, my children,*
Will cry to her own sick heart,
    My faithful, my children,
    My lovers who never hurt me,
    You also are Ireland.

And it may be that Ireland
Crying it so, will take courage
To tread on the forward track.

This, O comrade of mine,
This were your recompense.

INSCRIPTION FOR A FOUNTAIN
ERECTED IN MEMORY OF MABEL DEARMER WHO
DIED IN SERBIA AND OF CHRISTOPHER DEARMER
KILLED AT SUVLA BAY

Proud of the war, all glorious went the son:
Loathing the war, all mournful went the mother.
Each had the same wage when the day was done:
Tell me, was either braver than the other?

They lay in mire, who went so comely ever:
Here, when you wash, let thought of them abide.
They knew the parching thirst of wound and fever:
Here, when you drink, remember them who died.

W.B. YEATS
1865–1939

Born in Dublin to a Protestant ascendancy family, Yeats was a central figure of the Irish Literary Revival. In 1922 he was appointed to the Irish Senate, and in 1923 he was awarded the Nobel Prize for Literature.

AN IRISH AIRMAN FORESEES HIS DEATH

I know that I shall meet my fate
Somewhere among the clouds above;
Those that I fight I do not hate,
Those that I guard I do not love;
My country is Kiltartan Cross,
My countrymen Kiltartan's poor,
No likely end could bring them loss
Or leave them happier than before.
Nor law, nor duty bade me fight,
Nor public men, nor cheering crowds,
A lonely impulse of delight
Drove to this tumult in the clouds;
I balanced all, brought all to mind,
The years to come seemed waste of breath,
A waste of breath the years behind
In balance with this life, this death.

ON BEING ASKED FOR A WAR POEM

I think it better that in times like these
A poet's mouth be silent, for in truth
We have no gift to set a statesman right;
He has had enough of meddling who can please
A young girl in the indolence of her youth,
Or an old man upon a winter's night.

EASTER 1916

I have met them at close of day
Coming with vivid faces
From counter or desk among grey
Eighteenth-century houses.
I have passed with a nod of the head
Or polite meaningless words,
Or have lingered awhile and said
Polite meaningless words,
And thought before I had done
Of a mocking tale or a gibe
To please a companion
Around the fire at the club,
Being certain that they and I
But lived where motley is worn:
All changed, changed utterly:
A terrible beauty is born.

That woman's days were spent
In ignorant good-will,
Her nights in argument
Until her voice grew shrill.

What voice more sweet than hers
When, young and beautiful,
She rode to harriers?
This man had kept a school
And rode our wingèd horse;
This other his helper and friend
Was coming into his force;
He might have won fame in the end,
So sensitive his nature seemed,
So daring and sweet his thought.
This other man I had dreamed
A drunken, vainglorious lout.
He had done most bitter wrong
To some who are near my heart,
Yet I number him in the song;
He, too, has resigned his part
In the casual comedy;
He, too, has been changed in his turn,
Transformed utterly:
A terrible beauty is born.

Hearts with one purpose alone
Through summer and winter seem
Enchanted to a stone
To trouble the living stream.
The horse that comes from the road,
The rider, the birds that range
From cloud to tumbling cloud,
Minute by minute they change;
A shadow of cloud on the stream
Changes minute by minute;
A horse-hoof slides on the brim,
And a horse plashes within it;
The long-legged moor-hens dive,
And hens to moor-cocks call;
Minute by minute they live:
The stone's in the midst of all.

Too long a sacrifice
Can make a stone of the heart.
O when may it suffice?
That is Heaven's part, our part
To murmur name upon name,
As a mother names her child
When sleep at last has come
On limbs that had run wild.
What is it but nightfall?
No, no, not night but death;
Was it needless death after all?
For England may keep faith
For all that is done and said.
We know their dream; enough
To know they dreamed and are dead;
And what if excess of love
Bewildered them till they died?
I write it out in a verse —
MacDonagh and MacBride
And Connolly and Pearse
Now and in time to be,
Wherever green is worn,
Are changed, changed utterly:
A terrible beauty is born.

September 25, 1916

SIXTEEN DEAD MEN

O but we talked at large before
The sixteen men were shot,
But who can talk of give and take,
What should be and what not
While those dead men are loitering there
To stir the boiling pot?

You say that we should still the land
Till Germany's overcome;
But who is there to argue that
Now Pearse is deaf and dumb?
And is their logic to outweigh
MacDonagh's bony thumb?

How could you dream they'd listen
That have an ear alone
For those new comrades they have found,
Lord Edward and Wolfe Tone,
Or meddle with our give and take
That converse bone to bone?

ON A POLITICAL PRISONER

She that but little patience knew,
From childhood on, had now so much
A grey gull lost its fear and flew
Down to her cell and there alit,
And there endured her fingers' touch
And from her fingers ate its bit.

Did she in touching that lone wing
Recall the years before her mind
Became a bitter, an abstract thing,
Her thought some popular enmity:
Blind and leader of the blind
Drinking the foul ditch where they lie?

When long ago I saw her ride
Under Ben Bulben to the meet,
The beauty of her country-side
With all youth's lonely wildness stirred,
She seemed to have grown clean and sweet
Like any rock-bred, sea-borne bird:

Sea-borne, or balanced on the air
When first it sprang out of the nest
Upon some lofty rock to stare
Upon the cloudy canopy,
While under its storm-beaten breast
Cried out the hollows of the sea.

REPRISALS

Some nineteen German planes, they say,
You had brought down before you died.
We called it a good death. Today
Can ghost or man be satisfied?
Although your last exciting year
Outweighed all other years, you said,
Though battle joy may be so dear
A memory, even to the dead,
It chases other thought away,
Yet rise from your Italian tomb,
Flit to Kiltartan cross and stay
Till certain second thoughts have come
Upon the cause you served, that we
Imagined such a fine affair:
Half-drunk or whole-mad soldiery
Are murdering your tenants there.
Men that revere your father yet
Are shot at on the open plain.

Where may new-married women sit
And suckle children now? Armed men
May murder them in passing by
Nor law nor parliament take heed.
Then close your ears with dust and lie
Among the other cheated dead.

from MEDITATIONS IN TIME OF CIVIL WAR

V

THE ROAD AT MY DOOR

An affable Irregular,
A heavily-built Falstaffian man,
Comes cracking jokes of civil war
As though to die by gunshot were
The finest play under the sun.

A brown Lieutenant and his men,
Half dressed in national uniform,
Stand at my door, and I complain
Of the foul weather, hail and rain,
A pear tree broken by the storm.

I count those feathered balls of soot
The moor-hen guides upon the stream,
To silence the envy in my thought;
And turn towards my chamber, caught
In the cold snows of a dream.

VI

THE STARE'S NEST BY MY WINDOW

The bees build in the crevices
Of loosening masonry, and there
The mother birds bring grubs and flies.
My wall is loosening; honey-bees,
Come build in the empty house of the stare.

We are closed in, and the key is turned
On our uncertainty; somewhere
A man is killed, or a house burned,
Yet no clear fact to be discerned:
Come build in the empty house of the stare.

A barricade of stone or of wood;
Some fourteen days of civil war;
Last night they trundled down the road
That dead young soldier in his blood:
Come build in the empty house of the stare.

We had fed the heart on fantasies,
The heart's grown brutal from the fare;
More substance in our enmities
Than in our love; O honey-bees,
Come build in the empty house of the stare.

III

Come gather round me, players all:
Come praise Nineteen-Sixteen,
Those from the pit and gallery
Or from the painted scene
That fought in the Post Office
Or round the City Hall,
Praise every man that came again,
Praise every man that fell.

From mountain to mountain ride the fierce horsemen.

Who was the first man shot that day?
The player Connolly,
Close to the City Hall he died;
Carriage and voice had he;
He lacked those years that go with skill,
But later might have been
A famous, a brilliant figure
Before the painted scene.

From mountain to mountain ride the fierce horsemen.

Some had no thought of victory
But had gone out to die
That Ireland's mind be greater,
Her heart mount up on high;
And yet who knows what's yet to come?
For Patrick Pearse had said
That in every generation
Must Ireland's blood be shed.

From mountain to mountain ride the fierce horsemen.

POLITICS

*'In our time the destiny of man presents its
meanings in political terms.'*

THOMAS MANN

How can I, that girl standing there,
My attention fix
On Roman or on Russian
Or on Spanish politics?
Yet here's a travelled man that knows
What he talks about,
And there's a politician
That has read and thought,
And maybe what they say is true
Of war and war's alarms,
But O that I were young again
And held her in my arms.

Æ

1867–1935

Æ (George Russell) was born in County Armagh and educated in Dublin. A writer and artist, he was involved with the Irish Literary Revival and was editor of the *Irish Homestead* and the *Irish Statesman*. His *Collected Poems* was published in 1913.

ON BEHALF OF SOME IRISHMEN
NOT FOLLOWERS OF TRADITION

They call us aliens, we are told,
Because our wayward visions stray
From that dim banner they unfold,
The dreams of worn-out yesterday.
The sum of all the past is theirs,
The creeds, the deeds, the fame, the name,
Whose death-created glory flares
And dims the spark of living flame.
They weave the necromancer's spell,
And burst the graves where martyrs slept,
Their ancient story to retell,
Renewing tears the dead have wept.
And they would have us join their dirge,
This worship of an extinct fire
In which they drift beyond the verge
Where races all outworn expire.
The worship of the dead is not
A worship that our hearts allow,
Though every famous shade were wrought
With woven thorns above the brow.
We fling our answer back in scorn:
'We are less children of this clime
Than of some nation yet unborn

Or empire in the womb of time.
We hold the Ireland in the heart
More than the land our eyes have seen,
And love the goal for which we start
More than the tale of what has been.'
The generations as they rise
May live the life men lived before,
Still hold the thought once held as wise,
Go in by the same ancient door.
We leave the easy peace it brings:
The few we are shall still unite
In fealty to unseen kings
Or unimaginable light.
We would no Irish sign efface,
But yet our lips would gladlier hail
The firstborn of the Coming Race
Than the last splendour of the Gael.
No blazoned banner we unfold –
One charge alone we give to youth,
Against the sceptred myth to hold
The golden heresy of truth.

SALUTATION

To the Memory of Some I Knew Who
Are Dead and Who Loved Ireland

Their dream had left me numb and cold,
    But yet my spirit rose in pride,
Refashioning in burnished gold
    The images of those who died,
Or were shut in the penal cell.
    Here's to you, Pearse, your dream, not mine,
But yet the thought, for this you fell,
    Has turned life's waters into wine.

You who have died on Eastern hills
    Or fields of France as undismayed,
Who lit with interlinked wills
    The long heroic barricade,
You, too, in all the dreams you had,
    Thought of some thing for Ireland done.
Was it not so, Oh, shining lad,
    What lured you, Alan Anderson?

I listened to high talk from you,
    Thomas MacDonagh, and it seemed
The words were idle, but they grew
    To nobleness by death redeemed.
Life cannot utter words more great
    Than life may meet by sacrifice,
High words were equalled by high fate,
    You paid the price. You paid the price.

You who have fought on fields afar,
    That other Ireland did you wrong
Who said you shadowed Ireland's star,
    Nor gave you laurel wreath nor song.
You proved by death as true as they,
    In mightier conflicts played your part,
Equal your sacrifice may weigh,
    Dear Kettle, of the generous heart.

The hope lives on age after age,
    Earth with its beauty might be won
For labour as a heritage,
    For this has Ireland lost a son.
This hope unto a flame to fan
    Men have put life by with a smile,
Here's to you, Connolly, my man,
    Who cast the last torch on the pile.

You, too, had Ireland in your care,
Who watched o'er pits of blood and mire,
From iron roots leap up in air
Wild forests, magical, of fire;
Yet while the Nuts of Death were shed
Your memory would ever stray
To your own isle, Oh, gallant dead –
This wreath, Will Redmond, on your clay.

Here's to you, men I never met,
    Yet hope to meet behind the veil,
Thronged on some starry parapet;
    That looks down upon Innisfail,
And sees the confluence of dreams
    That clashed together in our night,
One river, born from many streams,
    Roll in one blaze of blinding light.

CONTINUITY

No sign is made while empires pass.
The flowers and stars are still His care,
The constellations hid in grass,
The golden miracles in air.

Life in an instant will be rent
Where death is glittering blind and wild –
The Heavenly Brooding is intent
To that last instant on Its child.

It breathes the glow in brain and heart,
Life is made magical. Until
Body and spirit are apart
The Everlasting works Its will.

In that wild orchid that your feet
In their next falling shall destroy,
Minute and passionate and sweet
The Mighty Master holds His joy.

Though the crushed jewels droop and fade
The Artist's labours will not cease,
And of the ruins shall be made
Some yet more lovely masterpiece.

CHIVALRY

I dreamed I saw that ancient Irish queen,
Who from her dun, as dawn had opened wide,
Saw the tall foemen rise on every side,
And gazed with kindling eye upon the scene,
And in delight cried, 'Noble is their mien.'
'Most kingly are they,' her own host replied,
Praising the beauty, bravery, and pride
As if the foe their very kin had been.
And then I heard the innumerable hiss
Of human adders, nation with poisonous breath
Spitting at nation, as if the dragon rage
Would claw the spirit, and I woke at this,
Knowing the soul of man was sick to death
And I was weeping in the Iron Age.

GODS OF WAR
1914

Fate wafts us from the pygmies' shore:
We swim beneath the epic skies:
A Rome and Carthage war once more,
And wider empires are the prize;
Where the beaked galleys clashed; lo, these
Our iron dragons of the seas!

High o'er the cloudy battle sweep
The winged chariots in their flight:
The steely creatures of the deep
Cleave the dark waters' ancient night:
Below, above, in wave, in air,
New worlds for conquest everywhere.

More terrible than spear or sword
Those stars that burst with fiery breath:
More loud the battle cries are poured
Along a hundred leagues of death.
So do they fight.   How have ye warred,
Defeated Armies of the Lord?

This is the Dark Immortal's hour,
His victory, whoever fail;
His prophets have not lost their power:
Caesar and Attila prevail.
These are your legions still, proud ghosts,
These myriad embattled hosts.

How wanes Thine empire, Prince of Peace!
With the fleet circling of the suns
The ancient gods their power increase;
Lo, how Thine own anointed ones
Make holy all Thy soul abhorred,
The hate on which Thy love had warred.

Who dreamed a dream mid outcasts born
Could overbrow the pride of kings?
They pour on Christ the ancient scorn.
His Dove its gold and silver wings
Has spread.   Perhaps it nests in flame
In outcasts who abjure His name.

Choose ye your rightful gods, nor pay
Lip reverence that the heart denies.
O Nations, is not Zeus to-day,
The thunderer from the epic skies,
More than the Prince of Peace?   Is Thor
Not nobler for a world at war?

They fit the dreams of power we hold,
Those gods whose names are with us still,
Men in their image made of old
The high companions of their will.
Who build in air an empire's pride –
Would they pray to the Crucified?

O outcast Christ, it was too soon
For flags of battle to be furled
While life was yet at the hot noon.
Come in the twilight of the world:
Its kings may greet Thee without scorn
And crown Thee then without a thorn.

BATTLE ARDOUR

Unto what heaven wends this wild ecstasy?
Is the fired spirit light upon its wings,
Self being outcast, as the diver flings
His garment so that every limb be free?
Is it an instant of eternity
Attained because no earthly terror clings?
Not now it battles for the rights of kings.
This ecstasy is all its own; to be
Quit of itself, mounted upon the power
That, like Leviathan, breaks from the deep
Primeval and all conquering.   He dies!
Yet has he conquered in that very hour.
He and his foeman the same tryst do keep.
His foemen are his brothers in the skies.

WASTE

All that heroic mood,
The will to suffer pain,
Were it on beauty spent,
An intellectual gain:

Had a fierce pity breathed
O'er wronged or fallen life,
Though strife had been unwise
We were not shamed by strife:

Had they but died for some
High image in the mind,
Not spilt the sacrifice
For words hollow as wind!

Darkened the precious fire:
The will we honour most
Spent in the waste!   What sin
Against the Holy Ghost!

APOCALYPTIC

1915

Our world beyond a year of dread
Has paled like Babylon or Rome.
Never for all the blood was shed
Shall life return to it as home.
No peace shall e'er that dream recall;
The avalanche is yet to fall.

Laugh, you whose dreams were outlawed things.
The sceptre from the tyrant slips.
Earth's kings are met by those wild kings
Who swept through the Apocalypse.
Ere the first awful hand be stayed,
The second shall have clutched the blade.

On the white horse is one who rides
Until earth's empires are o'erthrown,
And a red rider yet abides
Whose trumpet call is still unblown,
Whose battlefield shall be the grave
Either for master or for slave.

Once in a zodiac of years
Earth stirs beneath her heaving crust,
And high and low, unheeding tears,
Are equal levelled with the dust.
Laugh, slave, the coming terror brings
Thee to that brotherhood with kings.

Laugh too, you warriors of God,
The tyrants of the spirit fail.
The mitred head shall no more nod
And multitudes of men be pale.
When empires topple here below
The heavens which are their shadows go.

If the black horse's rider reign,
Or the pale horse's rider fire
His burning arrows, with disdain
Laugh.   You have come to your desire,
To the last test which yields the right
To walk amid the halls of light.

You, who have made of earth your star,
Cry out, indeed, for hopes made vain:
For only those can laugh who are
The strong Initiates of Pain,
Who know that mighty god to be
Sculptor of immortality.

TRAGEDY

This, of all fates, would be the saddest end;
That that heroic fever, with its cry
From Children unto Mother, 'Here am I!'
Should lose the very faith it would defend;
That the high soul through passion should descend
To work the evil it had willed must die.
If it won so, would that be victory,
That tragic close? Oh, hearken, foe or friend!
Love, the magician, and the wizard Hate,
Though one be like white fire and one dark flame,
Work the same miracle, and all are wrought
Into the image that they contemplate.
None ever hated in the world but came
To every baseness of the foe he fought.

STATESMEN

They tell us that they war on war.   Why do
    they treat our wit with scorn?
The dragon from the dragon seed, the breed
    was true since life was born.
When has the lioness conceived the lamb be-
    neath her tawny side?
When has the timid dove been born the off-
    spring of the eagle's pride?
When Cherubim smite at their Light, oh!
    yes, we may believe this thing.
When Eblis risen in revolt casts from its shades
    their awful king.

We know how from the deeds men do a sudden
 blackness blinds the soul,
How kindled by their sacrifice lights up the
 instant aureole.
The thought, the deed, breed always true.
 Shall nations not the law obey?
Has not the Mighty Father store within His
 Treasure House to pay?
The noble and the base beget their kin, and
 empires ere they pass
See their own mirrored majesty arise within
 Time's looking-glass.
The pride that builded Babylon of Egypt was
 the mighty child:
The beauty of the Attic soul in many a lovely
 city smiled.
The empire that is built in pride shall call
 imperial pride to birth,
And with that shadow of itself must fight for
 empire of the earth.
Fight where ye will on earth or sea, beneath
 the wave, above the hills,
The foe ye meet is still yourselves, the blade
 ye forged the sword that kills.

EVA GORE-BOOTH
1870–1926

Gore-Booth was born in Sligo, the younger sister of Constance
Markievicz. She was involved in the Suffragette movement and
became a social worker in Manchester, later campaigning for
prison reform. *Poems of Eva Gore-Booth: Complete Edition* was
published in 1929.

EASTER WEEK

Grief for the noble dead
Of one who did not share their strife,
And mourned that any blood was shed,
Yet felt the broken glory of their state,
Their strange heroic questioning of Fate
Ribbon with gold the rags of this our life.

CHRISTMAS EVE IN PRISON

Do not be lonely, dear, nor grieve
This Christmas Eve.
Is it so vain a thing
That your heart's harper, Dark Roseen,
A wandering singer, yet a queen,
Crownèd with all her seventeen stars,
Outside your prison bars
Stands carolling?

TO C.M. ON HER PRISON BIRTHDAY

February, 1917

What has time to do with thee,
Who hast found the victor's way
To be rich in poverty,
Without sunshine to be gay,
To be free in a prison cell?
Nay on that undreamed judgment day,
When on the old world's scrap-heap flung,
Powers and empires pass away,
Radiant and unconquerable
Thou shalt be young.

COMRADES

To Con

The peaceful night that round me flows,
    Breaks through your iron prison doors,
Free through the world your spirit goes,
    Forbidden hands are clasping yours.

The wind is our confederate,
    The night has left her doors ajar,
We meet beyond earth's barrèd gate,
    Where all the world's wild rebels are.

FRANCIS SHEEHY-SKEFFINGTON

Dublin, April 26, 1916

No green and poisonous laurel wreath shall shade
 His brow, who dealt no death in any strife,
Crown him with olive who was not afraid
 To join the desolate unarmed ranks of life.

Who did not fear to die, yet feared to slay,
 A leader in the war that shall end war,
Unarmed he stood in ruthless Empire's way,
 Unarmed he stands on Acheron's lost shore.

Yet not alone, nor all unrecognized,
 For at his side does that scorned Dreamer stand,
Who in the Olive Garden agonized,
 Whose Kingdom yet shall come in every land,

When driven men, who fight and hate and kill
 To order, shall let all their weapons fall,
And know that kindly freedom of the will
 That holds no other human will in thrall.

PINEHURST

1916

Dew-pearlèd cobwebs glitter on green boughs,
    Beneath our feet the grass is wet with dew,
It seems as if this clear dawn must arouse
    Our broken world to something strange and new.

Deep in the high-built fortress of the pines,
    Lost to her stars dark night imprisoned lies,
Near my hushed soul in peace a white rose shines,
    Like a new dream down flung from ancient skies.

Alas, the bugles on the distant plain –
    The guns break forth with their insistent din,
The dews of noon-day leave a crimson stain
    On grass, that all men's feet must wander in.

Oh, singing splendour of the morning furled
    About the souls of trees, the hearts of flowers,
Have you no dream of beauty for the world –
    This bitter bloodstained world we men call ours?

LORD DUNSANY
1878–1957

Edward Plunkett (later the eighteenth Baron of Dunsany) was born in London and educated at Eton and Sandhurst. A Boer War veteran, he also fought in the trenches in the First World War and served in the Home Guard during the Second World War. Involved in the Irish Literary Revival, he wrote novels, fantasy stories, poems and drama and was a lecturer and broadcaster.

THE MEMORIAL

I saw a pear-tree on a garden wall
    Stretching its arms quite fifteen feet each way.
There was no garden near, nor house at all:
    Flower and field and farm were passed away.
Many memorials can the Kaiser boast,
Yet this may stand for him as well as most.

A DIRGE OF VICTORY

Lift not thy trumpet, Victory, to the sky,
    Nor through battalions nor by batteries blow,
    But over hollows full of old wire go,
Where, among dregs of war, the long-dead lie
With wasted iron that the guns passed by
    When they went eastward like a tide at flow;
    There blow thy trumpet that the dead may know,
Who waited for thy coming, Victory.

It is not we that have deserved thy wreath.
 They waited there among the towering weeds:
The deep mud burned under the thermite's breath,
 And winter cracked the bones that no man heeds:
Hundreds of nights flamed by: the seasons passed.
And thou hast come to them at last, at last!

SONGS FROM AN EVIL WOOD

I

There is no wrath in the stars,
 They do not rage in the sky;
I look from the evil wood
 And find myself wondering why.

Why do they not scream out
 And grapple star against star,
Seeking for blood in the wood,
 As all things round me are?

They do not glare like the sky
 Or flash like the deeps of the wood;
But they shine softly on
 In their sacred solitude.

To their happy haunts
 Silence from us has flown,
She whom we loved of old
 And know it now she is gone.

When will she come again
    Though for one second only?
She whom we loved is gone
    And the whole world is lonely.

And the elder giants come
    Sometimes, tramping from far,
Through the weird and flickering light
    Made by an earthly star.

And the giant with his club,
    And the dwarf with rage in his breath,
And the elder giants from far,
    They are the children of Death.

They are all abroad to-night
    And are breaking the hills with their brood,
And the birds are all asleep,
    Even in Plugstreet Wood.

II

Somewhere lost in the haze
    The sun goes down in the cold,
And birds in this evil wood
    Chirrup home as of old;

Chirrup, stir and are still,
    On the high twigs frozen and thin.
There is no more noise of them now,
    And the long night sets in.

Of all the wonderful things
    That I have seen in the wood,
I marvel most at the birds,
    At their chirp and their quietude.

For a giant smites with his club
    All day the tops of the hill,
Sometimes he rests at night,
    Oftener he beats them still.

And a dwarf with a grim black mane
    Raps with repeated rage
All night in the valley below
    On the wooden walls of his cage.

III

I met with Death in his country,
    With his scythe and his hollow eye
Walking the roads of Belgium.
    I looked and he passed me by.

Since he passed me by in Plug Street,
    In the wood of the evil name,
I shall not now lie with the heroes,
    I shall not share their fame;

I shall never be as they are,
    A name in the land of the Free,
Since I looked on Death in Flanders
    And he did not look at me.

TO THE FALLEN IRISH SOLDIERS

Since they have grudged you space in Merrion Square,
    And any monument of stone or brass,
    And you yourselves are powerless, alas,
And your own countrymen seem not to care;
Let then these words of mine drift down the air,
    Lest the world think that it has come to pass
    That *all* in Ireland treat as common grass
The soil that wraps her heroes slumbering there.

Sleep on, forgot a few more years, and then
    The ages, that I prophesy, shall see
Due honours paid to you by juster men,
    You standing foremost in our history,
Your story filling all our land with wonder,
Your names, and regiments' names, like distant thunder.

THOMAS MacDONAGH
1878–1916

MacDonagh was born in Tipperary but moved to Dublin, where he joined the Gaelic League and taught at St Enda's school under Pádraic Pearse. He joined the Irish Republican Brotherhood (IRB) and was later executed for his role in the 1916 Easter Rising. His first poetry collection, *Through the Ivory Gate*, was published in 1902.

IN ABSENCE

Last night I read your letters once again –
Read till the dawn filled all my room with grey;
Then quenched my light and put the leaves away,
And prayed for sleep to ease my heart's great pain.
But ah! that poignant tenderness made vain
My hope of rest – I could not sleep or pray
For thought of you, and the slow, broadening day
Held me there prisoner of my throbbing brain.

Yet I did sleep before the silence broke,
And dream, but not of you – the old dreams rife
With duties which would bind me to the yoke
Of my old futile, lone, reluctant life:
I stretched my hands for help in the vain strife,
And grasped these leaves, and to this pain awoke.

AFTER A YEAR

After a year of love
Death of love in a day;
And I who ever strove
To hold love in sure life
Now let it pass away
With no grief and no strife.

Pass – but it holds me yet;
Love, it would seem, may die;
But we can not forget
And can not be the same,
As lowly or as high,
As once, before this came.

Never as in old days
Can I again stoop low;
Never, now fallen, raise
Spirit and heart above
To where once life did show
The lone soul of my love.

None would the service ask
That she from love requires,
Making it not a task
But a high sacrament
Of all love's dear desires
And all life's grave intent.

And if she asked it not? –
Should I have loved her then? –
Such love was our one lot
And our true destiny.
Shall I find truth again? –
None could have known but she.

THE POET CAPTAIN

They called him their king, their leader of men, and he
    led them well
For one bright year and he vanquished their foe,
Breaking more battles than bards may tell,
Warring victoriously, – till the heart spake low
And said – Is it thus? Do not these things pass? What
    things abide?
They are but the birds from the ocean, the waves of the tide;
And thou art naught beside, – grass and a form of clay.
And said – The Ligurian fought in his day, –
In vain, in vain! Rome triumphs. He left his friends to the fight,
And their victory passed away,
And he like a star that flames and falls in the night.

But after another year they came to him again,
And said – Lead us forth again. Come with us again.
But still he answered them – You strive against fate in vain.
They said – Our race is old. We would not have it pass.
Ere Rome began we are, a gentle people of old,
Unsavage when all were wild.
And he – How Egypt was old in the days that were old,
Yet is passed, and we pass.
They said – We shall have striven, unreconciled.
And he went with them again, and they conquered again.
Till the same bare season closed his unquiet heart
To all but sorrow of life – This is in vain! Of yore
Lo, Egypt was, and all things do depart,
This is in vain! And he fought no more.

He conned the poems that poets had made in other days,
And he loved the past that he could pity and praise.
And he fought no more, living in solitude,
Till they came and called him back to the multitude,

Saying – Our olden speech and our old manners die.
He went again, and they raised his banner on high:
Came Victory, eagle-formed, with wings wide flung,
As with them a while he fought, with never a weary thought,
    and with never a sigh,
That their children might have again their manners and
    ancient tongue.

But again the sorrow of life whispered to his soul
And said – O little soul, striving to little goal!
Here is a finite world where all things change and change!
And said – In Mexico a people strange
Loved their manners and speech long ago when the world
    was young!
Their speech is silent long – What of it now? – Silent and dead
Their manners forgotten, and all but their memory sped!
And said – What matter? Heart will die and tongue;
Or if they live again they live in a place that is naught,
With other language, other custom, different thought.
He left them again to their fight, and no more for him
    they sought.
But they chose for leader a stern sure man
That looked not back on the waste of story:
For his country he fought in the battle's van,
And he won her peace and he won her glory.

A DREAM OF HELL

Last night I dreamt I was in hell;
In waking dread I dream it yet;
I feel the gloom, my brow is wet;
My soul is prisoner of the spell.

Hell, gloomy, still, – no fire, no cry.
Flames were a joy and shrieks delight.
And sounds of woe and painful light
Were bliss to gloom without a sigh.

I dreamt that moments passed like years
In dumb blind darkness whelmed and drowned,
In silence of a single sound,
In grief eternal void of tears.

A single sound I heard all night
Pulse through the stillness like a sob:
I heard the weary changeless throb
Of dead damned hearts the silence smite.

No change, no end; no end, no change –
As in a death house when the door
Is closed, and to return no more
One form is gone, when stillness strange

Creeps in and in one dim room stays,
The widow, who with sleepless eyes
Has watched long, hears with dull surprise
A ticking she has heard for days.

So heard I myriad heart-beats blend
Into one mighty changeless knell,
The throb-song of the silent hell;
No end, no change; no change, no end.

In silence, solitude and gloom,
With working brain and throbbing heart,
Remembering things that cannot start
To life again out of the tomb,

Remembering, ruing, day by day,
And year by year, and age by age,
In sorrow without tear or rage
Watching the moments pass away,

I found thee – of all mortals thee! –
Buried in hell for endless time,
Buried in hell for unknown crime,
Who ever wert a saint to me.

I found thee there – I know not how –
And thou wilt never know that I,
Thy pitying friend of earth, was nigh –
My pity ne'er can reach thee now.

OF A POET PATRIOT

His songs were a little phrase
    Of eternal song,
Drowned in the harping of lays
    More loud and long.

His deed was a single word,
    Called out alone
In a night when no echo stirred
    To laughter or moan.

But his songs new souls shall thrill,
    The loud harps dumb,
And his deed the echoes fill
    When the dawn is come.

FOR VICTORY

An old man weeps
And a young man sorrows
While a child is busy with his gladness.
The old shall cheer
And the young shall battle, –
The child shall tremble for their gladness.

O Victory
How fair thou comest,
Young though the ages are thy raiment!
Thy song of death
How sweet thou singest,
Coming in that splendour of thy raiment!

All flaming thou
In grandeur of the Fianna
Or crowned with the memory of Tara!
In the fame of Kings,
In the might of chieftains,
Bound in the memory of Tara!

Sweet little child
To thee the victory –
Thou shalt be now as the Fianna!
For thee the feast,
For thee the lime-white mansions,
And the hounds on the hills of Fianna!

WILLIAM ORPEN
1878–1931

Born in Stillorgan, County Dublin, Orpen studied at the Dublin Metropolitan School of Art and Slade School of Fine Art, London. He travelled to the front as Britain's official war artist during the First World War and was the official painter for the Paris Peace Conference. Knighted in 1918, he was elected member of the Royal Academy, London, in 1919.

THE CHURCH, ZILLEBEKE
October 1918

'Mud
Everywhere –
Nothing but mud.
The very air seems thick with it,
The few tufts of grass are all smeared with –
Mud!
The Church a heap of it;
One look, and weep for it.
That's what they've made of it –
Mud!
Slimy and wet,
Churned and upset;
Here Bones that once mattered
With crosses lie scattered,
Broken and battered,
Covered in mud,
Here, where the Church's bell
Tolled when our heroes fell
In that mad start of hell –
Mud!
That's all that's left of it – mud!'

PÁDRAIC H. PEARSE
1879–1916

Born in Dublin, Pearse qualified as a barrister and joined the Gaelic League in 1898, editing its newspaper, *An Claidheamh Soluis*. He founded the bi-lingual school St Enda's in 1908 and joined the IRB in 1913. He was later executed for his part as a leader of the 1916 Rising. As well as poetry, Pearse wrote short stories, plays and political essays.

THE MOTHER

I do not grudge them: Lord, I do not grudge
My two strong sons that I have seen go out
To break their strength and die, they and a few,
In bloody protest for a glorious thing,
They shall be spoken of among their people,
The generations shall remember them,
And call them blessed;
But I will speak their names to my own heart
In the long nights;
The little names that were familiar once
Round my dead hearth.
Lord, thou art hard on mothers:
We suffer in their coming and their going;
And tho' I grudge them not, I weary, weary
Of the long sorrow – And yet I have my joy:
My sons were faithful, and they fought.

THE FOOL

Since the wise men have not spoken, I speak that am only a fool;
A fool that hath loved his folly,
Yea, more than the wise men their books or their counting
    houses or their quiet homes
Or their fame in men's mouths;
A fool that in all his days hath done never a prudent thing,
Never hath counted the cost, nor recked if another reaped
The fruit of his mighty sowing, content to scatter the seed;
A fool that is unrepentant, and that soon at the end of all
Shall laugh in his lonely heart as the ripe ears fall to the
    reaping-hooks
And the poor are filled that were empty,
Tho' he go hungry.
I have squandered the splendid years that the Lord God gave
    to my youth
In attempting impossible things, deeming them alone worth
    the toil.
Was it folly or grace? Not men shall judge me, but God.

I have squandered the splendid years:
Lord, if I had the years I would squander them over again,
Aye, fling them from me!
For this I have heard in my heart, that a man shall scatter
    not hoard,
Shall do the deed of to-day, nor take thought of to-morrow's teen,
Shall not bargain or huxter with God; or was it a jest of Christ's
And is this my sin before men; to have taken Him at His word?

The lawyers have sat in council, the men with the keen,
long faces,
And said, 'This man is a fool,' and others have said, 'He
blasphemeth';
And the wise have pitied the fool that hath striven to give a life
In the world of time and space among the bulks of actual things,
To a dream that was dreamed in the heart, and that only the
heart could hold.

O wise men, riddle me this: what if the dream come true?
What if the dream come true? and if millions unborn shall dwell
In the house that I shaped in my heart, the noble house of my
thought?
Lord, I have staked my soul, I have staked the lives of my kin
On the truth of Thy dreadful word. Do not remember
my failures,
But remember this my faith.

And so I speak.
Yea, ere my hot youth pass, I speak to my people and say:
Ye shall be foolish as I; ye shall scatter, not save;
Ye shall venture your all, lest ye lose what is more than all;
Ye shall call for a miracle, taking Christ at His word.
And for this I will answer, O people, answer here and hereafter,
O people that I have loved shall we not answer together?

THE REBEL

I am come of the seed of the people, the people that sorrow,
That have no treasure but hope,
No riches laid up but a memory
Of an Ancient glory.

49

My mother bore me in bondage, in bondage my mother
    was born,
I am of the blood of serfs;
The children with whom I have played, the men and women
    with whom I have eaten,
Have had masters over them, have been under the lash
    of masters,
And, though gentle, have served churls;
The hands that have touched mine, the dear hands whose touch
    is so familiar to me,
Have worn shameful manacles, have been bitten at the wrist
    by manacles,
Have grown hard with the manacles and the task-work
    of strangers,
I am flesh of the flesh of these lowly, I am bone of their bone,
I that have never submitted;
I that have a soul greater than the souls of my people's masters,
I that have vision and prophecy and the gift of fiery speech,
I that have spoken with God on the top of His holy hill.

And because I am of the people, I understand the people,
I am sorrowful with their sorrow, I am hungry with their desire:
My heart has been heavy with the grief of mothers,
My eyes have been wet with the tears of children.
I have yearned with old wistful men,
And laughed or cursed with young men;
Their shame is my shame, and I have reddened for it,
Reddened for that they have served, they who should be free,
Reddened for that they have gone in want, while others have
    been full,
Reddened for that they have walked in fear of lawyers and
    of their jailers
With their writs of summons and their handcuffs,
Men mean and cruel!
I could have borne stripes on my body rather than this shame
    of my people.

And now I speak, being full of vision;
I speak to my people, and I speak in my people's name to the
  masters of my people.
I say to my people that they are holy, that they are august,
  despite their chains,
That they are greater than those that hold them, and stronger
  and purer,
That they have but need of courage, and to call on the name
  of their God,
God the unforgetting, the dear God that loves the peoples
For whom He died naked, suffering shame.
And I say to my people's masters: Beware,
Beware of the thing that is coming, beware of the risen people,
Who shall take what ye would not give. Did ye think to conquer
  the people,
Or that Law is stronger than life and than men's desire to be free?
We will try it out with you, ye that have harried and held,
Ye that have bullied and bribed, tyrants, hypocrites, liars!

CHRISTMAS 1915

O King that was born
To set bondsmen free,
In the coming battle,
Help the Gael!

THE WAYFARER

The beauty of the world hath made me sad,
This beauty that will pass;
Sometimes my heart hath shaken with great joy
To see a leaping squirrel in a tree,
Or a red lady-bird upon a stalk,
Or little rabbits in a field at evening,
Lit by a slanting sun,
Or some green hill where shadows drifted by
Some quiet hill where mountainy man hath sown
And soon would reap; near to the gate of Heaven;
Or children with bare feet upon the sands
Of some ebbed sea, or playing on the streets
Of little towns in Connacht,
Things young and happy.
And then my heart hath told me:
These will pass,
Will pass and change, will die and be no more,
Things bright and green, things young and happy;
And I have gone upon my way
Sorrowful.

MARY DEVENPORT O'NEILL
1879–1967

O'Neill was born in County Galway and studied at the Dublin Metropolitan School of Art. A playwright and poet with an interest in modernist poetic techniques, she kept a literary salon in Rathgar and collaborated with Yeats. Her *Prometheus and Other Poems* was published in 1929.

DEAD IN WARS AND IN REVOLUTIONS

It is cold without flesh, without bones,
To cover the soul.
No blood or nerves to take the shock, but woes
Beat on the unprotected soul.

We are naked shades within our span of life,
A gap in living fabric,
A blot, a flaw.
Cold, cold without flesh, without bones;
Cold without flesh, without bones, to cover the soul.

We can perceive the sun, but not through warmth –
We have no bodies.
Not through colour nor through brightness –
We've no eyes.
Not through the increase of life
Which to life it brings.
What the sun pours
On our stript souls
Is the dark inverted essence of all these things.

We know when music plays,
But we are shades;
Sounds cannot caress our ears,
And rhythm tells us only
That we have no limbs –
No muscles clean as silk to swing our joints,
No lovely ivory joints that turn and slide:
We are weightless shades,
We wait upon the wind.
Tonight the music and the wind combine
And dead things dance,
Dead leaves and dust and ghosts.

No time, no night and day –
We crave for bodily cares or even pain
To give our dreadful souls a holiday.
Our souls outcast
From kindly human insincerity
Are whitening in the savage glare of truth.

THOMAS KETTLE
1880–1916

A prominent politician and prolific writer, Kettle was born in Dublin and educated at University College Dublin. A professor at the National University (UCD), he was an active member of the Irish Parliamentary Party and the Irish Volunteers. He fought with the Irish Brigade during the First World War and was killed in action.

TO MY DAUGHTER BETTY,
THE GIFT OF GOD

In wiser days, my darling rosebud, blown
To beauty proud as was your mother's prime,
In that desired, delayed, incredible time,
You'll ask why I abandoned you, my own,
And the dear heart that was your baby throne,
To dice with death. And, oh! they'll give you rhyme
And reason: some will call the thing sublime,
And some decry it in a knowing tone.
So here, while the mad guns curse overhead,
And tired men sigh, with mud for couch and floor,
Know that we fools, now with the foolish dead,
Died not for flag, nor King, nor Emperor,
But for a dream, born in a herdsman's shed,
And for the secret Scripture of the poor.

In the field, before Guillemont, Somme
September 4, 1916

BLANAID SALKELD
1880–1959

Born in Chittagong, India, Salkeld was raised in Dublin. She acted with the Abbey Theatre and her Dublin literary salon was attended by writers including Patrick Kavanagh and Flann O'Brien. Salkeld's poetry collections include *Hello, Eternity* (1933) and *The Fox's Covert* (1935).

CASUALTIES

Who would think the Spanish war
Flared like new tenure of a star,
The way our rhymes and writings are?
That Hilliard spilled his boxer's blood
Through Albacete's snow and mud,
And smiled to comrade death, Salud.
That Charlie Donnelly, small, frail,
And flushed with youth, was rendered pale –
But not with fear: in what queer squalor
Was smashed up his so ordered valour,
That rhythm, that steely earnestness,
That peace of poetry, to bless
Discordant thoughts of divers men –
Blue gaze that burned up lie and stain,
Put out by death.
I keep my breath:
So many grow upon my stem,
I cannot take their sap from them.
But to right charity, with spurs,
Through spite's asperity infernal –
My verity of verse
Is nothing else
But rattle of light shells
With no kernel,

Since Dublin boys have striven, and are
Knit to that alien soil, where war
Burns like the inception of a star.

WINIFRED M. LETTS
1882–1972

Poet, novelist, children's writer and playwright, Letts was born in England and raised and educated in Dublin. She worked as a nurse during the First World War and her groundbreaking poetry collection, *Hallowe'en and Poems of the War*, was published in 1916.

HALLOW-E'EN, 1914

'Why do you wait at your door, woman,
    Alone in the night?'
'I am waiting for one who will come, stranger,
    To show him a light.
He will see me afar on the road
    And be glad at the sight.'

'Have you no fear in your heart, woman,
    To stand there alone?
There is comfort for you and kindly content
    Beside the hearthstone.'
But she answered, 'No rest can I have
    Till I welcome my own.'

'Is it far he must travel to-night,
    This man of your heart?'
'Strange lands that I know not and pitiless seas
    Have kept us apart,
And he travels this night to his home
    Without guide, without chart.'

'And has he companions to cheer him?'
    'Aye, many,' she said.
'The candles are lighted, the hearthstones are swept,
    The fires glow red.
We shall welcome them out of the night –
    Our home-coming dead.'

THE CALL TO ARMS IN OUR STREET

There's a woman sobs her heart out,
    With her head against the door,
For the man that's called to leave her,
    – God have pity on the poor!
        But it's beat, drums, beat,
        While the lads march down the street,
        And it's blow, trumpets, blow,
        Keep your tears until they go.

There's a crowd of little children
    Who march along and shout,
For it's fine to play at soldiers
    Now their fathers are called out.
        So it's beat, drums, beat;
        But who'll find them food to eat?
        And it's blow, trumpets, blow,
        Ah! the children little know.

There's a mother who stands watching
    For the last look of her son,
A worn poor widow woman
    And he her only one.
        But it's beat, drums, beat,
        Though God knows when we shall meet;
        And it's blow, trumpets, blow:
        We must smile and cheer them so.

There's a young girl who stands laughing,
  For she thinks a war is grand,
And it's fine to see the lads pass,
  And it's fine to hear the band.
    So it's beat, drums, beat,
    To the fall of many feet;
    And it's blow, trumpets, blow,
    God go with you where you go
    To the war.

CASUALTY

John Delaney of the Rifles has been shot.
  A man we never knew,
  Does it cloud the day for you
  That he lies among the dead
Moving, hearing, heeding not?

No history will hold his humble name.
  No sculptured stone will tell
  The traveller where he fell;
  That he lies among the dead
Is the measure of his fame.

When our troops return victorious shall we care
  That deaf to all the cheers,
  Lacking tribute of our tears,
  He is lying with the dead
Stark and silent, God knows where?

John Delaney of the Rifles – who was he?
  A name seen on a list
  All unknown and all unmissed.
  What to us that he is dead? –
Yet he died for you and me.

SCREENS

(in a hospital)

They put the screens around his bed;
    A crumpled heap I saw him lie,
White counterpane and rough dark head,
    Those screens – they showed that he would die.

They put the screens about his bed;
    We might not play the gramophone,
And so we played at cards instead
    And left him dying there alone.

The covers on the screen are red,
    The counterpanes are white and clean; –
He might have lived and loved and wed
    But now he's done for at nineteen.

An ounce or more of Turkish lead,
    He got his wounds at Suvla Bay;
They've brought the Union Jack to spread
    Upon him when he goes away.

He'll want those three red screens no more,
    Another man will get his bed,
We'll make the row we did before
    But – Jove! – I'm sorry that he's dead.

THE DESERTER

There was a man, – don't mind his name,
Whom Fear had dogged by night and day.
He could not face the German guns
And so he turned and ran away.

Just that – he turned and ran away,
But who can judge him, you or I?
God makes a man of flesh and blood
Who yearns to live and not to die.
And this man when he feared to die
Was scared as any frightened child,
His knees were shaking under him,
His breath came fast, his eyes were wild.
I've seen a hare with eyes as wild,
With throbbing heart and sobbing breath.
But oh! it shames one's soul to see
A man in abject fear of death.
But fear had gripped him, so had death;
His number had gone up that day,
They might not heed his frightened eyes,
They shot him when the dawn was grey.
Blindfolded, when the dawn was grey,
He stood there in a place apart,
The shots rang out and down he fell,
An English bullet in his heart.
An English bullet in his heart!
But here's the irony of life, –
His mother thinks he fought and fell
A hero, foremost in the strife.
So she goes proudly; to the strife
Her best, her hero son she gave.
O well for her she does not know
He lies in a deserter's grave.

DEAD

In misty cerements they wrapped the word
My heart had feared so long: dead ... dead ... I heard
But marvelled they could think the thing was true
Because death cannot be for such as you.
So while they spoke kind words to suit my need
Of foolish idle things my heart took heed,
Your racquet and a worn-out tennis shoe,
Your pipe upon the mantel, – then a bird
Upon the wind-tossed larch began to sing
And I remembered how one day in Spring
You found the wren's nest in the wall and said
'Hush! ... listen! I can hear them quarrelling ...'
The tennis court is marked, the wrens are fled,
But you are dead, belovèd, you are dead.

ARNOLD BAX (DERMOT O'BYRNE)
1883–1953

Dermot O'Byrne was the pseudonym of the English composer Arnold Bax. Bax lived in Ireland for long periods and was influenced by the Celtic Revival, learning Gaelic and supporting the 1916 Rising. 'A Dublin Ballad – 1916' was banned by the British censor in Ireland, while his 'Shells at Oranmore' was reprinted on the fiftieth anniversary of the 1916 Rising.

MARTIAL LAW IN DUBLIN

By day this sunlit citadel of death
Flashes the arrogance of your bayonets,
Sharp biting gleams that sear our pride like teeth
Of the old dragonish sowing that begets
Even to-day as dangerous a birth
As ever bristled up from ancient earth.

Also by dusk we're home at your desire
To meditate upon your iron might.
Fool, have you padlocks for our inner fire?
Are there not long deep hours before the night
Flaming with signs of Her whose solemn eyes
Make empty all your brutish masteries?

SHELLS AT ORANMORE
April, 1916

Across this threatening tranquillity
Where are but ice-ground rocks for pasturage
Strange lumps of death came shrieking from the sea,
And still the earth's cold entrails quake with rage
That such a thing could be.

Never before had such a song been sung,
Never again perhaps while ages run
Shall the old pride of rock and wind be stung
By such an insolence winged across the sun,
So mad a challenge flung!

Man, have you roused again the unruly hosts
Sprung from the stony loins of rock and shale,
The flinty propagation of stark ghosts
Peopling these harshest townlands of the Gael,
These last wind-weary coasts?

THE IRISH MAIL
(Paddington)

That dank May-night her cheek was pale
Though she knew naught of Gall and Gael,
Mere lonely youth was all her pain
When I went out into the rain.

And at the platform barrier
There was disordered drunken stir;
My dream and ache I shouldered through
A mob of Khaki men and blue.

Red brutish faces smeared with sweat
Surged up like evil masks to set
Their hideousness to hound away
The wistful wonder of the day.

They mixed lewd talk of girls with beer;
One tattooed monster with a leer
Began to sentimentalize
About some Kathleen's arms and eyes.

Some child in Waterford, no doubt,
Or Cove of Cork or thereabout
Who met this thing from off the sea
And drained the lees of misery.

And others bragged between the roars
And hiccoughs round the carriage doors
They'ld soon make Paddy taste the rod
Of their fine empire's gilded god.

Before the mail-van on the ground
Damp packages were littered round,
And by the fogged and tawny flare
I read the place-names written there.

The first name held the labouring sigh
Of torn sands and the gannet's cry,
And the second wrought in me
Like cradle music of the Sidhe.

The third stung like an old sweet pain
Smiling through the Kerry rain,
More masterful to burn and bless
Than all the long day's tenderness.

And in my soul the hot tears strove
For the sad cleavage of my love,
My wounded land and your dark head
Sundered till all this love is dead.

Doors banged. A voice yelled vinously
'Kiss a damned Irish girl for me!'
A hoarse howl – and the train was gone
To harry the confusion on.

Easter 1916

A DUBLIN BALLAD — 1916

O write it up above your hearth
And troll it out to sun and moon,
To all true Irishmen on earth
Arrest and death come late or soon.

Some boy-o whistled *Ninety-eight*
One Sunday night in College Green,
And such a broth of love and hate
Was stirred ere Monday morn was late
As Dublin town had never seen.

And god-like forces shocked and shook
Through Irish hearts that lively day,
And hope it seemed no ill could brook.
Christ! for that liberty they took
There was the ancient deuce to pay!

The deuce in all his bravery,
His girth and gall grown no whit less,
He swarmed in from the fatal sea
With pomp of huge artillery
And brass and copper haughtiness.

He cracked up all the town with guns
That roared loud psalms to fire and death,
And houses hailed down granite tons
To smash our wounded underneath.

And when at last the golden bell
Of liberty was silenced, – then
He learned to shoot extremely well
At unarmed Irish gentlemen!

Ah! where were Michael and gold Moll
And Seumas and my drowsy self?
Why did fate blot us from the scroll?
Why were we left upon the shelf,

Fooling with trifles in the dark
When the light struck so wild and hard?
Sure our hearts were as good a mark
For Tommies up before the lark
At rifle practice in the yard!

Well, the last fire is trodden down,
Our dead are rotting fast in lime,
We all can sneak back into town,
Stravague about as in old time,

And stare at gaps of grey and blue
Where Lower Mount Street used to be,
And where flies hum round muck we knew
For Abbey Street and Eden Quay.

And when the devil's made us wise
Each in his own peculiar hell,
With desert hearts and drunken eyes
We're free to sentimentalize
By corners where the martyrs fell.

D.L. KELLEHER
1883–1958

Born in Cork, Kelleher first studied medicine, then literature, at Queen's College Cork. After graduating, he taught English literature in Dublin and Liverpool, and became a journalist in England. He is the author of a number of travel books and plays.

AN UPPER ROOM

*(In any town of the world
where patriots have striven)*

The noises of the street come up subdued,
And in some curious blend that has a new
Strange meaning in the mumbled many-hued
Soft spoken ghosts of words that have passed through
The talk of other generations gone before,
Until, it seems, one might push in my door
And say, 'I fought in such a year, but you forgot.
This house, this street, this town would flourish not
For you today if I had never been,
If I had never seen what I have seen.'
And as the door shuts out again the street
Hums with its mumbling noises from below
Where still those generations, to and fro,
Mysteriously greet.

THOMAS CARNDUFF
1886–1956

Carnduff was born in Belfast, the son of an army schoolmaster. He worked in the shipyards and served as a private in the Royal Engineers during the First World War. He published two books of poetry and several essays on culture and politics, and wrote plays for radio and for theatre.

GRAVES OF GALLIPOLI
(A few lines to 'Mr Turk')

There's a little stretch of country
Which lies along your beach.
Where some Christian lads are resting
Just within the crescent's reach:
There's a little cross above each mound.
Below it sleep the brave.
Who died for Britain's honour –
In Gallipoli's graves.

We don't want your bally country.
Nor your sun-scorched desert land;
You can keep your smug-faced friendship.
And your blood-besmeared hand:
You can raise your crescent banners.
You can give Mohammed praise;
But we don't forget our comrades
Of Gallipoli days.

You can wave your arms in triumph,
You can yell until you choke,
You can scheme of ridding Turkey
Of a galling Christian yoke;

While your warlike spirits rising,
And your crescent banners wave,
Don't forget the lion's watching
O'er Gallipoli's graves.

No heathen hand shall sacrilege
The Graves of Britain's dead,
No Turkish mob or Kamel horde
On Christian bones be fed.
You numbered us in thousands –
We'll come in countless waves,
If you claim our silent brothers,
In Gallipoli's graves.

MY LAND

She is my land and I love her,
And the stars that shine above her,
Love her too:
Sure with joy they shone around her,
When their jewelled lights first found her
Wet with dew.

She's a dear land with a story,
Steeped in history, wrapped in glory,
Through the years.
Crowning castles, grey and aged,
War-worn banners, torn and faded,
With her tears.

MESSINES, 17TH JUNE, 1917
(A Memory)

It seems but yesterday since we,
With flashing eye and naked sword
Uncowed by hell's artillery
Kept faith with country and with God.

'Twas June, and nature stood revealed
In all its beauty, yet we knew
To-morrow's sun would surely yield
The meadowed fields a crimson hue.

We thought of home – the hills of Down
Seemed far away, and yet we saw
With dreamy eyes Slieve Donard's crown
Erect above the clouds of war.

Beyond Messines our vision swept
O'er white-foamed sea and golden strand,
And silently each spirit kept
A tryst beneath the crimson land.

YPRES, SEPTEMBER, 1917
(A Memory)

'Tis sunset and the crimson glow
Spreads like a flaming fan
Across the sky, the white clouds flow
Transparent in its span.

Light breezes, scented with North Sea spray,
Breathe murmurs of remorse,
And leafless shell-scarred branches sway
Above each mangled corpse.

The ancient towers of Ypres loom grim
Athwart the crimson sky,
They silhouette their gaunt dark rim,
As if in mute reply.

Below the ramparts lie the plain
As far as eye can see.
Its beauty scarred with gory stain,
Of man's artillery.

'Neath Zillebeke's green fossilled lake
Pale ghostly faces gleam,
And round its slimy bottom rake,
The embers of their dream.

THE GRAVES OF THE UNKNOWN

I see a shattered farmhouse
With a murky stream hard by;
A field of yellow grass that once
Was pleasing to the eye.
Now poisoned with the battle fumes,
The listless blades are blown
Across a little mound of earth,
That holds a brave unknown.

Each morning at the break of dawn
God sends a little ray
Of happy sunshine o'er the hill,
To bid him time of day:
It seems to cast a halo where
A rough cross stands alone,
To the memory of a soldier lad –
A Britisher – Unknown.

O cold and damp the earthen bed
Which holds his mangled form.
Yet peaceful lies the pillowed head
Immune from wind and storm;
And often when the twilight fades
Across the sea from home.
A gentle breeze will stir the grass,
Above the brave unknown.

The scene is changed – I see a throng
Within a city square,
A grave and solemn multitude
In deep and earnest prayer:
A cenotaph, bedecked with flowers,
A flag half-mast is flown –
A nation's thought in glory crowns
The Graves of the unknown.

JOSEPH MARY PLUNKETT
1887–1916

Plunkett was born in Dublin, the son of a papal count. A member of the Gaelic League and co-founder of the *Irish Review* and the Irish Theatre, Plunkett was one of the main military strategists behind the 1916 Rising, a part for which he was executed.

WHEN I AM DEAD

When I am dead let not your murderous tears
Deface with their slow dropping my sad tomb
Lest your grey head grow greyer for my doom
And fill its echoing corridors with fears:
Your heart that my stone monument appears
While yet I love – O give it not to gloom
When I am dead, but let some joy illume
The ultimate Victory that stings and sears.

Already I can hear the stealthy tread
Of sorrow breaking through the hush of day;
I have no hope you will avert my dread,
Too well I know, that soon am mixed with clay,
They mourn the body who the spirit slay
And those that stab the living weep the dead.

THE CLAIM THAT HAS THE
CANKER ON THE ROSE

The claim that has the canker on the rose
Is mine on you, man's claim on Paradise
Hopelessly lost that ceaselessly he sighs
And all unmerited God still bestows;

The claim on the invisible wind that blows
The flame of charity to enemies
Not to the deadliest sinner, God denies –
Less claim than this have I on you, God knows.

I cannot ask for any thing from you
Because my pride is eaten up with shame
That you should think my poverty a claim
Upon your charity, knowing it is true
That all the glories formerly I knew
Shone from the cloudy splendour of your name.

NEW LOVE

The day I knew you loved me we had lain
Deep in Coill Doraca down by Gleann na Scath
Unknown to each till suddenly I saw
You in the shadow, knew oppressive pain
Stopping my heart, and there you did remain
In dreadful beauty fair without a flaw,
Blinding the eyes that yet could not withdraw
Till wild between us drove the wind and rain.
Breathless we reached the brugh before the west
Burst in full fury – then with lightning stroke
The tempest in my heart roared up and broke
Its barriers, and I swore I would not rest
Till that mad heart was worthy of your breast
Or dead for you – and then this love awoke.

BEFORE THE GLORY OF YOUR LOVE

Before the glory of your love
The beauty of the world is bowed
In adoration, and to prove
Your praises every Truth is proud:

Each silent witness testifies
Your wonder by its native worth
And dumbly its delight denies
That your wild music may have birth:

Only this madman cannot keep
Your peace, but flings his bursting heart
Forth to red battle, – while they weep
Your music who have held apart.

TO GRACE

On the morning of her christening,
April 7th, 1916

The powerful words that from my heart
Alive and throbbing leap and sing
Shall bind the dragon's jaws apart
Or bring you back a vanished spring;
They shall unseal and seal again
The fount of wisdom's awful flow,
So this one guerdon they shall gain
That your wild beauty still they show.
The joys of Spring leap from your eyes,
The strength of dragons in your hair,
In your young soul we still surprise
The secret wisdom flowing there;

But never word shall speak or sing
Inadequate music where above
Your burning heart now spreads its wing
In the wild beauty of your Love.

SEE THE CROCUS' GOLDEN CUP

See the crocus' golden cup
Like a warrior leaping up
At the summons of the spring,
'Guard turn out!' for welcoming
Of the new elected year.
The blackbird now with psalter clear
Sings the ritual of the day
And the lark with bugle gay
Blows reveillé to the morn,
Earth and heaven's latest born.

FRANCIS LEDWIDGE
1887–1917

Ledwidge was born in Slane, County Meath. He worked as a labourer until his poetry came to the attention of Lord Dunsany, who became his patron. Ledwidge enlisted in the Royal Inniskilling Fusiliers in 1914 and was killed in action.

THE CALL TO IRELAND

It's time to be up and be doing,
To be up and be doing now;
For, lo, anywhere around you,
From the vale to the mountain's brow,
The grass grows up through the harrow,
And the weather rusts on the plough.
Oh, let us be up and be doing
The work that is calling us now.

We have fought so much for the nation
In the tents we helped to divide;
Shall the cause of our common fathers
On our hearthstones lie denied?
For the price of a field we have wrangled
While the weather rusted the plough,
'Twas yours and 'twas mine, but 'tis ours yet
And it's time to be fencing it now.

There is gall in the cups of our children,
But ours is the goblet of wine.
They are crying away in the future:
Is their cause neither yours nor mine?
Better they die in their mothers
Than our shame be writ on their brow,
If we will not be up and be doing
The work that is calling us now.

IN THE MEDITERRANEAN —
GOING TO THE WAR

Lovely wings of gold and green
Flit about the sounds I hear,
On my window when I lean
To the shadows cool and clear.

Roaming, I am listening still,
Bending, listening overlong,
In my soul a steadier will,
In my heart a newer song.

THOMAS MacDONAGH

He shall not hear the bittern cry
In the wild sky where he is lain,
Nor voices of the sweeter birds
Above the wailing of the rain.

Nor shall he know when loud March blows
Thro' slanting snows her fanfare shrill,
Blowing to flame the golden cup
Of many an upset daffodil.

But when the Dark Cow leaves the moor,
And pastures poor with greedy weeds,
Perhaps he'll hear her low at morn
Lifting her horn in pleasant meads.

AFTER COURT MARTIAL

My mind is not my mind, therefore
I take no heed of what men say,
I lived ten thousand years before
God cursed the town of Nineveh.

The Present is a dream I see
Of horror and loud sufferings,
At dawn a bird will waken me
Unto my place among the kings.

And though men called me a vile name,
And all my dream companions gone,
'Tis I the soldier bears the shame,
Not I the king of Babylon.

WAR

Darkness and I are one, and wind
And nagging thunder, brothers all,
My mother was a storm. I call
And shorten your way with speed to me.
I am Love and Hate and the terrible mind
Of vicious gods, but more am I,
I am the pride in the lover's eye,
I am the epic of the sea.

TO MRS JOSEPH PLUNKETT

You shall not lack our little praise
If such can win your fair renown.
The halcyon of your lost days
We shall replace with living crown.

We see you not as one of us
Who so lament each little thing,
You profit more by honest loss,
Who lost so much, than song can sing.

This you have lost, a heart which bore
An ideal love, an ideal shame,
And earned this thing, for evermore
A noble and a splendid name.

A SOLDIER'S GRAVE

Then in the lull of midnight, gentle arms
Lifted him slowly down the slopes of death,
Lest he should hear again the mad alarms
Of battle, dying moans, and painful breath.

And where the earth was soft for flowers we made
A grave for him that he might better rest,
So, Spring shall come and leave it sweet arrayed,
And there the lark shall turn her dewy nest.

THE IRISH IN GALLIPOLI

Where Aegean cliffs with bristling menace front
The Threatening splendour of that isley sea
Lighted by Troy's last shadow, where the first
Hero kept watch and the last Mystery
Shook with dark thunder, hark the battle brunt!
A nation speaks, old Silences are burst.

Neither for lust of glory nor new throne
This thunder and this lightning of our wrath
Waken these frantic echoes, not for these
Our Cross with England's mingle, to be blown
On Mammon's threshold; we but war when war
Serves Liberty and Justice, Love and Peace.

Who said that such an emprise could be vain?
Were they not one with Christ Who strove and died?
Let Ireland weep but not for sorrow. Weep
That by her sons a land is sanctified
For Christ Arisen, and angels once again
Come back like exile birds to guard their sleep.

O'CONNELL STREET

A noble failure is not vain,
But hath a victory its own.
A bright delectance from the slain
Is down the generations thrown.

And, more than Beauty understands,
Has made her lovelier here, it seems.
I see white ships that crowd her strands,
For mine are all the dead men's dreams.

HOME

A burst of sudden wings at dawn,
Faint voices in a dreamy noon,
Evenings of mist and murmurings,
And nights with rainbows of the moon.

And through these things a wood-way dim,
And waters dim, and slow sheep seen
On uphill paths that wind away
Through summer sounds and harvest green.

This is a song a robin sang
This morning on a broken tree,
It was about the little fields
That call across the world to me.

PATRICK MACGILL
c. 1890–1963

MacGill was born in Glenties, County Donegal. He worked as an itinerant labourer until his poetry collection, *Gleanings from a Navvy's Scrapbook*, was published in 1911. He fought with the London Irish Rifles during the First World War and was wounded at the Battle of Loos in 1915.

IT'S A FAR, FAR CRY

It's a far, far cry to my own land,
    A hundred leagues or more,
To moorlands where the fairies flit
    In Rosses and Gweedore,
Where white-maned waves come prancing up
    To Dooran's rugged shore.

There's a cabin there by a holy well,
    Once blessed by Columbcille,
And a holly bush and a fairy fort
    On the slope of Glenties Hill,
Where the dancing feet of many winds
    Go roving at their will.

My heart is sick of the level lands,
    Where the wingless windmills be,
Where the long-nosed guns from dusk to dawn
    Are speaking angrily;
But the little home by Glenties Hill,
    Ah! that's the place for me.

A candle stuck on the muddy floor
    Lights up the dug-out wall,
And I see in its flame the prancing sea
    And the mountains straight and tall;
For my heart is more than often back
    By the hills of Donegal.

I OFT GO OUT AT NIGHT-TIME

I oft go out at night-time
    When all the sky's a-flare
And little lights of battle
    Are dancing in the air.

I use my pick and shovel
    To dig a little hole,
And there I sit till morning –
    A listening-patrol.

A silly little sickle
    Of moon is hung above;
Within a pond beside me
    The frogs are making love:

I see the German sap-head;
    A cow is lying there,
Its belly like a barrel,
    Its legs are in the air.

The big guns rip like thunder,
    The bullets whizz o'erhead,
But o'er the sea in England
    Good people lie abed.

And over there in England
  May every honest soul
Sleep sound while we sit watching
  On listening patrol.

BEFORE THE CHARGE
(Loos, 1915)

The night is still and the air is keen,
  Tense with menace the time crawls by,
In front is the town and its homes are seen,
  Blurred in outline against the sky.

The dead leaves float in the sighing air,
  The darkness moves like a curtain drawn,
A veil which the morning sun will tear
  From the face of death. – We charge at dawn.

THE LONDON LADS
(While standing to arms in billets,
La Beuvriere, July, 1915.)

Along the road in the evening the brown battalions wind,
With the trenches' threat of death before, the peaceful
    homes behind;
And luck is with you or luck is not as the ticket of fate
    is drawn,
The boys go up to the trench at dusk, but who will come
    back at dawn?

The winds come soft of an evening o'er the fields of golden
   grain,
The good sharp scythes will cut the corn ere we come
   back again;
The village girls will tend the grain and mill the Autumn
   yield
While we go forth to other work upon another field.

They'll cook the big brown Flemish loaves and tend the
   oven fire,
And while they do the daily toil of barn and bench and byre
They'll think of hearty fellows gone and sigh for them in
   vain –
The billet boys, the London lads who won't come
   back again.

THE DUG-OUT

Deeper than the daisies in the rubble and the loam,
   Wayward as a river the winding trenches roam,
Past bowed, decrepit dug-outs leaning on their props,
   Beyond the shattered village where the lightest limber stops;

Through fields untilled and barren, and ripped by shot and shell, –
   The bloodstained braes of Souchez, the meadows of Vermelles,
And poppies crown the parapet that rises from the mud –
   Where the soldiers' homes – the dug-outs – are built of clay
   and blood.

Our comrades on the level roofs, the dead men, waste away
   Upon the soldiers' frontier homes, the crannies in the clay;
For on the meadows of Vermelles, and all the country round,
   The stiff and still stare at the skies, the quick are underground.

A SOLDIER'S PRAYER

Givenchy village lies a wreck, Givenchy Church is bare,
No more the peasant maidens come to say their vespers
    there.
The altar rails are wrenched apart, with rubble littered o'er,
The sacred, broken sanctuary-lamp lies smashed upon the
    floor;
And mute upon the crucifix He looks upon it all –
The great white Christ, the shrapnel-scourged, upon the
    eastern wall.

He sees the churchyard delved by shells, the tombstones
    flung about,
And dead men's skulls, and white, white bones the shells have
    shovelled out;
The trenches running line by line through meadow fields
    of green,
The bayonets on the parapets, the wasting flesh between;
Around Givenchy's ruined church the levels, poppy-red,
Are set apart for silent hosts, the legions of the dead.

And when at night on sentry-go, with danger keeping tryst,
I see upon the crucifix the blood-stained form of Christ
Defiled and maimed, the merciful on vigil all the time,
Pitying his children's wrath, their passion and their crime.
Mute, mute He hangs upon His Cross, the symbol of
    His pain,
And as men scourged Him long ago, they scourge Him once
    again –
There in the lonely war-lit night to Christ the Lord I call,
'Forgive the ones who work Thee harm. O Lord, forgive
    us all.'

THOMAS MacGREEVY
1893–1967

MacGreevy was born in Kerry and moved to Dublin in 1910, where he worked for the Irish Land Commission. He was Second Lieutenant in the Royal Field Artillery during the First World War, after which he studied at Trinity College Dublin (TCD), becoming director of the National Gallery of Ireland in 1950. MacGreevy is considered to be the first Irish modernist poet.

NOCTURNE

To Geoffrey England Taylor, 2nd Lieutenant, RFA
'Died of wounds.'

I labour in a barren place,
Alone, self-conscious, frightened, blundering;
Far away, stars wheeling in space,
About my feet, earth voices whispering.

DE CIVITATE HOMINUM

To A.S.F.R.

The morning sky glitters
Winter blue.
The earth is snow-white,
With the gleam snow-white answers to sunlight,
Save where shell-holes are new,
Black spots in the whiteness –

A Matisse ensemble.

The shadows of whitened tree stumps
Are another white.

And there are white bones.

Zillebeke Lake and Hooge,
Ice gray, gleam differently,

Like the silver shoes of the model.

The model is our world,
Our bitch of a world.
Those who live between wars may not know
But we who die between peaces
Whether we die or not.

It is very cold
And, what with my sensations
And my spick and span subaltern's uniform,
I might be the famous brass monkey,
The *nature morte* accessory.

Morte . . . !
'Tis still life that lives,
Not quick life –

There are fleece-white flowers of death
That unfold themselves prettily
About an airman
Who, high over Gheluvelt,
Is taking a morning look round,
All silk and silver
Up in the blue.

I hear the drone of an engine
And soft pounding puffs in the air
As the fleece-white flowers unfold.

I cannot tell which flower he has accepted
But suddenly there is a tremor,
A zigzag of lines against the blue
And he streams down
Into the white,
A delicate flame,
A stroke of orange in the morning's dress.

My sergeant says, very low, 'Holy God!
'Tis a fearful death.'

Holy God makes no reply
Yet.

THE SIX WHO WERE HANGED

The sky turns limpid green.
The stars go silver white.
They must be stirring in their cells now –

Unspeaking likely!

Waiting for an attack
With death uncertain
One said little.

For these there is no uncertainty.

The sun will come soon,
All gold.

'Tis you shall have the golden throne –

It will come ere its time.
It will not be time,
Oh, it will not be time,
Not for silver and gold,
Not with green,
Till they all have dropped home,
Till gaol bells all have clanged,
Till all six have been hanged.

And after?
Will it be time?

There are two to be hanged at six o'clock,
Two others at seven,
And the others,
The epilogue two,
At eight.
The sun will have risen
And two will be hanging
In green, white and gold,
In a premature Easter.

The white-faced stars are silent,
Silent the pale sky;
Up on his iron car
The small conqueror's robot
Sits quiet.
But *Hail Mary! Hail Mary!*
They say it and say it,
These hundreds of lamenting women and girls
Holding Crucified Christs.

Daughters of Jerusalem . . .

Perhaps women have Easters.

There are very few men.
Why am I here?

At the hour of our death
At this hour of youth's death,
Hail Mary! Hail Mary!
Now young bodies swing up
Then
Young souls
Slip after the stars.
Hail Mary! Hail Mary!

Alas! I am not their Saint John –

Tired of sorrow,
My sorrow, their sorrow, all sorrow,
I go from the hanged,
From the women,
I go from the hanging;
Scarcely moved by the thought of the two
    to be hanged,
I go from the epilogue.

Morning Star, Pray for us!

What, these seven hundred years,
Has Ireland had to do
With the morning star?

And still, I too say,
Pray for us.

Mountjoy, March, 1921

AUSTIN CLARKE
1896–1974

Clarke was born in Dublin and educated at UCD, where he met writers of the Irish Literary Revival and became a lecturer in English. In addition to writing poetry, plays and three novels, Clarke was a radio broadcaster and a literary journalist.

THE SUBJECTION OF WOMEN

Over the hills the loose clouds rambled
From rock to gully where goat or ram
Might shelter. Below, the battering-ram
Broke in more cottages. Hope was gone
Under the legendary Maud Gonne,
For whom a poet lingered, sighed,
Drove out of mist upon a side-car,
Led back the homeless to broken fence,
Potato plot, their one defence,
And, there, despite the threat of Peelers,
With risky shovel, barrow, peeling
Their coats off, eager young men
Jumped over bog-drain, stone, to mend or
Restore the walls of clay; the police
Taking down names without a lease.
O she confronted the evictors
In Donegal, our victory.
When she was old and I was quickened
By syllables, I met her. Quickens
Stirred leafily in Glenmalure
Where story of Tudor battle had lured me.
I looked with wonder at the sheen
Of her golden eyes as though the Sidhe
Had sent a flame-woman up from ground
Where danger went, carbines were grounded.

Old now by luck, I try to count
Those years. I never saw the Countess
Markievicz in her green uniform,
Cock-feathered slouch hat, her Fianna form
Fours. From the railings of Dublin slums,
On the rickety stairs the ragged slumped
At night. She knew what their poverty meant
In dirty laneway, tenement,
And fought for new conditions, welfare
When all was cruel, all unfair.
With speeches, raging as strong liquor,
Our big employers, bad Catholics,
Incited by Martin Murphy, waged
War on the poorest and unwaged them.
Hundreds of earners were batoned, benighted,
When power and capital united.
Soon Connolly founded the Citizen Army
And taught the workers to drill, to arm.
Half-starving children were brought by ship
To Liverpool from lock-out, hardship.
'Innocent souls are seized by kidnappers,
And proselytisers. Send back our kids!'
Religion guffed.
                    The Countess colled
With death at sandbags in the College
Of Surgeons. How many did she shoot
When she kicked off her satin shoes?

Women rose out after the Rebellion
When smoke of buildings hid the churchbells,
Helena Maloney, Louie Bennett
Unioned the women workers bent
At sewing machines in the by-rooms
Of Dublin, with little money to buy
A meal, dress-makers, milliners,
Tired hands in factories.

Mill-girls
In Lancashire were organised,
Employers forced to recognise them:
This was the cause of Eva Gore-Booth,
Who spoke on platform, at polling-booth,
In the campaign for Women's Suffrage,
That put our double beds in a rage,
Disturbed the candle-lighted tonsure.
Here Mrs Sheehy-Skeffington
And others marched. On a May day
In the Phoenix Park, I watched, amazed,
A lovely woman speak in public
While crowding fellows from office, public
House, jeered. I heard that sweet voice ring
And saw the gleam of wedding ring
As she denounced political craft,
Tall, proud as Mary Wollstonecraft.
Still discontented, our country prays
To private enterprise. Few praise
Now Dr Kathleen Lynn, who founded
A hospital for sick babes, foundlings,
Saved them with lay hands. How could we
Look down on infants, prattling, cooing,
When wealth had emptied so many cradles?
Better than ours, her simple Credo.

Women, who cast off all we want,
Are now despised, their names unwanted,
For patriots in party statement
And act make worse our Ill-fare State.
The soul is profit. Money claims us.
Heroes are valuable clay.

SIX SENTENCES

BLACK AND TANS

No man can drink at any public-house
In Dublin but these roarers look for trouble
And break an open door in – Officer,
When spirits are at hand, the clock is moon:
Command these men, dreadful as what they hold,
Nor think the pockets of a pious poet
Have something worse in them than this poor curse.

CIVIL WAR

I

I could not praise too hot a heart
Or take a bellows to that blaze,
Yet, knowing I would never see him,
I gave my hand to Liam Mellowes.

II

They are the spit of virtue now,
Prating of law and honour,
But we remember how they shot
Rory O'Connor.

TO JAMES STEPHENS

Now that the iron shoe hangs by a nail
Once more and nobody has cared a damn,
Stick to the last of the leprechaun – I, too,
Have meddled with the anvil of our trade.

NO RECOMPENSE

Quality, number and the sweet divisions
Of reason may forget their schoolmen now,
And door-chill, body's heat, a common ill,
Grow monstrous in our sleep: I have endured
The enmity of my own mind that feared
No argument; but O when truth itself
Can hold a despairing tongue, what recompense
To find my name in any mortal mouth?

THE TALES OF IRELAND

The thousand tales of Ireland sink: I leave
Unfinished what I had begun nor count
As gain the youthful frenzy of those years;
For I remember my own passing breath,
Man's violence and all the despair of brain
That wind and river took in Glenasmole.

THE LAST REPUBLICANS

Because their fathers had been drilled,
Formed fours among the Dublin hills,
They marched together, countermarched
Along the Liffey valley, by larch-wood,
Spruce, pine road. Now, what living shout
Can halt them? Nothing of their faces
Is left, the breath has been blown out
Of them into far lonely places.

Seán Glynn pined sadly in prison. Seán
McNeela, Tony Darcy, John
McGaughey died on hunger-strike,
Wasting in the ribbed light of dawn.
They'd been on the run, but every dyke
Was spy. We shame them all. George Plant,
Quick fighter and a Protestant,
Patrick McGrath and Richard Goss,
Maurice O'Neill with Thomas Harte
Were executed when Dev's party
Had won the county pitch-and-toss,
Pat Dermody, John Kavanagh
John Griffith, John Casey, black-and-tanned.
At Mountjoy Gaol, young Charlie Kerins
Was roped; we paid five pounds to Pierpoint,
The Special Branch castled their plans,
Quicklimed the last Republicans.

from RIGHTFUL RHYMES

III

THE PLOT

So, in accordance with the plot,
MacDonagh, Plunkett, Pearse, were shot.
Campbell dropped dead in a mountainy spot,
Stephens, lifting the chamber pot.
O Conaire went, a ragged sot.
Higgins was coffined in a clot.
Twice-warned, when must I join our lot?

V

Maurice was in an Exhibition Hall
Where crowds of men and fashionable women
In bosoming dresses, embroidered shawl,
    Were moving. But a silent form
Was waiting in a corner. Up marble stairs,
He hurries from mirrored hall to hall, by glimmer
Of statues in niches. The Watcher stares,
    Red tabs upon his uniform.

Again he mounts the steps, alone,
Self-followed from mirrors to hall, the crowd
Of visitors waltzing below,
    And looking from the bannisters
Upon the billiard tables, playerless,
Green-shaded, saw the Watcher with a frown
Behind a pillar, standing motionless
    Casting the shadow of a policeman.

Once, wandering from a hollow of asphodel,
Still flowering at mid-night, he saw the glint of
Gigantic row of columns beyond the dell,
    Templed, conical, unbedecked
And knew they were the holy ictyphalli
Curled hair for bushwood, bark or skin
Heavily veined. He worshipped, a tiny satyr,
    Mere prick beneath those vast erections.

Joyously through a gateway, came a running
Of little Jewish boys, their faces pale
As ivory or jasmine, from Lebanon
    To Eden. Garlanded, caressing,
Little girls ran with skip and leap. They hurried,
Moon-pointing, beyond the gate. They passed a pale
Of sacred laurel, flowers of the future. Love
    Fathered him with their happiness.

Always in terror of Olympic doom,
He climbed, despite his will, the spiral steps
Outside a building to a cobwebbed top-room.
    There bric-à-brac was in a jumble,
His forehead was distending, ears were drumming
As in the gastric feved of his childhood.
Despite his will, he climbed the steps, stumbling
    Where Mnemosyne lay in dust.

Dreaming, as sunlight idled, Maurice believed
He darted by with sticks of gelignite,
Unbarracked County Limerick, relieved
    His fellows, fought to the last bullet.
Daring Republican of hillside farm-yards,
Leader of raiding parties, digging at night,
He blew up lorries, captured British arms.
    Rain-hid, he cycled to Belmullet.

Drowsily Maurice was aware
Of someone by his bed. A melancholy
Man, sallow, with black moustache, sat there.
    'Where am I?' Voice was hollow.
The other brooded: 'Think.' His gaze
Was so reproachful, what was his guilt?
Could it be parricide? The stranger
    Still murmured: 'Think … Think.'

X

In Winter around the fire,
Soldiers at a camp
After the long rout.
Brass helmet tipped with coal
By the fender and fire-guard.
A history-book lying on the floor.

In the dark, secured,
They lie. Every night
The news is going into the past:
The airman lost in Mozambique,
Far shouting at the General Election
And the Great War ending
In drums, processions
And a hooded Preacher
At the Pro-Cathedral.

They lie, in the dark,
Watching the fire, on the edge
Of a storybook jungle: they watch
The high boots of the colonists.

The scales are broken.
Justice cannot reach them:
All the uproar of the senses,
All the torment of conscience,
All that twists and breaks.
Without memory or insight,
The soul is out of sight
And all things out of sight
And being half gone they are happy.

They lie in bed, listening
To the sleet against the bars, train
That whistles from the country. A horse-car
Waits under the oil-lamp at the station
And turns into a drosky.

AT THE HOUSE OF COMMONS

Foot-handed, I waited in the Lobby,
Poor relative from Athlone or lob
In boots, for the Father of the House.
Too soon I would hear his greeting: 'How do
You do?' and ask him weakly:
'Sir, can I write for your new Weekly?'
Quickly I saw him talling before me
With a smile, then, frown: T.P. O'Connor
In summer-grey frockcoat. Three, four,
Members came out. One glanced from the conning
Tower of a submarine in the foam-race,
Marked me; a small man, determined, chubbed.
I recognised him – Mr Churchill,
And drew back, servile as our race.
Darkly, that young-man-killing Warlock,
Lord Kitchener who had no Last Post –
Drowned finger pointing from a ripped poster –
Asked: 'What did *you* do in the Great War?'

MONK GIBBON
1896–1987

Born in Dublin and educated at Oxford University, William Monk Gibbon served in the First World War until he was invalided out in 1918. His collected poems, *This Insubstantial Pageant*, was published in 1951. He also wrote novels, travel books, essays and literary criticism, including a memoir of Yeats.

SOLDIERING

We have hardened our hearts within us, our hearts are
    grown very hard;
Hard words in our mouths are spoken, hard are the roads
    we tread;
We have forgotten softness; we have put by those things;
Hard days, hard nights, before us – and a hard bed.

The five steps up to a doorway, a path through the fields
    at dusk,
Hard thoughts have taken their places, hard are the jests
    we make.
All that might bring remembrance, all that might
    wake regret,
Our hearts are hardened against them – lest they
    should break.

LOST HOPES

(To any stranger)

And you,
And you,
Look at me, gaze into my eyes and tell me
How many hopes you buried in stark graves,
In little narrow graves,
Such as a dog has, or a pauper.
And you,
What tender, delicate, graceful child was yours
In what grave lain?

Sound, trump!
Yield up your content, coffins. Reintegrate,
Pale ghosts!
No! earth, lie heavy,
Lest at that sound too many walk abroad,
And mine amongst them.

ICI

(A recollection of the First World War)

'Ici' – presumably christened
With the aid of a Parlez-vous,
When asked for the French equivalent
Of 'Here! Come Here!', and who knew

Some broken-hearted old lady
Would never see her again,
Now that our unit was moving
And her stolen pet was gone –

Sits on the box of a wagon,
Or gambols free at each halt.
It was too late to return her
When we learnt of the culprit's fault –

Proud as a tiny princess,
In a coat that was silver-curled,
She perched beside her abductor
As if she had bought the world.

Venus and Mars ignore her,
She could whirl, curvet and prance:
But, as a mere camp-follower,
They leave her to take her chance.

Presently a lustful mongrel
Makes her, perforce, his friend;
Rapes her, to our embarrassment,
For three whole days on end.

The midget form on the box-seat
Swelled and grew less elate,
She seemed – like millions around her –
A little puzzled by fate.

Her litter in due course arriving,
It proved beyond her strength
To deal with this new situation;
Endurance failed her at length.

Patient and uncomplaining,
Breathing a sigh at most,
We watched the princess yield up
Her little canine ghost.

Great events are forgotten
In the changing tides of time:
But Ici haunts me, sixty-six years on,
As I write this trivial rhyme.

C.S. LEWIS
1898–1963

Born in Belfast and educated in England, Lewis served with the Somerset Light Infantry in France during the First World War and was wounded in 1917. He studied at Oxford University and was a fellow and tutor there until 1954, when he became Professor of Medieval and Renaissance English at Cambridge University. His poetry collections include *Spirits in Bondage* (1919).

FRENCH NOCTURNE
(Monchy-Le-Preux)

Long leagues on either hand the trenches spread
And all is still; now even this gross line
Drinks in the frosty silences divine,
The pale, green moon is riding overhead.

The jaws of a sacked village, stark and grim,
Out on the ridge have swallowed up the sun,
And in one angry streak his blood has run
To left and right along the horizon dim.

There comes a buzzing plane: and now, it seems
Flies straight into the moon. Lo! where he steers
Across the pallid globe and surely nears
In that white land some harbour of dear dreams!

False, mocking fancy! Once I too could dream,
Who now can only see with vulgar eye
That he's no nearer to the moon than I
And she's a stone that catches the sun's beam.

What call have I to dream of anything?
I am a wolf. Back to the world again,
And speech of fellow-brutes that once were men
Our throats can bark for slaughter: cannot sing.

VICTORY

Roland is dead, Cuchulain's crest is low,
The battered war-gear wastes and turns to rust,
And Helen's eyes and Iseult's lips are dust
And dust the shoulders and the breasts of snow.

The faerie people from our woods are gone,
No Dryads have I found in all our trees.
No Triton blows his horn about our seas
And Arthur sleeps far hence in Avalon.

The ancient songs they wither as the grass
And waste as doth a garment waxen old,
All poets have been fools who thought to mould
A monument more durable than brass.

For these decay: but not for that decays
The yearning, high, rebellious spirit of man
That never rested yet since life began
From striving with red Nature and her ways.

Now in the filth of war, the baresark shout
Of battle, it is vexed. And yet so oft
Out of the deeps, of old, it rose aloft
That they who watch the ages may not doubt.

Though often bruised, oft broken by the rod,
Yes, like the phoenix, from each fiery bed
Higher the stricken spirit lifts its head
And higher – till the beast become a god.

APOLOGY

If men should ask, Despoina, why I tell
Of nothing glad nor noble in my verse
To lighten hearts beneath this present curse
And build a heaven of dreams in real hell,

Go you to them and speak among them thus:
'There were no greater grief than to recall,
Down in the rotting grave where the lithe worms crawl,
Green fields above that smiled so sweet to us.'

Is it good to tell old tales of Troynovant
Or praises of dead heroes, tried and sage,
Or sing the queens of unforgotten age,
Brynhild and Maeve and virgin Bradamant?

How should I sing of them? Can it be good
To think of glory now, when all is done,
And all our labour underneath the sun
Has brought us this – and not the thing we would?

All these were rosy visions of the night,
The loveliness and wisdom feigned of old.
But now we wake. The East is pale and cold,
No hope is in the dawn, and no delight.

DEATH IN BATTLE

Open the gates for me,
Open the gates of the peaceful castle, rosy in the West,
In the sweet dim Isle of Apples over the wide seas breast,
Open the gates for me!

Sorely pressed have I been
And driven and hurt beyond bearing this summer day,
But the heat and the pain together suddenly fall away,
All's cool and green.

But a moment agone,
Among men cursing in fight and toiling, blinded I fought,
But the labour passed on a sudden even as a passing thought,
And now – alone!

Ah, to be ever alone,
In flowery valleys among the mountains and silent
    wastes untrod,
In the dewy upland places, in the garden of God,
This would atone!

I shall not see
The brutal, crowded faces around me, that in their toil
    have grown
Into the faces of devils – yea, even as my own –
When I find thee,

O Country of Dreams!
Beyond the tide of the ocean, hidden and sunk away,
Out of the sound of battles, near to the end of day,
Full of dim woods and streams.

EILEEN SHANAHAN
1901–1979

Born and educated in Dublin, Shanahan worked as a secretary in the League of Nations in Geneva, but returned to Dublin in 1940 when France was invaded, and lived in England thereafter. Most of her work remains unpublished.

FREE STATE

O Ireland once as Rosaleen
Your woes were heard across the sea
But now assuaged, we've lost a queen
And found instead a bourgeoisie.

1925

PASTORALE, 1946

The merry skeleton lay on the ground,
Eased of his flesh, so happy dead
To fill himself with flowers instead of bread.
The sun poured through
The wind his bones made sweet
While the incredible financier
Drove by the fields of wheat
In lands unravaged, winner of all wars,
Seeking to feed the satisfied.
But he whose humble breathing was denied
Forgot the child flower-spattered at his side,
The fleshless son he sooner died to save
And dying left him neither bread nor grave.

JIMMY KENNEDY
1902–1984

Kennedy was born in Omagh and educated at TCD. He served as a captain in the British Army's Royal Artillery during the Second World War. His songs have been performed by Louis Armstrong, Nat King Cole and Elvis Presley.

WE'RE GOING TO HANG OUT THE WASHING ON THE SIEGFRIED LINE

We're going to hang out the washing on the Siegfried Line.
Have you any dirty washing, mother dear?
We're gonna hang out the washing on the Siegfried Line
'cause the washing day is here.

Whether the weather may be wet or fine
We'll just rub along without a care.
We're going to hang out the washing on the Siegfried Line
If the Siegfried Line's still there.

Mother dear I'm writing you from somewhere in France,
Hoping to find you well,
Sergeant says I'm doing fine, a soldier and a pal
Here's a song that we don't sing, this'll make you laugh.

We're going to hang out the washing on the Siegfried Line.
Have you any dirty washing, mother dear?
We're gonna hang out the washing on the Siegfried Line
'cause the washing day is here.

Whether the weather may be wet or fine
We'll just rub along without a care.
We're going to hang out the washing on the Siegfried Line
If the Siegfried Line's still there.

PATRICK MacDONOGH
1902–1961

Born into a Protestant middle-class family in Dublin,
MacDonogh was educated at TCD and worked in public
relations at the Guinness brewery, Dublin. His five collections
of poetry include *Over the Water* (1943) and *One Landscape
Still* (1958).

OVER THE WATER

Through weeks of this windy April with horror hawking reason
Reiterated boasting of thrush and blackbird wakened
Anger and lonely hatred that they in their happy season
Cared less for her lost grieving than rapt unknowing faces
She scanned in brittle streets. But oh! returning soon,
Curlew and plover only were brothers to her sorrow
Crying from lonely tillage to a house of empty rooms,
They and that ragged heron who laboured up to tree-tops
Leaving reed-broken silver before her troubled movements.

May brought the south to mellow April's harsh brightness,
But brought no timid stirring of hope to my darling,
There where the wild duck convoys her young from reedy islands
Through narrows wharfed by lilies, she saw their shadows darken,
Cruciform on the water when foul birds from the sea
Came in for prey. But I had comfort slogging
Hard roads with marching hundreds, lulling a private grief,
Dulling in rhythmic stupor the fierce assaults of longing
And dreading memory less than lacerated feet.

Though noon will drowse in roses her young days carry coolness
Cropped from Meath's dawning acres or stolen from shadows
Under Dunboyne's tall hedges that lately shut the moon
From those more lucky lovers whom flitting dusk had gathered

In gentle couples. Here skies have scarcely room
To house their clouds of bombers, yet had I but my darling,
We'd mix our hate with pity for stripling airmen doomed
To their own strange damnation, and in a night of horror
Softly we'd lie together under a bomber's moon.

WAR WIDOW

These are the self-same ways you walked, crazy with grief,
Waking this sleeping water to hear your stumbling woes,
Blind with importunate tears when the wild duck rose from
      the lake,
And hoping your heart might break before the fall of the leaf.
But sight was stark in the dawn, and the heart refused to break,
And, thronged or alone, it ached until, with the star-bright sloes,
The pains of the dying year were lost in the pangs of spring
And, breaking from blinding lilies, the clamorous drake arose –
But the wild duck moaned in the ozier bed, spreading a
      wounded wing.

These are the willow boughs that wept, casting wild shade,
When, with protesting murmurs, you saw in love's disguise
The face of the warring world, as the moon came over the hill,
And the individual heart, the innocent life betrayed
By nobleness of mind serving a brutal will.
Then the quivering branch was still, and stillness grew in
      your eyes,
Struggling no more against grief and, lifting your listening head
To hear the wild duck moaning, you laughed your gay goodbyes,
From a heart that you hoped was dying to a love already dead.

Break no more from the willow branch emblems of grief,
For you that were death's rival must take a live love soon,
Drowning in curtained laughter the wild duck's endless moan,
And walking no more alone in woods where a falling leaf
Brings him again from the sky who journeyed proud and alone,
Doomed like the conquering drone, shattered in blazing noon –
Give him again to death! for your time draws near to break
This grief-charmed ghostly circle, your six-years' honeymoon,
And the dead leaves mixed in the waking earth fell for the
    live leaf's sake.

FRANCIS STUART
1902–2000

Born in Australia to Protestant parents from County Antrim, Stuart was raised in Ireland and educated in England. He smuggled arms for the IRA during the Irish Civil War and was subsequently interned. During the Second World War he lectured at Berlin University. He also broadcast on Berlin radio which led to his imprisonment by the Allies. During his long and prolific writing career he authored novels, poetry and journalism.

MORNING IN A TOWN
UNDER BOMBARDMENT

The yellow lamp-light sheds itself
Over the patterned walls and gleaming delf
And darker blood impartially
And irresponsible as is the sea.

The lamp-light in the quiet room
Gleams like the paint on Eastern tomb,
And from the East the unwelcome dawn
Falls on the outside blind that hangs half torn.

1918

IN TIME OF WAR

I had no peace when there was peace,
I had no light when all was lit
By the world's glittering wealth and ease.
I saw a noisy swarm of bees
Around the empty hive of death.

It is evening, it is late,
And I, like a bird on the bough,
A raven black as ink,
Or an owl, secret and slow,
Folded and still and blind,
In the depths of the forest wait
For words to fade from the mind
And the sun of day sink.

IRELAND

Over you falls the sea light, festive yet pale,
As though from the trees hung candles alight in a gale
To fill with shadows your days, as the distant beat
Of waves fills the lonely width of many a western street.
Bare and grey and hung with berries of mountain ash,
Drifting through ages with tilted fields awash,
Steeped with your few lost lights in the long Atlantic dark,
Sea-birds' shelter, our shelter and ark.

Berlin, 1943

THE TREES IN THE SQUARE

I see from the Linden trees out in the square
(I see without looking, with only a glance at them)
More than from hours of people, of books and talk,
How to pass through these deathly days, how to walk
Over this desert of ours, both in leaf and bare.

Balanced above the earth on my own strong stem.
In their loose centre, in their blown breast
There is shadow, they slant their leaves to the sun
And are green, but within there is rest
Beyond green, beyond words and worlds.

Berlin, 1944

BERLIN, 1944

Last night in that cafe
In a city in the middle of Europe,
Poised on the brink
Of the storm that was to be the end
To all that we know or think,
For a flash when I heard you say
A book's name: *Gone With the Wind*,
All was flowing, fleeting, slipping away
Until nothing was left, nothing was sure
But ourselves in the half-empty cafe,
We so rich, so frighteningly poor,
Your black eyes so hauntingly bright,
And only a moment left, an hour, a night.

OUT OF THE SWIM

My prison codes are branded on my arm
No long detentions, six shortish spells in all
Which doesn't shame me though it does me harm
And no-one phones and no-one comes to call.

The mattress broken, the garden is in brambles,
To those not in the know it seems a shambles.
I'm guilty yes, but oh I have compassion
And am of course completely out of fashion.

COOGAN'S WOOD

They played till the dusk of summer in the wood
By the stream full of boulders under the hill;
And now like a shadow and bell within my blood
Their cries and the wood in the dusk are throbbing still.

Fold me once more, dark leaves, shelter the earth
And men from the desert heat and fevered din
Of war. Sweetness blooms there and there sways mirth
And deep in the stream-lit dusk peace blossoms within.

Ah, children do you go there summer days
Or are you too old now still to race and cry
From pool to pool? And is it only I
Who turn once more along those dusky ways
Into that wood, into that world, from one
Where life is shrunk to what can be fired from a gun?

EWART MILNE
1903–1987

Milne was born and educated in Dublin. He served as an ambulance driver for the British Medical Unit during the Spanish Civil War. His first of many volumes of poems, *Forty North Fifty West*, was published in 1938.

SPEECH ON BEHALF OF INISHFAIL

It is time we, the Irish, men and women,
It is time we should praise the great Russians,
The men and women of Lenin and Stalin.

It is time we should honour without stint
Their partisan fighters and nameless heroes
And our hearts leap up before their slain.

That girl planting a sunflower seed
Lovingly in a garden's ruins
Is our sister of Kiltartan plain.

That old woman blessing herself in the snows,
Embracing her soldiers, her sons, her Red Army men,
That old woman is our mother freed.

Now that the blackbird hunts the fowler
And lures him by its song to doom,
Now should we speak and praise the true ones

Who hold the bridgehead by the river
Running redder than the fuchsia:
Now by the Shannon praise the Sarsfields of the Don.

THINKING OF ARTOLAS

Sirs and Senoras, let me tell you a story.
A story neither of long ago nor faraway
But close enough now and to you unhappily.
We will call it Going-Into-History
And you all know History is a cruel country
Where tiger terraces crouch drinking rivers waterless
And sheep immobilised by sombrero shepherds' piping ...
It could be set in Estremadura or Cordova,
Time crawling like inches and napoleonic wars
Dogeared in textbooks seeming the latest in strategy –
At least until recently. Or as Shaw might have said
The life force gets going but man has his lag ...
True. And to gain on his lag must man lose his leg,
And truncate himself, as in Estremadura?

Well, at Casada's we ate ortolans elsewhere we drank coffee.
In the Gran Via in the Colon we went into conference.
All day the starlings on the Ramblas whispered,
All day the dead air pacified the street,
Fat pigeons swaggered on the Plaza Catalunya.
It was easy enough to analyse an ortolan,
Conjure pigeon into pie: translate con leche ...

But the starlings worried me, and their whispering,
I could never understand their whispering.
It weaved breathlessly up and up like the Coulin –
Or like that dissonance outsoaring ecstacy, heard
Near any roadside or beside any bed, disrupting the
Lovers enlaced, singing with no sound and saying
'O the world is bright and empty.'

At Madrid we dined with the newspaper bunch.
So-and-so shouted they all called him a Fascist –
There *had* been whispers – but he didn't care
He shouted for Empire. That was all right
Empire shouted for him – one supposes, somewhere.
All day I was a method of analysis … Did my heart, Tomas,
Or your depthless eyes tell me analysis was cowardly
While Los Madrilenos were barricading their old
    Madrid out?
… All day So-and-so the Fascist was blustering.
I analysed his quality as extreme
Scatology and efficiency walking backwards, with a shrug …
But sadly I knew the whispering starlings
Wintering would rise from the Plaza Catalunya
Before I returned.

With Jarama held they brought him in, the tankist.
From his Georgian hair the blood smiled through,
And smiled on the paving and from the verandah
Smiled as it dripped and adventured below …
In parks they dream of penny murder non-intervention –
He took the hammered blow and said Salud –
All day my heart with love was helpless, all day I knew
He had gone further than I towards finding a synthesis.
With Jarama held his wound wore on, the Georgian
Who held a dawnstar and not nettles as we do –
Whisper, starlings, whisper! Be incorruptible and saying
'O the world is bright and always living'.

Sirs and Senoras, let me end my story –
I show you earth, earth formally,
And Two on guard with the junipers.
Two, Gael and Jew side by side in a trench
Gripping antique guns to flick at the grasshoppers
That zoomed overhead and the moon was rocking.

Two who came from prisonment, Gael because of Tone,
Jew because of human love, the same for Jew as German –
Frail fragments both, chipped off and forgotten readily ...

I set them together, Izzy Kupchik and Donnelly;
And of that date with death among the junipers
I say only, they kept it: and record the exploded
Spreadeagled mass when the moon was later
Watching the wine that baked earth was drinking.
Such my story, Sirs and Senoras. Whether you like it
Or pay a visit to your vomitorium, is all one ...
Perhaps you'll like junipers and a moon steadied,
High baked earth and night's formalism,
Remembering that History is always a cruel country
And crueller man than April.

THE WIND OF BOMBERS MOON

Who shall sing you among the island peoples,
Who shall know you when the sea bursts and delivers?
Shall there be one to greet you wading the shore marshes,
Rising before you in extended flight the indignant
    water-birds?

Only the child and the morning know you.
The sun's brassy violence knows. Yes, and I sing you,
Hearing faintly among dry bones your new world
    symphony.
But only girl and boy will savour your rhapsodic
    abundance.

I want to hear their shout along these battered squares,
Where a pillared dust is blown like cinder ash on Pompeii;
Here I want your profile etched: a landscape bright
    with sound.
I want your laughter lightening darkened street and street.

I want the curlews back that innocently blurr the moon.
Who shall sing you when the pitted pain has passed?
The bridge of skeleton and stench be built that brings
    you near,
Soldier and airman freed and skies like foreheads clear,
    serene.

SIERRAN VIGIL

Where the lazy wall is down
Where the lemon leaf is poisoned
Where the road is holed: where gloom of
Cloud and sky is blessing: we

Speaking no good word for war
For heroics, for the kingly dust,
Exalting not the self-evident murder,
Turn: not assuming hope: turn, offering hands.

Where blue is war zone's leading light
Where blue lights plead for morning: where
Doorways wince the darkness out:
We there, ill-starred too, offer hands.

Guitarists who with *Yi Yi Yi*
Haunted melody with reflection
Heed now the rifles' acid action
And find through fingering a new notation.

The boy with the goats takes over, takes power.
The boy with the goats, green Gabriel still,
Dyes the terraced hillsides with his Never ...
And in his river

Here where the lazy wall is down
Here where the lemon leaf is poisoned
Where the road is holed, is trustless,
We, remembering love, kill cruelly ...

Kill cruelty. *Hi* and you nestle in gunfire, poet!
Hi and you mow down forests briefly.
Hi and you gain the cunning touch
That low on Andalusian evenings strikes your match.

For this is the act, the chorus argument.
This is the work we have said is to do.
This is the thing now trust and fear both fail
We have resorted to:

Though no man here is hero, and we
Line up defending the unheroic unalterably.
Who taught us War? This time
Those who did not begin will finish it ...

For Chico's sake, for Chica's pride ...

And where the lazy wall is down
Where the lemon leaf is poisoned
Where the road is holed, is trustless,
Here shall we grow the olive, and the orange blithely.

GEORGE BUCHANAN
1904–1989

A poet and novelist, Buchanan was raised in County Antrim but moved to London and became a journalist. He served in the RAF during the Second World War. Buchanan's poetry collections include *Conversation with Strangers* (1959) and *Inside Traffic* (1976).

ON FILM

Here are the snapshots of history. Look at Hitler
before his servile crowd, the troops marching
half-asleep in a cocky synchronous footwork,
statesmen jumping up and down on the steps of a building.
We're slightly ashamed to have lived
through such documentaries. Victory, revolution,
the rise of the masses – out of the high-flown texts
they drop to a visual scrapbook usually depressing
or cruel or utterly desperate. Watching, we lose
admiration for those glorified conquests, expansion
        of frontiers,
the low objectives of nations.

ON THE DEAD KILLED
IN TWO WORLD WARS

The number of the killed
was a minor consideration. They were thoughts
in the thinking of a High Command
accustomed to shoots on the moors. Uniformed crowds
ran on the wet ground:

game flushed by their officers for German guns.
Oh monuments, mention of bravery,
the stone-carved glory!

In the Second War they were on shipboard
or wings
or wheels,
machine-parts in a military industry,
more sparingly killed; and less trouble was taken
over the granite memorials.

Today the sun rises
on a different country. Those wars have gone into the
    wet grass.
The armies are forgotten. We have even forgotten
the causes for which the armies died.

New wars
are flame creeping on coloured mapsheets. Is peaceful
    intention
to be found only in noisy crowds in the square?
Can the sum-total of nobodies be taken as
the serious thinker whose advice will everywhere
carry the day?

KILWAUGHTER
(to C.H.L.B.)

He didn't believe, as suggested,
that God was dead; couldn't quite
mock the roadside slogans WHERE
WILL YOU SPEND ETERNITY?

Freshness came from the hillside hedges
and jocose people not downcast
under those trickling roofs. In the damp
rectory inquisitive sons, singing
at the piano, finding a foothold
in the high trees, playing at the
river, made unexpected arguments,
a generation further on –
where the event was a downfall, as disease
took empires to the artillery-
conditioned mud.

The small boys clambered on rocks and
the sky was occupied by
a benign spectator. They valued
unploughed land, the crookedness
of a stream, books on the exotic
past, barbarian procedures
as well as plantlike ecstasy;
sang hymns in church; but time
was the enemy. Carefully
in the white light they sloughed off
protective faiths, moved to
skin and bones. The subtle tame
took over from the wild, and acts
of thoughts from country wandering.
The human sea was calling, to leave
the superabundance of grass for
dry minds. The poets grew up
to be recruited for another war.

POETS OF THE NEXT CENTURY

Poets of the next century, forgive
our plaints at two world wars and pandemonium on an
    island of Japan.
Was it not natural to be nervous
of what a bomb can do? and not stop worrying
about a further wave of droppings from the air?
The biggest risk was to have trust in others.
Would we dare? We counted on others' fears and ours.
We wouldn't be the first to exclude the bomb from
    our defence.
No one argued for
mutual reliance all round.

WAR PILOT

If he should not come back from a flight,
would he exist only in the memory
of a friendly woman? Did the clergy promise
a better end? She says 'I'll love you as if you were
to live always. What else do you expect?
Do you suppose the Group Captains remember
or officials at the Air Ministry?' –
He returns next day in the pink morning.
Preoccupied with fate he asks 'Am I dead?
Is this the other side?'

C. DAY LEWIS
1904–1972

Day Lewis was born in County Laois and educated at Oxford University, where he was Professor of Poetry from 1951–6. He was appointed Poet Laureate of England in 1968. As well as writing poetry he translated works by Virgil and wrote detective novels under a pseudonym. His *Collected Poems* was published in 1954.

BOMBERS

Through the vague morning, the heart preoccupied,
A deep in air buried grain of sound
Starts and grows, as yet unwarning –
The tremor of baited deepsea line.

Swells the seed, and now tight sound-buds
Vibrate, upholding their paean flowers
To the sun. There are bees in sky-bells droning,
Flares of crimson at the heart unfold.

Children look up, and the elms spring-garlanded
Tossing their heads and marked for the axe.
Gallant or woebegone, alike unlucky –
Earth shakes beneath us: we imagine loss.

Black as vermin, crawling in echelon
Beneath the cloud-floor, the bombers come:
The heavy angels, carrying harm in
Their wombs that ache to be rid of death.

This is the seed that grows for ruin,
The iron embryo conceived in fear.
Soon or late its need must be answered
In fear delivered and screeching fire.

Choose between your child and this fatal embryo.
Shall your guilt bear arms, and the children you want
Be condemned to die by the powers you paid for
And haunt the houses you never built?

NEWSREEL

Enter the dream-house, brothers and sisters, leaving
Your debts asleep, your history at the door:
This is the home for heroes, and this loving
Darkness a fur you can afford.

Fish in their tank electrically heated
Nose without envy the glass wall: for them
Clerk, spy, nurse, killer, prince, the great and the defeated,
Move in a mute day-dream,

Bathed in this common source, you gape incurious
At what your active hours have willed –
Sleep-walking on that silver wall, the furious
Sick shapes and pregnant fancies of your world.

There is the mayor opening the oyster season:
A society wedding: the autumn hats look swell:
An old crocks' race, and a politician
In fishing-waders to prove that all is well.

Oh, look at the warplanes! Screaming hysteric treble
In the long power-drive, like gannets they fall steep.
But what are they to trouble –
These silver shadows to trouble your watery,
    womb-deep sleep?

See the big guns, rising, groping, erected
To plant death in your world's soft womb.
Fire-bud, smoke blossom, iron seed projected –
Are these exotics? They will grow nearer home.

Grow nearer home – and out of the dream-house stumbling
One night into a strangling air and the flung
Rags of children and thunder of stone niagaras tumbling,
You'll know you slept too long.

WATCHING POST

A hill flank overlooking the Axe valley.
Among the stubble a farmer and I keep watch
For whatever may come to injure our countryside –
Light-signals, parachutes, bombs, or sea-invaders.
The moon looks over the hill's shoulder, and hope
Mans the old ramparts of an English night.

In a house down there was Marlborough born. One night
Monmouth marched to his ruin out of that valley.
Beneath our castled hill, where Britons kept watch,
Is a church where the Drakes, old lords of this countryside,
Sleep under their painted effigies. No invaders
Can dispute their legacy of toughness and hope.

Two counties away, over Bristol, the searchlights hope
To find what danger is in the air tonight.
Presently gunfire from Portland reaches our valley
Tapping like an ill-hung door in a draught. My watch
Says nearly twelve. All over the countryside
Moon-dazzled men are peering out for invaders.

The farmer and I talk for a while of invaders:
But soon we turn to crops – the annual hope,
Making of cider, prizes for ewes. Tonight
How many hearts along this war-mazed valley
Dream of a day when at peace they may work and watch
The small sufficient wonders of the countryside.

Image or fact, we both in the countryside
Have found our natural law, and until invaders
Come will answer its need: for both of us, hope
Means a harvest from small beginnings, who this night
While the moon sorts out into shadow and shape our valley,
A farmer and a poet, are keeping watch.

July, 1940

WHERE ARE THE WAR POETS?

They who in folly or mere greed
Enslaved religion, markets, laws,
Borrow our language now and bid
Us to speak up in freedom's cause.

It is the logic of our times,
No subject for immortal verse –
That we who lived by honest dreams
Defend the bad against the worse.

THE DEAD

They lie in the Sunday street
Like effigies thrown down after a fête
Among the bare-faced houses frankly yawning revulsion,
Fag-ends of fires, litter of rubble, stale
Confetti-sprinkle of blood. Was it defeat
With them, or triumph? Purification
Or All Fools' Day? On this they remain silent.
Their eyes are closed to honour and hate.

We cannot blame the great
Alone – the mad, the calculating or effete
Rulers. Whatever grotesque scuffle and piercing
Indignant orgasm of pain took them,
All that enforced activity of death
Did answer and compensate
Some involuntary inaction, soft option, dream retreat.
Each man died for the sins of a whole world:
For the ant's self-abdication, the fat-stock's patience
Are sweet goodbye to human nations.

Still, they have made us eat
Our knowing words, who rose and paid
The bill for the whole party with their uncounted
      courage.
And if they chose the dearer consolations
Of living – the bar, the dog race, the discreet
Establishment – and let Karl Marx and Freud go hang,
Now they are dead, who can dispute their choice?
Not I, nor even Fate.

WILL IT BE SO AGAIN?

Will it be so again
That the brave, the gifted are lost from view,
And empty, scheming men
Are left in peace their lunatic age to renew?
Will it be so again?

Must it be always so
That the best are chosen to fall and sleep
Like seeds, and we too slow
In claiming the earth they quicken, and the old usurpers reap
What they could not sow?

Will it be so again –
The jungle code and the hypocrite gesture?
A poppy wreath for the slain
And a cut-throat world for the living? that stale imposture
Played on us once again?

Will it be as before –
Peace, with no heart or mind to ensue it,
Guttering down to war
Like a libertine to his grave? We should not be surprised: we
    knew it
Happen before.

Shall it be so again?
Call not upon the glorious dead
To be your witnesses then.
The living alone can nail to their promise the ones who said
It shall not be so again.

IN THE SHELTER

In a shelter one night, when death was taking the air
Outside, I saw her, seated apart – a child
Nursing her doll, to one man's vision enisled
With radiance which might have shamed even death to
    its lair.

Then I thought of our Christmas roses at home – the dark
Lanterns comforting us a winter through
With the same dusky flush, the same bold spark
Of confidence, O sheltering child, as you.

Genius could never paint the maternal pose
More deftly than accident had roughed it there,
Setting amidst our terrors, against the glare
Of sunshaded bulb and whitewashed brick, that rose.

Instinct was hers, and an earthquake hour revealed it
In flesh – the meek-laid lashes, the glint in the eye
Defying wrath and reason, the arms that shielded
A plaster doll from an erupting sky.

No argument for living could long sustain
These ills: it needs a faithful eye, to have seen all
Love in the droop of a lash and tell it eternal
By one pure bead of its dew-dissolving chain.

Dear sheltering child, if again misgivings grieve me
That love is only a respite, an opal bloom
Upon our snow-set fields, come back to revive me
Cradling your spark through blizzard, drift and tomb.

REMEMBERING CON MARKIEVICZ

Child running wild in woods of Lissadell:
Young lady from the Big House, seen
In a flowered dress, gathering wild flowers: Ascendancy
    queen
Of hunts, house-parties, practical jokes – who could foretell
(*Oh fiery shade, impetuous bone*)
Where all was regular, self-sufficient, gay
Their lovely hoyden lost in a nation's heroine?
Laughterless now the sweet demesne,
And the gaunt house looks blank on Sligo Bay
A nest decayed, an eagle flown.

The Paris studio, your playboy Count
Were not enough, nor Castle splendour
And fame of horsemanship. You were the tinder
Waiting a match, a runner tuned for the pistol's sound,
Impatient shade, long-suffering bone.
In a Balally cottage you found a store
Of Sinn Fein papers. You read – maybe the old sheets
    can while
The time. The flash lights up a whole
Ireland which you have never known before,
A nest betrayed, its eagles gone.

The road to Connolly and Stephen's Green
Showed clear. The great heart which defied
Irish prejudice, English snipers, died
A little not to have shared a grave with the fourteen.
Oh fiery shade, intransigent bone!
And when the Treaty emptied the British jails,
A haggard woman returned and Dublin went wild to
    greet her.
But still it was not enough: an iota
Of compromise, she cried, and the Cause fails.
Nest disarrayed, eagles undone.

Fanatic, bad actress, figure of fun –
She was called each. Ever she dreamed,
Fought, suffered for a losing side, it seemed
(The side which always at last is seen to have won),
Oh fiery shade and unvexed bone.
Remember a heart impulsive, gay and tender,
Still to an ideal Ireland and its real poor alive.
When she died in a pauper bed, in love
All the poor of Dublin rose to lament her
A nest is made, an eagle flown.

PATRICK KAVANAGH
1904–1967

Kavanagh was born into a large farming family in Inniskeen, County Monaghan. In 1939 he moved to Dublin, where he worked as a journalist. His seminal poem, *The Great Hunger*, was published in 1942. He is the author of seven poetry collections, as well as novels and autobiographies.

from THE GREAT HUNGER

X

Their intellectual life consisted in reading
Reynolds' News or the *Sunday Dispatch*,
With sometimes an old almanac brought down from
    the ceiling
Or a school reader brown with the droppings of thatch.
The sporting results or the headlines of war
Was a humbug profound as the highbrow's Arcana.
Pat tried to be wise to the abstraction of all that
But its secret dribbled down his waistcoat like a drink from
    a strainer.
He wagered a bob each way on the Derby,
He got a straight tip from a man in a shop –
A double from the Guineas it was and thought himself
A master mathematician when one of them came up
And he could explain how much he'd have drawn
On the double if the second leg had followed the first.
He was betting on form and breeding, he claimed,
And the man that did that could never be burst.
After that they went on to the war, and the generals
On both sides were shown to be stupid as hell.
If he'd taken *that* road, they remarked of a Marshal,
He'd have … O they knew their geography well.

This was their university. Maguire was an undergraduate
Who dreamed from his lowly position of rising
To a professorship like Larry McKenna or Duffy
Or the pig-gelder Nallon whose knowledge was amazing.
'A treble, full multiple odds ... That's flat porter ...
My turnips are destroyed with the blackguardly crows ...
Another one ... No, you're wrong about that thing I was
    telling you ...
Did you part with your filly, Jack? I heard that you sold her...'
The students were all savants by the time of pub-close.

from LOUGH DERG

I

Then there was war, the slang, the contemporary touch,
The ideologies of the daily papers.
They must seem realer, Churchill, Stalin, Hitler,
Than ideas in the contemplative cloister.
The battles where ten thousand men die
Are more significant than a peasant's emotional problem.
But wars will be merely dry bones in histories
And these common people real living creatures in it
On the unwritten spaces between the lines.
A man throws himself prostrate
And God lies down beside him like a woman
Consoling the hysteria of her lover
That sighs his passion emptily:
'The next time, love, you shall faint in me.'

. . . .

All happened on Lough Derg as it is written
In June nineteen forty-two
When the Germans were fighting outside Rostov.
The poet wrote it down as best he knew,
As integral and completed as the emotion
Of men and women cloaking a burning emotion
In the rags of the commonplace will permit him.
He too was one of them. He too denied
The half of him that was his pride
Yet found it waiting, and the half untrue
Of this story is his pride's rhythm.

The turnips were a-sowing in the fields around Pettigo
As our train passed through.
A horse-cart stopped near the eye of the railway bridge.
By Monaghan and Cavan and Dundalk
By Bundoran and by Omagh the pilgrims went;
And three sad people had found the key to the lock
Of God's delight in disillusionment.

BEYOND THE HEADLINES

Then I saw the wild geese flying
In fair formation to their bases in Inchicore,
And I knew that these wings would outwear the wings of war,
And a man's simple thoughts outlive the day's loud lying.

Don't fear, don't fear, I said to my soul:
The Bedlam of Time is an empty bucket rattled,
'Tis you who will say in the end who best battled,
Only they who fly home to God have flown at all.

EPIC

I have lived in important places, times
When great events were decided: who owned
That half a rood of rock, a no-man's land
Surrounded by our pitchfork-armed claims.
I heard the Duffys shouting 'Damn your soul'
And old McCabe, stripped to the waist, seen
Step the plot defying blue cast-steel –
'Here is the march along these iron stones'.
That was the year of the Munich bother. Which
Was most important? I inclined
To lose my faith in Ballyrush and Gortin
Till Homer's ghost came whispering to my mind.
He said: I made the *Iliad* from such
A local row. Gods make their own importance.

I HAD A FUTURE

O I had a future,
A future.

Gods of the imagination bring back to life
The personality of those streets,
Not any streets
But the streets of nineteen-forty.

Give the quarter-seeing eyes I looked out of,
The animal-remembering mind,
The fog through which I walked towards the mirage
That was my future.

The women I was to meet,

They were nowhere within sight.

And then the pathos of the blind soul,
Who without knowing stands in its own kingdom.

Bring me a small detail
How I felt about money,
Not frantic as later,
There was the future.

Show me the stretcher-bed I slept on
In a room on Drumcondra Road.
Let John Betjeman call for me in a car.

It is summer and the eerie beat
Of madness in Europe trembles the
Wings of the butterflies along the canal.

O I had a future.

PÁDRAIC FALLON
1905–1974

Fallon was born in County Galway but moved to Dublin as a teenager, where he became a member of Æ's literary circle. He wrote many radio plays as well as short stories and literary journalism. His *Collected Poems* was published in 1974.

HEROES 1916

Occasionally talking
Of cities seen,
          not from a wave-top in
A mother of pearl morning, showering spires
Left over by the gods,
            but other, the dream was other, and

I watched them, common men, fall back
Into place, the big rhythms
Peeling off,
          soon to sit
Shabby, wingless, on grass heels, between
The turnip drills

And heroes must die
On their feet, in their own
Enormous footprints, out there on the sky,
Each man unique, and man alone,

Not gossiping
Of cities seen in
The passing smoke,

Birmingham, Coventry, Liverpool,

Their day done.

DARDANELLES 1916

Last night in stomped
Our Connaught Ranger, Private Patrick Carty
On his way:
            Fully accoutred now, a ramp
Of belts and bandoliers, a bayonet
Wags at his side with no wound yet, the heavy
Haversack sits high:

            Filling the back kitchen, squinting
Down from the roofbeams, shyly
Shaking hands all round the family, smiling;
Me he picks up and by God kisses me.

            Up there under
The brown-white plaster an unknown soldier's face
Is weeping.

            Do I remember more? The urchin daughters
Bold for once and peeping
Washed and ribboned through the door to wave
Him off on the Mail, the 4.15, and away
Where muted now in a long sand he lies, if not
Entirely melted into
The steadfast bony glare of Asia Minor.

BRIAN COFFEY
1905–1995

Coffey was born in Dublin and educated at UCD, where he met
and collaborated with Denis Devlin. He travelled to Paris in the
1930s, where he became involved with other Irish modernists,
including Thomas MacGreevy and Samuel Beckett. A poet,
translator, editor and publisher, his *Poems and Versions
1929–1990* was published in 1991.

from DEATH OF HEKTOR

6

Homer   where born where buried of whom the son
what journeys undertaken not known   His work
abides witness to unfaltering sad gaze constrained
A harp he uses   background for verses sung
He pared no fingernails not indifferent   not masked
Light we suppose once had entered eyes to brand memory
with noon's exact flame of sun mirrored in wind-stirred sea
Black night for death   Colours of morning evening for life
the rose the glaucous the amethystine wave-work carpeting
maimed anatomy black white red of man at war
screams the women keening patience the emptied hearts
His ears open to spoken word and words down time like
    wind-blown sand
words of triumph unsleeping enmities wound-up spells malice
swirl of sound continual mixed in a perfect ear
surfacing coherent truer than history all and everything

Prudent Homer who survived to make his poems
did he keep unsaid wordly in innermost anguished heart
what would not have pleased his client banqueters
not reached by resonance the hearts of self-approving lords
yet at last might reach our raddled selves

7

Tradition   Scholars   Establishment   Well-filled heads
now in vain hope of the definitive critic supreme
A versus B versus C followed by later K reaching perhaps P
on the way towards the unseen lighthouse Z
They say   Let them say   What poems have They made

Priam watching from Troy Wall fearful felt the glare
light like Sirius white on the slaughter plain
nimbus   Achilles spher'd round with battle glory
luminous like Cuchullain figure of War Itself
belly-ripper head-splitter neck-lopper
skewering fighters commoners heroes alike
with ash-tree spear gift of his father weapon unique
what none but he could lift shake and throw
tossing from it corpses to river Xanthus choking it
cursing the dying mocking the dead   action man galore
of slaughter   mindless glory   embodied hatred's stench
    of blood
cool malice   merciless   Achaean paramount
true professional   he stares out his own death imminent
golden hair image of manhood for vain victorian dead souls
Achilles fleet of foot unloving he worships gory spoils
his unawakened spirit impassive under doom

Achilles then unsated moves on Hektor troubled by
    second thoughts
either seek safety in Troy or keep the esteem of fellow
    heroes
They had followed him   then fled   now all would go
    Fate's way
on this fixed day of the tenth year of Troy besieged

And we are forced to see godlike Achilles with aiding gods
induce Hektor to the test he is doomed to fail
and Achilles sent his pierced foe to darkness with jeering words
promising his corpse would be food for dogs and fowl
promising absence of due burial unremittable disgrace
and Hektor dead the pallid Greeks draw near
to stab a once feared foe   Then piercing ankles and
    threading thong
through Achilles fixed corpse to chariot head to trail on
    ground
and mounting beast hero scourged beast as if to flight
and making a whirlwind of dust around them as it drew
and the dust filled and knotted Hektor's black-brown curls
which sight all Troy with father mother wife mourn to see

Glory for Achilles   Glory for Greeks   Hektor dishonoured

And
Doom now in the air like a cloudy mushroom swags
    above Troy

14

Homer has shown us how indeed it was
By what he has not said we judge ourselves
He showed us hero bad compassion none hero good
idolatry of spoil   fightmanship   glory

His liking Hektor we infer from how he shows
Hektor's home wife child frightening helmet crest
and how he shows Greek self-styled heroes
at slaughter and jealous play

False picture false childhood standards war not human
    not good
Conflict it is struggle dismembering steel unmanning bolt
unworthying by unworthy grinning foe who'd eat one raw

15

And he gave us his Andromache lamenting
like any woman victim of any war robbed of her world
her husband her child her friends her linen her pots and
    pans
the years it took to put a home together living against the
    grain
of great deeds   her woman's life   in her heart
much held fast   word hidden for all

SAMUEL BECKETT
1906–1989

Beckett was born in Foxrock, Dublin. After graduating from TCD he moved to Paris, where he met James Joyce. His poetry collection, *Echo's Bones and Other Precipitates*, was published by George Reavey's Europa Press in 1935. When the Second World War broke out, Beckett joined the French Resistance, and he was a member of the Irish Red Cross in France after the war. He was awarded the Nobel Prize for Literature in 1969.

SAINT-LÔ

Vire will wind in other shadows
unborn through the bright ways tremble
and the old mind ghost-forsaken
sink into its havoc

1946

SHEILA WINGFIELD
1906–1992

Wingfield was born into an Anglo-Jewish ascendancy family and married the last Viscount of Powerscourt. Wingfield is the author of eight collections of poetry and three memoirs.

from MEN IN WAR

Shouts rang up the street
War War it has come
Like leaves they were blown:
A spear from its corner
A summons on paper
Or buckle to thumb:

In the dark of a room
Old fears were known
By wrinkled up cheeks
And by young wives
Bent back at the waist
To kiss them alone:

But light were their feet
As thoughts were broken
And barriers thrown –
Out of copse out of brake
Out of field they were flown
To the tap of the drum.

Goodbye the milkcart pony
Standing in the sun;
The creaking basket
Of a baker's round;
And summer's garden besom
Sweeping on the ground
Then pausing; work unfinished
And work done.

Goodbye to the inn's warmth
Of views on sport and crop,
Where each man's talk
Is well known as his gait;
Goodbye to what the village
Knows and hears; to that late
Word at the lit door
Of a small shop.

Goodbye to emptiness
That loiters up and down
To show its friends
The new pup on a string,
Or with some tight-held flowers
Goes mutely visiting,
On Sundays, in the cleanness
Of a town.

All this is gone, a lost age,
Gust-torn like a picture page
That flutters, sidles down, then lies:
For a new sight now stings men's eyes
As, carried in a wind that sweeps
Them over shores and crags – what steeps
They'll view, how take a city's height,
Where their force will next alight

Or like a spark will strike the sea,
Into what gates they bring a key –
Not one among the many knows.
But blowing hope, a trumpet echoes
Under arch of colonnade;
And shivering but unafraid
Other families will roll
With bedding and with bamboo pole,
Plank cart and piebald pony,
Jerking over hills and *li*.
Look at them, at march or rest:
A gipsy walking gave the breast
To this one, and he likes to feel
Peril snapping at his heel;
While he, that Dublin bucko there,
At Liffey's edge who'd spit and swear,
Now whistles 'Killaloe' quite plain
Through the drenching Flemish rain;
Another, that in passing smiles
With pleasure at the red-curled tiles
Of homes; or he whose limbs are free,
Or knobbed like Kentish cobnut tree;
Pale Yorkshireman with eager gullet
And lank wrist – each one is yet
That god the Mexicans have sung
Who was in Paradise made young.
You will have heard some call them mad.
But whether any of them had
A doubt, which for a moment stood
Shy as roebuck in a wood
Before it fled in startled haste,
Is forgotten and effaced;
Or whether, to the night air
Extending patiently and where

Lyra throbs and Lynx spies
And Draco's coils anatomize,
Men turned for help, with dry lips,
Pumping heart, wet fingertips
And gulping breath – historian
Or plaque will never say. All I can
Tell is, that as clouds which seem
Too soft may harden till they gleam
Like iron shields, then clash their scorn
Downward, by veined anger torn;
As fire through Leinster's bowels ranged;
Or as the French king's blood was changed
Who saw the Englishmen at Cressy;
As a pibroch's wail would free
Some heavy sword from off its strap
Forcing the plaids to a tight wrap;
As on a gentle morning, youths
To whom a lute, a rose, were truths,
Fought from thick-rigged galleass
With savagery that saved the Mass;
As those by nature wise and mild,
Twelve provinces of forest and wild
Rivers, terrors, ravines crossed
And mountains, half their number lost,
On the Long March which lasted three days
And a year: so war will braze
My metal. I declare, that with the oldest
Of our ills pressed on me, borne on me like
A storm which no mere plan can shift
Or strength dispel, with danger turned
From a low thunder rolling in the hills
To an immediate hurt, I am aware
No time but now ever existed,
This was I meant for, here I am man:
Which – before a fox saw villages
Die out when the Euphrates changed its bed,

Or lazy air first woke to tower,
Or hunters could hear northern winds,
While grasses whipped their legs, or moaned in rocks –
Men learned, men knew, men felt, men understood.
   The fact is proved and clear, that war
   Rescinds what mattered, rends each form.
My hand, no longer casual and loose-plucking
Under a filtering of trellised leaves,
   With careful and slight trigger act
   Gives vast effect; wishes once scattered,
Vague as any drift of gipsies, have now
Gathered from their road and ditch and plain
   Into one march of power; thoughts that were
   Finches starting from a thicket
Wing to where the eagle and the sun
Beat fiercely in a far and dazzled reach,
   High from the ground's indignity.
   Witness how David, rid of foes,
Grieves most; and Caesar sets up Pompey's statue;
Over Alps how emperors can boast
   In fight and Holy, then, be crowned.
   O praise events that led me to this
Fate, whose searchlight-cone, or glint on hilt
Points out the place where I can show my whole
   And candid self: let me be great,
   Bold, gilt by that esteem
Each lover longs for in a woman's eyes
To flood his soul with bliss and to uphold
   Supreme compulsion and desire
   With governance, salvation, succour,
Monstrous commands, and favour. Let me die:
Cut out my heart and hold it to the sun
   In fury; may its blood run slowly
   Under root and stone of time,
To rise in temples where ash-whitened Shiva,
The abhorred, renews by fire; and urge

Crusaders in far massacre
To tread the winepress of the Lord.

Brothers, this is our cloud, our hidden night.
We, being obscured ourselves, know nothing,
    In this darkness find no frame,
    No ladder to climb in clear air,
No tap or chip of bricks on a bright day;
But lean together as if chained to pillars,
    Under scourge from the whole world.
    And now not I, but at all cost
The other, must be saved from harm. Look how
In chaos they are carrying a boy
    On strong arms, with safe steps, or lifting
    In the half-drowned enemy,
Their names lost like a voice in the storm, shown
On the scroll of the sea, hushed in passages
    And space of air, of empty windy
    Air, or shouted in a noise
Uncurling to implacable explosion
And then vanished, gone. Note, in this turmoil,
    How it's strange as myth to meet
    A man who sows his land in calm,
A pigeon nest, joy of a watermill:
For in our blood we feel the heavy pace
    Of cataracts and, in our limbs,
    The tremor of small leaves that shake
Beside them, on their banks, perpetually.
We are a madness, shrill over the ground,
    We are the bass notes' melancholy;
    We are the men who pulled Lorca
Between shrubs, beyond night-shadowed houses;
We are a man dragged and killed on the outskirts
    Of a town in Spain. We also know
    Much of the horror and the numbness –
Snow to the waist – of the defense of Moscow;

A shelterwarden's knack of seeming mild,
    His inner rage. Another time,
      Close under the soil we go
In trenches, huddled in a reek of furs,
Like pictures in a bestiary: for cunning,
    Fellowship and cruelty
      Live in my palms and shins and back;
And glitter-eyed, like flocks at night, are those
Who camp in dips and hollows of a field.
    Each thing that stirs, warily
      Is watched and feared and felt and spied,
And silence, or the din of gunfire, guessed
For signs. Sappers have kneeled; they tap and wait
    And listen for the faintest sounds,
      Then know their fate. O smile O cry
For minutes hang on rumours of a rumour,
Hours fall to a wreck, and seconds beat
    As in Cassandra's pulsing neck
      With my defeat or with your doom,
With answer to our two encountered ranks,
With hurts, much longing, sickness and huge dread.

But look, how this one's glad and how he grips
His steel; nothing astounds and all is safe,
    Lightfooted, as once in a lad
      Angel led and dog at heel.
With talent for his pith, fame in his eye,
He makes design and chance, by strength of touch,
    Agree like music on the map
      Of high campaign towards his end.
Then will the Incas blaze near to, like suns.
Rochelle unbend itself. Madrid give in.
    A prodigy. But in the haste,
      And in the clamour and the sweat,
This sharp acclaim is his own shout, the ray's
Behind his blink of tears: he does not know

That over waste the dawn spilled out,
The street abandoned when he came.
But I – what I have done has come untied
In spite of all I've tried or said. For long
     I fail. I can do nothing right,
     But heap mistake upon mistakes;
While war's old cart goes slowly creaking on
Into the disillusionary years
     Of its real destiny, where later
     My own enemy will tread.
Where is my cause, that seems as cold as a blown
Mist? It was so firm, so solid. Must I think
     It's I have grown into a ghost?
     All is reversed; all is astray;
And reason an old mirror full of flaws.
Gestures that were heroic are remote
     As black clouds in a battle-piece;
     But they need rain in Barcelona
Where there's blood up to the second storeys.
God of hopes, how you misguide us. We,
     Who thought we had the heart and sinews
     Of strong beasts, of noble birds –
Head high the running stag, the great in pinion –
Find we emboss, with virtues and with oath,
     Only a blazon, cut in stone,
     And which the weathers chip and winds
Chafe. I'd said our coats would boast our pride –
But see, mine's foul and ragged with deceit
     Because, by Ronda bridge across
     The double cliffs that sheer to drop eight
Hundred feet, and from whose rocks so many
Pigeons flew, instead, the violated
     Nuns fall, fluttering.
     We thought, this is warm, this is different,
This abscinds us from all past fights, as we marched
          among haycocks

With some of the brambles ripe, but the same chill
    Lies on our hair, as in pale winter
    When the saplings are cut through.
Indeed, there's more of torture; and the crime
Of children with their peace hurled into air:
    More fault, more insult and more shame
    Than can be cleaned out from our core –
Unless Time, in its passage round the world,
Should, like an idle workman, make a halt.

FREDA LAUGHTON
1907–*n.d.*

Laughton was born in Bristol and studied art in London. She moved to Ireland in 1932 and her poetry collection, *A Transitory House*, was published in 1945.

THE BOMBED HOUSE

This house has lanes not corridors.
Some walls are cliffs, and some,
Whilst drunkenly dancing,
Committed suicide.

One night the inhabitants
Of this corybantic ruin,
One-time desirable residence
Replete with indigestible furniture,

Aroused without warning into death,
Found their bedroom passage
An unsuspected lane leading
Into the unimaginable.

LOUIS MACNEICE
1907–1963

MacNeice was born in Belfast, the son of a Church of Ireland
clergyman, and was educated at Oxford University. A poet,
critic and radio producer with the BBC, his seminal work,
Autumn Journal, was published in 1939. His radio plays include
The Dark Tower, broadcast in 1946.

AUBADE

Having bitten on life like a sharp apple
Or, playing it like a fish, been happy,

Having felt with fingers that the sky is blue,
What have we after that to look forward to?

Not the twilight of the gods but a precise dawn
Of sallow and grey bricks, and newsboys crying war.

CARRICKFERGUS

I was born in Belfast between the mountain and the gantries
    To the hooting of lost sirens and the clang of trams:
Thence to Smoky Carrick in County Antrim
    Where the bottle-neck harbour collects the mud which jams

The little boats beneath the Norman castle,
    The pier shining with lumps of crystal salt;
The Scotch Quarter was a line of residential houses
    But the Irish Quarter was a slum for the blind and halt.

The brook ran yellow from the factory stinking of chlorine,
    The yarn-mill called its funeral cry at noon;
Our lights looked over the lough to the lights of Bangor
    Under the peacock aura of a drowning moon.

The Norman walled this town against the country
    To stop his ears to the yelping of his slave
And built a church in the form of a cross but denoting
    The list of Christ on the cross in the angle of the nave.

I was the rector's son, born to the anglican order,
    Banned for ever from the candles of the Irish poor;
The Chichesters knelt in marble at the end of a transept
    With ruffs about their necks, their portion sure.

The war came and a huge camp of soldiers
    Grew from the ground in sight of our house with long
Dummies hanging from gibbets for bayonet practice
    And the sentry's challenge echoing all day long;

A Yorkshire terrier ran in and out by the gate-lodge
    Barred to civilians, yapping as if taking affront:
Marching at ease and singing 'Who Killed Cock Robin?'
    The troops went out by the lodge and off to the Front.

The steamer was camouflaged that took me to England –
    Sweat and khaki in the Carlisle train;
I thought that the war would last for ever and sugar
    Be always rationed and that never again

Would the weekly papers not have photos of sandbags
    And my governess not make bandages from moss
And people not have maps above the fireplace
    With flags on pins moving across and across –

Across the hawthorn hedge the noise of bugles,
    Flares across the night,
Somewhere on the lough was a prison ship for Germans,
    A cage across their sight.

I went to school in Dorset, the world of parents
    Contracted into a puppet world of sons
Far from the mill girls, the smell of porter, the salt-mines
    And the soldiers with their guns.

from THE CLOSING ALBUM

IV GALWAY

O the crossbones of Galway,
The hollow grey houses,
The rubbish and sewage,
The grass-grown pier,
And the dredger grumbling
All night in the harbour:
The war came down on us here.

Salmon in the Corrib
Gently swaying
And the water combed out
Over the weir
And a hundred swans
Dreaming on the harbour:
The war came down on us here.

The night was gay
With the moon's music
But Mars was angry
On the hills of Clare
And September dawned
Upon willows and ruins:
The war came down on us here.

from ENTERED IN THE MINUTES

I

BARCELONA IN WARTIME

In the Paralelo a one-legged
Man sat on the ground,
His one leg out before him,
Smiling. A sudden sound

Of crazy laughter shivered
The sunlight; overhead
A parrot in a window of aspidistras
Was laughing like the dead.

CONVOY

Together, keeping in line, slow as if hypnotised
Across the blackboard sea in sombre echelon
The food-ships draw their wakes. No Euclid could have devised
Neater means to a more essential end –
Unless the chalk breaks off, the convoy is surprised.

The cranks go up and down, the smoke-trails tendril out,
The precious cargoes creak, the signals clack,
All is under control and nobody need shout,
We are steady as we go, and on our flanks
The little whippet warships romp and scurry about.

This is a bit like us: the individual sets
A course for all his soul's more basic needs
Of love and pride-of-life, but sometimes he forgets
How much their voyage home depends upon pragmatic
And ruthless attitudes – destroyers and corvettes.

BOTTLENECK

Never to fight unless from a pure motive
And for a clear end was his unwritten rule
Who had been in books and visions to a progressive school
And dreamt of barricades, yet being observant
Knew that that was not the way things are:
This man would never make a soldier or a servant.

When I saw him last, carving the longshore mist
With an ascetic profile, he was standing
Watching the troopship leave, he did not speak
But from his eyes there peered a furtive footsore envy
Of these who sailed away to make an opposed landing –
So calm because so young, so lethal because so meek.

Where he is now I could not say; he will,
The odds are, always be non-combatant
Being too violent in soul to kill
Anyone but himself, yet in his mind
A crowd of odd components mutter and press
For compromise with fact, longing to be combined
Into a working whole but cannot jostle through
The permanent bottleneck of his highmindedness.

NEUTRALITY

The neutral island facing the Atlantic,
The neutral island in the heart of man,
Are bitterly soft reminders of the beginnings
That ended before the end began.

Look into your heart, you will find a County Sligo,
A Knocknarea with for navel a cairn of stones,
You will find the shadow and sheen of a moleskin mountain
And a litter of chronicles and bones.

Look into your heart, you will find fermenting rivers,
Intricacies of gloom and glint,
You will find such ducats of dream and great doubloons of
     ceremony
As nobody to-day would mint.

But then look eastward from your heart, there bulks
A continent, close, dark, as archetypal sin,
While to the west off your own shores the mackerel
Are fat – on the flesh of your kin.

THE ATLANTIC TUNNEL

(*a memory of 1940*)

America was ablaze with lights,
Eastward the sea was black, the ship
Black, not a cigarette on deck;
It was like entering a zigzag tunnel.

Old Irish nuns were returning home,
So were young men due for the call-up,
So were the survivors from the *Jervis Bay*;
The tunnel absorbed us, made us one.

But how many miles or days we did not
Know we were one, nor how many waves
Carried in code the words to prevent,
The words to destroy. We were just passengers,

As on this ship, so on our own
Lives, passengers, parasites, never
Entrusted with headphones or signals and out of
The code, yet not in the clear. The tunnel

Might be about to collapse, this whole
Zigzag might be a widening crack
Which led to the bottom before Belfast
Or Liverpool gave us reluctant welcome.

Meanwhile the dark ship rolled, a ball
Prattled and spun on a rolling table;
The sailors from the *Jervis Bay*
Called the score, were otherwise silent.

RUDDICK MILLAR
1907–1952

Born in Carrickfergus, County Antrim, Millar was a popular playwright and worked as a journalist and broadcaster. His *Collected Poems* was published in 1931.

THE SOMME
1st July, 1916

'Tis zero hour!
A word of swift command,
A shower of shrapnel,
And the valiant band
Begin the forward rush,
While, near at hand –
The stilled note of a thrush.

They stumble on,
These gallant boys in brown,
From Antrim and from Down,
On and yet on!

Then clash of steel,
Blood like the river's foam;
While women kneel
In some far Ulster home.

And so they die,
With 'No surrender' on their lips
These weavers of linen,
These builders of ships.

GEORGE REAVEY
1907–1976

Reavey was born in Russia, but his family fled to Belfast during the Russian Revolution. He was educated at Cambridge and moved to Paris in 1929. An important literary innovator, he founded the Europa Press, publishing his own *Nostradam* in 1935. He spent the Second World War first, briefly, in Madrid working for the British Council, and then in the Soviet Union, where he was posted with the Foreign Office.

THE SINKING OF THE SS JUTLAND
The Barents Sea
Night of May 2/3, 1942

Murmansk was still four days to go,
And Iceland's rocks behind;
Bear Island tried with Arctic snow,
And Norway blew ill-wind.

What sudden trials can explain
A sea so calm that day,
As always grey? Yet German planes
In ambush, steel-eyed, lay.

Two days the convoy had been tracked:
The third, torpedo bombers,
Rising wave on wave, attacked
And broke the white night's slumber.

Ta-ram ... the oerlikons and guns
Now beat a flamed tattoo,
And yet the planes kept coming on
As no birds ever do.

One plane now crossed so low, it hid
His captain's bridge from view:
It nosed to port; a black shape slid
Into the ocean's flue.

Right then the first torpedo hit
His ship about the screw;
Rear guns and gunners, all the kit,
Into grey waters flew.

The boat slewed gulping, split in two,
Her stern all wrenched and gone:
Along her sloping decks a few
Survivors limped and shone

In varnish of a hellish glow
Reflected from a ship
To port, shocked by another blow
Ablaze in bright-rouged lip

Of fuel wincing into flame
– No longer there to feed
The 'Hurricanes', but paint raw shame
Of faces, hands, that bleed.

The plane itself that crossed his brow,
Now burnt upon the waves,
And vanished with its crew in tow,
Clutched down by spectral graves.

And who had been a moment back
The raging lords of air,
Launching torpedoes in our track,
Defying all we dared,

Were now some enemies at least
Reaped down to bulge the drink,
But not before our brows were creased
With three ships in the sink.

That was a nightmare for our age
— A bloody battle blaze
In imagery of hell's rampage;
Until, through all this daze,

With crisscross play of tracers bright
And oerlikons, some jammed,
The convoy crackled out of sight.
Farewell, the sorely damned.

And o the silence densely hung
With signals black and white:
The leaden sky and ship that clung,
Hugging the mottled light.

And then she reared and flapped her wings
— A monstrous penguin sick
That spewed a cataract of things
For fish to find and pick.

Tanks broke their chains, explosives rolled:
It was a dreadful spree;
And we could hear the bell that tolled
Without man's agency.

In this cascade of hurtling things,
A figure seemed to show:
Was it a man who stumbles, clings
To every piece of tow?

Or was it you, an hour ago
Who looked unreal and green
As if transparently aglow
In light of worlds unseen?

Was it a ghost already sprung
Deep from the bowels of time;
A sprite with immaterial lung
To brand this wreck in rhyme?

Or was it mirage only seen
When midnight blanched is there;
A man unknown who might have been
A motion of the air?

One moment so: the next, a bare
And briefly sucking sea
Unfurled a sulking skyline where
The penguin used to be.

The vacuum mouth coughed up again
A floating mass of wood
And anything that bore the strain
Of sea in gobbling mood.

Grey waters flared to tangerine
And jerking objects spun:
A mash stirred up in a tureen.
There was no moon or sun.

Ay, where's the man, that sea-time friend,
A while ago who walked
And sudden met his silent end
– And almost as he talked?

The flaking plaster of the sky
Has made him white as foam;
And his blue eyes will never cry
With those he left at home.

Adrift, he reels the slippery chain
Of facts that brought the deluge;
Adrift in broken porcelain
– The wake of icebergs huge.

And while adagio icebergs ground
The organ of the mist,
He is musician blind and bound
For ever to their grist.

He was alone in that great cave
That only is himself,
Where every echo was a wave
And every wave his self.

And as his drowsy yearning grew,
Embracing all the earth,
The swell of leprous waters slew
The promise of new birth.

He asked salvation of the sky,
Of all things great that stirred,
But only silence, big of eye,
Surveyed him as he heard

The muffled rasping of an oar
Behind his furrowed head,
Which now was that tremendous door
Of refuge with the dead.

THE RAPE OF EUROPE

Ptolemy fades among the stars:
Goodbye the static world's seclusion,
Gunpowder-rent the seamless robe
Of one-way-world-safe-from-delusion.
New problems surge, invite divisions,
Engender systems, force decisions;
Earth spins, new planets simulate
The prophecies of Europe's fate;
And Europe in her madness builds,
Destroys, discovers, blends and spends
Her precious substance ages tilled;
Barters for gold and slaves, mean ends,
Her hard-won freedom, mind's content;
Betrays her mission, infects all lands
With envy, greed and discontent,
The consistent harvest of her hands;
And spreading still like foul plague,
Unchecked, corrupt, incontinent,
By rivers, oceans, waterways,
Through all the highways, towns, byways,
Of every chartered continent.

Poor Ptolemy, your vision's faded:
Aix, too, is fallen and dissolved,
The strongholds of the West invaded.
But who will speak and weld together
Expectant Europe, armed, air-raided,
Perplexed in this uncertain weather?
Involved, inconstant and determined,
In sawing winds', sharp whirlwinds' swirl,
She dares her destiny, stars' whirl.

HIROSHIMA AND AFTER

The bud of doom is locked above my head
Like a lamp hung in a receding room
Unlit – until the clocked second splits
The ravished hour and booms the magic daze
And the lilac-sundering light
Snaps the ravelment of a tragic ending
Stripping the beggar of his meagre rags
The scorched captains of the flash of hope
An upstart world of the flesh of marvels

Here are the bones of your delusion
The loom of power and tall pride
Crumbled in a meteor shower
The dust the scrap-heap and the licking flame
And O the crushed heart among the morning-glories
O wind O night O mind O light
O world discovered in a pulp of shame
In a room too small for such a flowering.

JOHN HEWITT
1907–1987

Hewitt was born in Belfast and educated at Queen's University. He worked in the Ulster Museum and later became Art Director of the Herbert Art Gallery, Coventry. In 1976 he was appointed as the first writer in residence at Queen's. He published eight collections of poetry and was a noted reviewer and art critic.

PORTSTEWART, JULY 1914

Portstewart. Nineteen fourteen. Willie's clutch –
our cousins, Cecil, Edna, Uncle, Aunt –
rented a house with us. There can't be much
remembered now which was significant:
the bathing pool, the jellyfish that stung,
and how the Chaplin film, unreeled, would fall
into an open basket; that is all,
that, and a chorus which the Pierrots sung.

The war broke out in Europe. Bishops blessed
the Austrians, the Russians. It was odd,
both benches hurled opposing prayers to God.
We thought that foolish, had more interest
in picnics at the strand, at Castlerock.
By August, back in Belfast, came the shock.

THE YCVS AND THE ULSTER DIVISION

Surprised one day, I watched Belfast's Lord Mayor
borne on gun-carriage, when Young Citizen
Volunteers in grey first took the air,
mere lads they looked, too soon they would be men.
And, some months later, we went down to see
our khaki soldiers marching to the docks
to sail away for France to keep us free;
our cheering then my memory often mocks.

For later still, as days limped past or flew,
the newsboys yelled hoarse tidings down the street
of Jutland's victory, Dardanelles' defeat,
and, propped on crutches, men in sloppy blue,
approached with awe, would tell us stories from
the shell-ploughed fields of Passchendaele and Somme.

BROWN'S BAY, ISLANDMAGEE,
SPRING 1917

Once, with my mother and my grandmother,
conscripted to lend a hand, fetch water, go
on errands to the farm. Our cottage there
clung to a ridge, where certain hours would show,
steaming at dawn, returning, in a row,
the black minesweepers file, each evening.
While out in France we struck them blow for blow,
at Europe's edge here, we were hazarding
that U-boats kept the issue still in doubt.
One morning, tasks accomplished, for a stroll
I climbed the turf and rocks round Skernaghan,
and fifty yards off, swelling like a shoal,
sea-surface broke, a conning tower thrust out.
I scrambled, frightened, from the waving man.

THE VOLUNTEER

My father's closest brother of his three
trained as an artist, by compulsion made
his living at the lithographic trade.
After adventures, Edinburgh, he
settled in Finchley with his family.
One Bangor holiday I saw him plain,
his tilted boater and his swagger cane,
a smiling man, he shared some jokes with me.

Months after war broke out he wrote to say
he had enlisted by deliberate choice,
not waiting for conscription, lest his boys
might think of that with shame some future day.
I still recall my father's countenance
that day we learned he had been killed in France.

NINETEEN SIXTEEN,
OR THE TERRIBLE BEAUTY

Once, as a boy of nine, he heard his teacher
back from his interrupted holiday,
a red-faced, white-haired man, repeating wildly
all he had seen of Dublin's rash affray:

'The abandoned motor cars, the carcasses
of army horses littering the street ...'
No more remains of all he must have told them
of that remote, ambiguous defeat.

It took those decades crammed with guns and ballads
to sanctify the names which star that myth;
and, to this day, the fierce infection pulses
in the hot blood of half our ghetto-youth.

Yet, sitting there, that long-remembered morning,
he caught no hint he'd cast an ageing eye
on angled rifles, parcels left in doorways,
or unattended cars, he'd sidle by.

ENCOUNTER NINETEEN TWENTY

Kicking a ragged ball from lamp to lamp,
in close November dusk, my head well down,
not yet aware the teams had dribbled off,
I collided with a stiffly striding man.

He cursed. I stumbled, glimpsing his sharp face,
his coat brushed open and a rifle held
close to his side. That image has become
the shape of fear that waits each Irish child.

Shock sent each reeling from the light's pale cone;
in shadow since that man moves out to kill;
and I, with thumping heart, from lamp to lamp,
still race to score my sad unchallenged goal.

TO THE MEMORY OF JAMES CONNOLLY

A dozen years have passed since then,
   The memory has died away
Of Connolly and the martyred men
   Who rose on Easter Day.

When I was six years old I heard
   Connolly address a Labour crowd –
I cannot recollect a word
   Yet I am very proud –

As one who stood upon the edge
Of Galilee to watch the ship
That waders pushed beyond the sedge
While bright oars flash and dip;

But not indeed as one who stood
Among the crowd on Calvary
To see Christ die for Brotherhood,
As Connolly died for me.

THE TROUBLES, 1922

The Troubles came; by nineteen twenty-two
we knew of and accepted violence
in the small streets at hand. With Curfew tense,
each evening when that quiet hour was due,
I never ventured far from where I knew
I could reach home in safety. At the door
I'd sometimes stand, till with oncoming roar,
the wire-cage Crossley tenders swept in view.

Once, from front bedroom window, I could mark
black shapes, flat-capped, across the shadowed street,
two policemen on patrol. With crack and spark
fierce bullets struck the kerb beneath their feet;
below the shattered streetlamp in the dark
blurred shadow crouched, then pattered quick retreat.

THE PRISONERS ON THE ROOF

A hundred yards along the other side
from where our house stood, ran the high gaol wall,
dark, grey and blank, with everything to hide
save at the clanging front gate where they call
with captured men in vans. So, once, just then,
the cells were crammed with gunmen – IRA;
their protest they asserted in a way
proclaimed, though they were captive, they were men.

For they had thrust and clambered to the roof,
and clattered, rattled chamber pot or pail –
all metal instruments they find in gaol –
to keep the town awake when all should sleep.
We heard the rumoured uproar, ran for proof;
and thought the ledge they danced on high and steep.

CAMARADAS Y COMPAÑEROS

Once years ago
we listened to Bilbao
on headphones after midnight

found Albacete on the map
pronounced Barcelona properly

applauded the red-sashed boys
and the blue whirling skirts of the jota
the innocent fife and drum

argued for and against the Anarchists
or slipped an unobtrusive note
to a secretive comrade collecting

for the International Brigade
maybe even stood a drink
to a gruff-voiced laughing Basque
from the rusting ship at the docks.

That is all long over now.
It was only for a short while;
we have forgotten if it lasted years or months.
The pages of the atlas turn.
We have momentarily memorised
many other placenames,
hear foreign stations more easily.

But sometimes
a name slips back to mind
from a book or magazine
like Jarama or Guadalajara
or a fragment of song
like the scent of an exotic flower
of the merry muleteers
or the formal dance of the spinners.

Or maybe an elderly man in a crowd
catches your eye, flashes a grin
and clenches his fist shoulder-high,
he fought in Spain and imagines
we remember it.

AUGUST 1939

On this day of crisis
when men march
and the avalanche waits for the shout
I try to make better English
of Wang's literal translation of verses
about the evening moon and the East Lake
by a Ming poet
painted on a small bowl
in the museum.

EPITAPH FOR A CONSCRIPT, 1940

I go to seek the peace we could not save
because we left it to the fool and knave,
will maybe find instead my father's grave.

MINOR POET'S DILEMMA, 1940

Caught in my prime in pitiful disaster,
my world's walls gape atilt, about to fall:
where must I turn for comfortable master
to fill the hush of terror's interval?

Say – Edward Thomas, who, when earth was breaking,
brooding on vole and hawthorn, deathward went,
or Roman Landor, brave at eighty, making
immortal quatrains of pure sentiment?

SECOND FRONT
DOUBLE SUMMERTIME, JULY 1943

The crazy clock two hours astray
defies the angle of the sun,
yet accurately ticks away
the dripping minutes one by one
that heap their grains to reach the date
our nibbled pencils testify,
and all the guns of Europe wait
for all the men who are to die.

STRANGERS AND NEIGHBOURS

The Jews of my childhood were
resident strangers and neighbours;
not like the flash gypsies
once a year with clothes pegs, lace and luck,
or the occasional organ-grinders
with earrings and beautiful parrots;
they lived among us doors away.

You recognised their features as foreign
and exaggerated their accent,
holding your nose with thumb and forefinger,
knew their names, Weiner, Eban, Lantin,
surprised at some with off-key names
like Gordon or Ross.

Though you played readily enough
with their youngsters after school,
you did not, as with your best friends,
run in and out of their houses,
which, anyway, smelt of hot olive oil.

They were often handsome when young,
but frequently ran to fat,
quickly losing their looks.
The grown men seldom had comfortable feet;
I thought they walked tired
because of their ancestor, the Wandering Jew,
with the black hat and the greasy ringlets.

They followed no handicraft or trade
except that of baking bread,
unleavened bread, their special biscuit
which a boy brought round once a week
on a bicycle. For the rest
they lent out money to poor people,
sold articles on instalments,
oblong objects wrapped in American cloth
like pictures, so we called them Pickey Jews.

They kept their Sunday on Saturday,
had a feast they called the Passover
and a silly New Year, not at the New Year,
called their flat-flooted minister
Rabbi; he wore a long beard.
Their coffins were cheaply constructed
of onion boxes and thin black cloth.

I have never been to Palestine,
Israel, where they are native,
so I do not know if labour
has made them more like us
or like the leathery peasants
I have seen in other countries,
bending in the large fields.

But I remember that the dark,
florid wives of the more prosperous
were demanding and loud in shops
and very conspicuous;
I cannot imagine what
a nation of these would be like.

Nevertheless, I have been to Auschwitz,
once when a delegate,
have passed through the prison gate
with the cast-iron Freedom motto,
walked along the straight paths round
the barracks of undressed brick.
(The Nazis blew up the furnace before they left.)
And I have felt my heart turn
and my eyes burn dry beyond tears
at the swathes and billows of human hair
in the long museum showcase,
inextricably tangled like a
vast sombre sand-churning wave,
grizzled tufts, plaits, ringlets,
blond, brown, black, lank, curling;
the cropped heads of that harvest
long gone into the furnace.

And once in Kafka's Prague, I
went into the ancient synagogue,
an architectural eccentricity,
a tiny Gothic Jewish church,
shrine not of saint but the Golem,
and, nearby, stepped where I could
among the close-stacked headstones
where the bony centuries huddle under the
bulging turf of the miniature graveyard
so many dead are poured into it:

and so I have some pity and much respect
for a patient enduring people.

When we found the famous Portuguese
synagogue in Amsterdam shut,
it was opened for us by the caretaker's
daughter that winter morning.
Inside the cold shell I saw
the grimy woodwork and the tarnished
candelabra, neglected as if
it was no longer a holy place.
So I was surprised when my friend,
who is not an orthodox Jew,
fumbled round the shelves and benches
until, in a corner, he found
a dusty skullcap, and carefully
put it on his bare head.

ULSTER WINTER (1942)

The army lorry, cold, anonymous,
Straining its plates and groaning heavily,
Bore me at speed along the winter road
Between black hedges under a grey sky.

Low on the left a flooded bog was fenced
With dark-tipped flags that here and there had gone
All over-ripe and harried by the wind
Into gay flaunting tufts of thistledown.

And on the right the higher ground assumed
The attributes of hills: the cresting trees,
Bare now and grey with evening's drifting mist,
Were vexed by starlings in daft companies.

Then, at a sudden corner, hedges gave
A grass bank topped by line of oak and beech
Above red arcs of wet decaying leaves,
And veined with ivy high as hand could reach.

I glanced at the young soldier by my side,
Gripping the wheel with a grubby-knuckled hand,
A cockney by his tongue, and wondered if
I spoke my thoughts he'd even understand.

For I am native, though my fathers came
From fatter acres over the grey sea:
The clay that hugs the rows of exile bones
Has shaped my phantom nationality.

TO THE PEOPLE OF DRESDEN

Your famous city stood, plucked out of time,
a dream-pavilion set in porcelain,
where the masked dancers paced in stately mime
with grace no later age can now attain.
Then towards disaster all seemed swiftly drawn,
your cruel firestorm fuelling men's fears,
to shards all shattered, all those dancers gone,
in the dark Europe of my middle years.

But now that darkness breaks, and I have stood,
shouldered with thousands in your Altmarkt Square,
to swear my silent oath of brotherhood,
and join my lonely prayer to your vast prayer
that by the common will of common men
no war shall ever darken day again.

DENIS DEVLIN
1908–1959

Devlin was born to Irish parents in Greenock, Scotland, and educated at UCD. He studied in Paris where he met Samuel Beckett and Thomas MacGreevy. One of the Irish modernist poets, his posthumous *Selected Poems* was published in the USA in 1963.

ANNAPOLIS

'No, we can't get a licence for liquor, being too near the
    church,'
Said the waiter. The church looked friends enough
On its humble, grassy hillock. So I said: 'Excuse me,
I must have a drink.' And I rambled on down West Street
To eat and drink at Socrates the Greek's.
On my right at the Raw Bar, a truckdriver drinking milk
And a Norwegian second mate glared at their faces
In the mirror. We floated on heat
Like paper boats boys prod in the bathroom.

The white-linen cadets walked with girls of good family
It was the feast-day of the Republic and the girls
In long dresses made a drawing room of the streets;
They were like sweet william and buttercups
Like petunia and sweet pea and silver moss,
The *haute couture* clapped a little askew
On their melodious immaturity.
As I said to the truckdriver: 'They are children.'
He flashed a sigh and said: 'Indeed they are.'

Imperceptibly darkness plucked its petals
You hear the coloured people's viola laughter
And starlight one never looks up to
Blurs the woollen trees
And the houses with no comment to make.
    A delicate drunk
Weaves his glass limbs together up the street.

The little, red-brick capital,
Its velvet, burgess elms,
Curls back into childhood
Trumpets and tricorns, arteries of fern.
I hold my breath for the expected
According to the mechanics of fairyland.

But then, it is not Hans Andersen, the monuments
Of power lour as in any London. Cadets conduct
Camera-fans to the Governor's residence
To the Capitol and the Revolutionary General

Leading ghosts on his enthusiastic stone horse.
In the porches, after dinner
Loud-bellied citizens swat flies.
The band blows open the Academy gates
And there a girl-dancer remotely
Flows to the dance.

THE TOMB OF MICHAEL COLLINS

To Ignazio Silone

I

Much I remember of the death of men,
But his I most remember, most of all,
More than the familiar and forgetful
Ghosts who leave our memory too soon –
Oh, what voracious fathers bore him down!

It was all sky and heather, wet and rock,
No one was there but larks and stiff-legged hares
And flowers bloodstained. Then, Oh, our shame
    so massive
Only a God embraced it and the angel
Whose hurt and misty rifle shot him down.

One by one the enemy dies off;
As the sun grows old, the dead increase,
We love the more the further from we're born!
The bullet found him where the bullet ceased,
And Gael and Gall went inconspicuous down.

II

There are the Four Green Fields we loved in boyhood,
There are some reasons it's no loss to die for:
Even it's no loss to die for having lived;
It is inside our life the angel happens
Life, the gift that God accepts or not,

Which Michael took with hand, with harsh, grey eyes,
He was loved by women and by men,
He fought a week of Sundays and by night
He asked what happened and he knew what was –
O Lord! how right that them you love die young!

He's what I was when by the chiming river
Two loyal children long ago embraced –
But what I was is one thing, what remember
Another thing, how memory becomes knowledge –
Most I remember him, how man is courage.

And sad, Oh sad, that glen with one thin stream
He met his death in; and a farmer told me
There was but one small bird to shoot: it sang
'Better Beast and know your end, and die
Than Man with murderous angels in his head.'

III

I tell these tales – I was twelve years old that time.
Those of the past were heroes in my mind:
Edward the Bruce whose brother Robert made him
Of Ireland, King; Wolfe Tone and Silken Thomas
And Prince Red Hugh O'Donnell most of all.

The newsboys knew and the apple and orange women
Where was his shifty lodging Tuesday night;
No one betrayed him to the foreigner,
No Protestant or Catholic broke and ran
But murmured in their heart: here was a man!

Then came that mortal day he lost and laughed at,
He knew it as he left the armoured car;
The sky held in its rain and kept its breath;
Over the Liffey and the Lee, the gulls,
They told his fortune which he knew, his death.

Walking to Vespers in my Jesuit school,
The sky was come and gone; 'O Captain, my Captain!'
Walt Whitman was the lesson that afternoon –
How sometimes death magnifies him who dies,
And some, though mortal, have achieved their race.

LITTLE ELEGY

I

I will walk with a lover of wisdom
A smile for Senator Destiny
But I shall gladly listen.

Her beauty was like silence in a cup of water
Decanting all but the dream matter.
The figures of reality
Stood about, Dantesque and pitiful.
Can anyone tell me her name?
I will love her again and again
Girl on skis, arrow and bow in one,
Masked in glass, graceful,
Hard as a word in season.

I saw a round, Bavarian goodman
And a Harvard student with a Mohican's lope
Colliding with huge nosegays
Then laughter burst above their flowers:

Absent of mind, they had their wits about them
I laughed at them both outright

And at simpering, peasant statues
Graces and gods would they be!
It was a heady springtime in Munich
Many I knew confided in me
Popu, the champion cyclist
Sigmund, deriding tyrants
And Carlos, who made love shyly
To a furtive, gentle girl
And came to my door, stammering,
'She loves me, you know.'

'She loves me, you know.'

But geography separated them
And geography keeps them apart
Now they live forgotten in each other's heart.

II

The sun was full on, the bird-breed
Gradually found their wings.
The baroque churches glowed like the Book of Kells.
We two, with butterbrot and sweetmilk
Over the snow beneath blue winds
Went far and wide.
Busy, alone, we all go far and wide
Who once listened to each other's
Fair vows and counsel.

Of those that go out of the cafés and the gardens
Some lie in prisons
Some die of unhappiness
Indeed, it is so!

This is all I can remember
Quarrelling, gusts of confidence
The class climbing through faun nights
And her I would meet
As though I were unconscious
In vacant, bright-columned streets
And beings in love's tunic scattered to the four winds
For no reason at all
For no reason that I can tell.

CONCENTRATION CAMPS

from Pierre Emmanuel (1916–1984)

Down in the steep pit sealed by sunlight
A little quivering mud and silence.
The whole man is dying here. Will
His tortured form reveal the secret that angels
Tremble with? the boldness of standing in the face
Of God, the daring of a suffering that provokes
The unimaginable accents God alone
Hears surging from the ages' depths to chill
The absurd hierarchies of His glory?

And you, anonymous hangman, whose function
Is to disfigure your own face,
Worn out by hate and sorrow, will you reach
Those shores of pure inhumanity where the Face of God
Is quite close and is hurt with love,
Behind the victims' translucid faces,
That the most hellish blasphemy would be less
Sacreligious than that face in filigree,
Yours! Who will confront you in eternity?

If (victim or hangman, what matter!) one heart should dare
Assume the guilt for all blood for love's sake,
If horror tore the sky and crime
Were God in a flash of infinite memory:
A prayer might then be raised, hands
Sing out a Tree upon the calcined shades,
A look could quench the love-thirst of the wounds,
A meaning flower out of the thorn and the lip, an essence
Unite crime and candour in a single cry
And God remembers himself in the triumphal pangs
Of the flesh, the blessed, the poor flesh.

But God knows not that it is He who dies:
So sweet to Him His suffering in men,
Whose grief confirms Him in His eternity.
Or perhaps He has never been but dead
In this flesh tortured to the very soul,
This flesh that cries Him living, that already
Offers itself for the resurrection of all flesh
In the terrifying joy of His presence.

LIAM MacGABHANN
1908–1979

MacGabhann was born on Valentia Island, County Kerry. A journalist and film critic, he was editor of *An Phoblacht* and worked for the *Irish Press*, the *Irish Times*, Radio Éireann and the *Sunday World*.

THE ROADS OF KERRY

A terrible reminder they will be to them,
These white crosses
Glowing in the dusk, by the roads of Kerry;
Pitiful, lovable names on them,
With mention of battalion and brigade,
And tender prayers in Gaelic
Like those that come to Kerry mothers' lips,
Who sit, lonely, by the turf-fires,
Or peer across half-doors into the dusk;
Dark eyes of mothers, questioning always,
Questioning dumbly
The death they died,
The horror and the glory and the shame,
But they are strong
These women of the hills of Kerry,
Strong in the memory of their splendid sons.

They who have seen the roadsides wet with blood,
And broken hands bound fast to one another,
And cold dead fingers, clutching rosaries.
They who have seen the coffins laid outside
The doors of churches where their sons had prayed.
They are strong and silent,
But their hearts are heavy.

And in the glooming hills,
By the dark lochs of the triumphant hills,
The men of Kerry, mindful, too are marching,
Softly together.

And there is great quiet
By the white crosses
Glowing in the wistful dusk
By the roads of Kerry.

CONNOLLY

The man was all shot through that came to-day
Into the barrack square;
A soldier I – I am not proud to say
We killed him there;
They brought him from the prison hospital.
To see him in that chair
I thought his smile would far more quickly call
A man to prayer.

Maybe we cannot understand this thing
That makes these rebels die;
And yet all things love freedom and the Spring
Clear in the sky!
I think I would not do this deed again
For all that I hold by;
Gaze down my rifle at his breast – but then
A soldier I.

They say that he was kindly – different, too
Apart from all the rest;
A lover of the poor; and all shot through
His wounds ill drest,

He came before us, faced us like a man,
Who knew a deeper pain
Than blows or bullets – ere the world began;
Died he in vain?

Ready present! And he just smiling – God!
I felt my rifle shake.
His wounds were opened out and round that chair
Was one red lake;
I swear his lips said 'Fire!' when all was still
Before my rifle spat
That cursed lead – And I was picked to kill
A man like that.

W.R. RODGERS
1909–1969

Born in Belfast, Rodgers studied at Queen's University and was ordained in 1935. He served as minister in Loughgall, County Armagh, until 1946 when he joined the BBC as a script writer. In 1953 he became a freelance writer and he moved to California in 1966. His *Awake! And Other Poems* was published in 1941.

WAR-TIME

Now all our hurries that hung up on hooks,
And all our heels that idly kicked in halls,
And all our angers that at anchor swung,
And all our youth long tethered to dole-lines,
And all our roots that rotted deep in dump,
Are recollected: in country places
Old men gather the children round them now,
As an old tree, when lopped of every bough,
Gathers the young leaves into itself, a frilled stump.

ESCAPE

The roads of Europe are running away from the war,
Running fast over the mined bridges and past the men
Waiting there, with watch, ready to maim and arrest them,
And strong overhead the long snorings of the planes' tracks
Are stretching like rafters from end to end of their power.
Turn back, you who want to escape or want to forget
The ruin of all your regards. You will be more free
At the thoughtless centre of slaughter than you would be
Standing chained to the telephone-end while the world cracks.

THE INTERNED REFUGEE

And I was left here in the darkened house,
Listening for the fat click of the softly-shut door,
Looking for the oiled glint and ghost of light
Sliding soundlessly along the wall toward me,
Knowing that round me They were mobilising
Their cold implacable forces slowly.

I shouted and none answered, one by one
My listening hopes crept back to me
Out of that dead place; mine was a lighted face
Looking into darkness, seen, but seeing nothing.

BRYAN MacMAHON
1909–1998

MacMahon was born in Listowel, County Kerry, where he worked as a schoolteacher for over forty years. He was later writer in residence at several American universities. As well as writing poetry, fiction and several plays, he wrote for radio and television and was a collector of music and song.

CORNER BOYS

Day in, day out,
The line of corner boys,
Ex-soldiers most,
Expectorate, expatiate,
On subtleties of scandal,
On ways of catching fish
In distant lands.
On housing schemes and strikes,
On handy ways of killing men,
On bawds.
On charms and spells
On mysteries of birth and death,
And ways of welding steel,
On inside alterations
Wrought by fever,
On constipation and on ailments
On pigeons and pagodas,
On rhombuses and razors …
God's truth! Who'd patronize the halls of Art
And schools of great renown,
When here,
A step beyond your door,
The gleanings of the globe
Are thrown into your lap?

Few finger-posts have trod the way they point,
Embittered, lonely, cynical,
What if they tell of maids
With awful malevolence
In their downfall?
These who have seen
the sun behind a minaret,
the strands of France,
the cobalt seas ...
While here,
Here the lonesome Kerry winds
Shriek up along the draughty streets,
And howl around the corner
Where the corner boys are growing grey,
Dreaming of sunny skies.

SEÁN JENNETT
1910–*n.d.*

Born in Yorkshire of Irish descent, Jennett worked as a typographer for Faber and Faber, who published his first poetry collection, *Always Adam*, in 1943. He also wrote travel books and *The Making of Books* (1951), an important guide to printing.

from ALWAYS ADAM

XXXVII
CAFÉ AU LAIT

We talked of war with light and easy lips,
jesting upon our action, this or that,
if it came to the last, and while we chattered
we drank our coffee in delicious sips
and watched the soft, contented café cat.

But then the woman in the wicker chair
cried Havoc! and suddenly I was afire
because I saw, under the skirts of light,
the corpses of our laughter and delight
smashed and dismembered, bloodily bespattered
across the red carpet ...

           And still the solemn stare
of all the sleepy cats in Oxfordshire.

1937

XXXVIII

CLERKS

Curve and grapple and growth of apple-red brick
close us, enwomb us, in rows under the lamps;
heads bent over books, tongues sucking enamelled pens,
we are the metal of war in warily peaceful camps.

But what if no cannon roars, no bullet is fired,
what if the world for peace loses the chance
for us of excitement and death in foreign fields,
ours for ever the brick and the walled-in, short-stopped
   glance:

ours eyes glazed with the dust of travelled dreams,
brains dazed, wandering feet chained in;
no marching songs in towns, by fabled streams,
nor danger of death, nor joy of ultimate sin.

1938

XL

THE NEWS WAS TOLD

Hearing the grouse call across the moor
their words' warning through the marble day
we climbed the steep rift through the heather,
you and I, the dreamed-of girl and boy:
   and in the east the tall guns burned.

The thin clouds flung across the early sky
were veils of cosmic dancers for us then
and the green wind along the level flower
the scarves' draught. Nearer and dearer than
   the dead rotting where the front was turned.

207

And yet we felt even in the marvellous air
the quick glitter of the million blades
and in the wind on the sharp-edged crag
the ache where the torn wound bleeds;
    yet dimly, not as the nerves feel.

But when we dropped into the smoking valley
and the news was told by the goggle-eyed
the blades were our blades, and the wound
was ours: we were the ones that died
    because the old world flared and fell.

1942

XLI
THE LODGER

Peace was the held of heart, the following love,
the unexpressible air of the sucking lung:
five senses cradled it in the common nerve
and in its sleep forgot it for too long.
O not until the knife-edge balance tilts
too far, and the bayonet burnishes the day
with its disciplined and sloping gleam
where hostile troops along the front deploy
do we of our dear element take care
or alter it to hold the modern place
it earns in change: we are always too slow
to hate the threat, too diffident to please
ourselves; and take the lodger in
who turns peace out of heart, and will remain.

1942

XLII

AUTUMN 1940

The days were glorious – we remember that
because the clear September of that year
was good for bombers. We remember it
because the sky screamed and we were mere
items of wreckage in the ruined day,
the half-face or the limbless or the dead,
the convenient basis for the hero's fame,
the rescued rubble in the hospital bed.

I was the man in the collapsing tower.
I was the body in the flooded shelter.
I was the mad objector shifting stone,
the conscious saint arising in his hour.
I was the bomber, the breaker and the welder.
I was the shattered and the exulting son.

1942

XLIII

WINTER 1940–1

And we remember the rain and sleet of winter
and the falling iron fountains of the guns,
the empty rattle on the dangerous roof,
the sudden birth and death of brilliant suns:
and then the flowering of the dark horizon
with rose of fire and red smoke-bordered petal,
the lovely vision of the gape of horror,
agony of collapse and sear of exploding metal.

And we, my dear, were there, the fellow flesh,
feeling the shear and sever of the bone,
feeling the horror enter at the eye;
but felt no hate: for those broken in that flash
pity and love. Lit by the flaring gun
a new Christ hung on the old Calvary.

1942

XLIV

For my love's sake bring me safe out of this
furnace of fire and fury of battering bomb,
I who wait unsheltered on the roof,
to-night no croucher of the catacomb:
myself safe home, who feel disfigurement
in curling nerve, imagination's flesh,
recognizing the occasion as it comes,
the scarred face or limb shattered in the flash.

I am the power, the splinterer of the stars:
what lizard voice is it lifts from the world
to split my dreams, what fierce desire or fear?

My voice is every silent prayer that stirs
in men who stand below this sky: the wild
phoenix emerging from its womb of fire.

1942

XLV
SUPERSTITIONS

The sailor seeing the octopus swim below
and the cool sails of the carrion shark
sees there the likely end, the last confusion,
the beak that waits the failure of his work,
    the bite that closes the whimpering of the nerve.

Turning to his familiar gun he sees
the thin medallion of his future hung
upon the sight, and down the rifled barrel
his path goes: where the high birds sing
    death swings, a cross, along the quiet curve.

In England still the summer flower is torn
to tell a silly girl the truth of love;
his smiling photograph is studied too
and bids anxiety no longer grieve
    since yet it hangs unfaded on the wall.

The sailor sweating at the smoking breach,
feeling the bomb strike and the sudden smart,
in extasy rejects the grasp of the sea
yet catches comfort where above his heart
    his fingers feel the crinkle of the caul.

1942

XLVI

Fighting in naked deserts he thought of home,
the soldier swallowed by the drouth of war,
of fields and heavy trees and quiet rivers
and the apple-hearted hollow forests where

211

the girders of the blackthorn blossomed over
in early spring: and thrushes loved to sing
through all the cool green shadows of the summer
their bell-dropping, water-falling song.

Here earth's bones lie bleached below the sun
and the barrenness of death fills up the eye
all day; and there is never any shelter
from the anger of the sky; nor any sign
of gentleness: grain grinding grain, the dry
sands drag across the days their burning shutter.

1942

XLVII
THE ADMIRALTY REGRETS TO ANNOUNCE ...

When sharp-toothed ache in the hollow bone
runs, and flesh to brother flesh
gropes blind along the circle sea
the chambers of the heart flood flush
    with fill of grief and the dead weight of doubt.

Where spills the common blood the passionate wound
opens and spills too; and the water
of the slurring sea fills up the gape
with pain early and with carrion later;
    nor lulling drives the devil out.

But in the evil of gradual death
the drowning spin where the dear ship dives
and end; and the keen edge of hate
beyond the margin of the closing waves
    is thrust, to cut the heart's love and its coiling shoot.

1942

L

THE SOLDIER

O waiter on quays, above the oily water,
the smooth swell of the sluggish yellow tide
slapping on beams under, your sight last
of home a packing straw bobbing on the slide
and heave of harbour, you and all your host
of uniformed companions, why leave
your heart of quiet land, your hearth of ease?
Is it because an extasy of love,
a Christ-like self-denying, drums and drives you?

Think of the girl who by the iron line
a diagram of love made for her grieving,
her waving white for you a flag: she
longer than you live will continue loving.
And hands that nursed you once, now lax, and shy
of comforting this stranger son, the soldier,
but with no less affection, you know how.
Is love the reason why you are the wielder
of all that robs a woman of her love?

Is it the snare of danger that attracts you,
or the persuasion of the patterned lie?
Cradle your reason in your secret breast,
cradle where Christ once in communion lay,
for if your faith shall fail the silent beast
that crouches in the rotting corpse shall tear
your soul, and for each idle human boast
drive in the crooked talons of despair.
Hold fast in faith: even the false may save you.

Yet not entirely free you when your finger
crooked from the stock, commands insistent death
and fires the vulture bullet through the valley.
O you who drag your days with living breath
from corpse to breathless corpse, in your own belly
shall feel the passionate wound of an old fable
of flagged crosses on a scar of hill, and feel
the bitterness of prayer. Now in the feeble
heart Christ gutters out, suffers again defeat.

1942

LI

Since men attracted by the lust of death
kill their dear love, and the wide breast of peace
stab through, how shall we teach the following age
the use of this, not long, expensive lease?
Since we destroy, shall not they too destroy,
by our example making worse destruction?
Now is the aching nail of all dead years,
and we for our sons are the cancerous friction.

Is there no help? The sickness breeds again
and makes men mad. Nor rest is cure.
Peace is a fallow field, bright with bayonets;
Christ's love grows guns, cross calls the sky its own:
and yet the careful womb, the issuing core
of time, breeds store. Our heritage is minutes.

1942

FOR THOMAS FLANAGAN

This breast of sea that suckled sullen war
from that far time when men first gave themselves
into the perilous hollow of a ship
and thrust their cockleshells to new horizons
breeds war again and rasps the steel
of death against the scaffold bone. Jackals
crunch the time with fangs of fire;
the mouths of fish gape, spiked and avid:
and the lax limb surrenders to the tooth,
the blind eye calls no fear up to the heart.

O in the icy waters of the north
under the floes he swings at rest
who drowned his turbulence in the restless sea
and fled the empty spaces of the land
that gave no purchase to his wandering feet
and would not have his strength and his small skill:
even when the spectre at the last
broke down the door and stood upon the sill
and silently walked through the sleepy room
and touched his enemies and claimed their souls.

THE LETTER

She has a letter, and the crinkled sheet
stands in her hands, facing its careless scrawl
to her face, and through her morning eyes
links with the eager question in the scroll
of brain: the words have power to move, to laugh
or weep, what though the wielder lacked in skill.

On nightmare seas the letter swung, yet came
to this small village and to her own door
to-day, swung on sea and flung in air
to her; and nerveless hands and aching bodies dare
the splitting world for this, the personal noun,
the I that means the living is her dear.

So though the danger of a world at war
lies over all, the coupling ego joins
still, and life springs from the ultimate fusion;
growing to future among the traps and gins
of a scarecrow world: but growing from barrenness
through shooting blades to harvest in other Junes.

MORNING

Now curls of mist swirl in the water-meadow
this cool morning, coming before summer heat
of sun, and curds crowd on the plangent chord
of the canal, or on the sloping, scarred
garth of hill slip, slide, supple, dissolving,
mouth's steamy breath, earth's shawl, night's remnant
    shadow.

Each neb of bush holds daedal webs of light
spun like glass in threads, bridging, brittle span,
from leaf to leaf; and spider mesh is strung
all round with water jewels; even the strong,
the tall trees bend, list under burden of
fine woof and warp, the thin chill stuff of night.

Through this the throb of engines thrills the brain
from sleep, as, in all-grey, wings slit the air
from Europe, from fire-spouting, under-sliding fields,
and in the sheet of mist, the dangerous folds
of vapour, eyes look for land, smooth-levelled lawn,
for rest of firm, familiar green and brown.

And when the sun with violent eye clears all
the cold away, the fogs and webs of dark,
that shutter off this island to its dream,
along the margin of the aerodrome
black bombers stand, silent, pitiful birds,
that lately raged over and split the fearful skull.

EXPLOSION

That rounding smoke drives out the souls of men,
creating nullity where once the mind had engined
and glad tongue wagged; on the cool light of evening
flinging the severed limb and rain of brain.

On that round pillow do the dead men lie
who made the shattering instruments of death,
who at their quick, precise machines all day
had fashioned for a thousand men their end.

Now in their own home is that grief attending
that should have waited in their neighbour's house;
their own wives weep, while other wives are glad,
seeing the angel pass for this time more.

But yet death drives and will not be directed
by every order of our ingenuity:
its force makes farce of our most careful plans
or shakes disaster from a careless finger.

LESLIE DAIKEN
1912–1964

Daiken was born in Dublin and educated at TCD before moving to London. He was a private in the Irish Army during the Emergency. A Republican socialist, he edited the *Irish Front* with Charles Donnelly. He is the author of two poetry collections and editor of the poetry anthology, *Good-Bye, Twilight* (1936).

NIGHTFALL IN GALWAY

Now when the buildings of all Europe don their sackcloth
And the places and the plazas prepare for raiders, all
    lamps hidden,
Night spreads her spangled quilt of silk on Galway City.

In Eyre Square beats the stillness of epilepsy, not the hush
that follows the convulsion of ambush.
The children chanting *Asher, asher, we all fall down*, have
faded into a motor engine filtering desolation.

And suddenly, from the throat of dream,
and about the stone ears of O Connaire on his plinth,
a lepracaun listening,
falls the husky song of drunkards like the call of a muezzin.

Sleep cancels the very water of this mystery.
Sleep freezes the water of our isolated peace.
Beauty throbs
unbeholden of ten thousand pairs of native eyes
    re-emigrant,
under April stars.

Till, waking to a blackbird's highborn singing
that trickles between brown clamps of turf like bastions,
the night's silk is become
a blaze of skylight.
A Church bell rings and a Spring morning unfolds
her hair of Andalusian jet, and combs it out, smiling.

DONAGH MacDONAGH
1912–1968

MacDonagh was born in Dublin, the son of poet and 1916
Rising leader, Thomas MacDonagh. Educated at UCD, he was
called to the bar in 1935 and made a district judge in 1941.
He published three collections of poetry, including *The Hungry
Grass* (1947), and several plays, and was a broadcaster on Radio
Éireann.

HE IS DEAD AND GONE, LADY...

(For Charles Donnelly, RIP)

Of what a quality is courage made
That he who gently walked our city streets
Talking of poetry or philosophy,
Spinoza, Keats.
Should lie like any martyred soldier
His brave and fertile brain dried quite away
And the limbs that carried him from cradle to death's
    outpost
Growing down into a foreign clay.

Gone from amongst us and his life not half begun
Who had followed Jack-o-Lantern truth and liberty
Where it led wavering from park-bed to prison cell
Into a strange land, dry misery,
And then into Spain's slaughter, sniper's aim
And his last shocked embrace of earth's lineaments.
Can I picture truly that swift end
Who see him dead with eye that still repents.

What end, what quietus, can I see for him
Who had the quality of life in every vein?
Life with its passion and poetry and its proud
Ignorance of eventual loss or gain.
This first fruit of our harvest, willing sacrifice
Upon the altar of his integrity
Lost to us; somewhere his death is charted –
Something has been gained by this mad missionary.

JUST AN OLD SWEET SONG

The pale, drooping girl and the swaggering soldier,
The row-dow-dow-dow of the stuttering drum,
The bugles, the charges, the swords are romantic
For those who survive when the bugles are dumb.

The lice of the trenches, the mortars, machine-guns,
The prisoners exchanged and the Christmas Day lull,
The no-man's-land raid and the swagger-stick rally
Are stirring, for when was a finished war dull?

The road-block, the ambush, the scrap on the mountain,
The slouch-hat, the trench-coat, the raid in the night,
The hand-grenade hefted, police-barracks burning
Ah, that was the life, and who's hurt in a fight?

The blitzkrieg, the landings, the victories, the losses,
The eyes blind with sand, the retreat, the alert,
Commando and D-Day, H-Hour and Block-buster
Have filed through the glass, and was anyone hurt?

A flash and a mushroom, a hole in the planet,
Strange growth in the flora, less fauna to feed.
Peace enters, the silence returns and the waters
Advance on the earth as the war tides recede.

CHARLES DONNELLY
1914–1937

Donnelly was born in County Tyrone and educated at UCD, where he became involved in republican politics. In 1936 he joined the International Brigade and fought in the Spanish Civil War, where he died in action. A collection of his work, *The Life and Poems*, which includes a memoir by his brother, Joseph, was published in 1987.

THE FLOWERING BARS

After sharp words from the fine mind,
protest in court,
the intimate high head constrained,
strait lines of prison, empty walls,
a subtle beauty in a simple place.

There to strain thought through the tightened brain,
there weave
the slender cords of thought, in calm,
until routine in prospect bound
joy into security,
and among strictness sweetness grew,
mystery of flowering bars.

THE TOLERANCE OF CROWS

Death comes in quantity from solved
Problems on maps, well-ordered dispositions,
Angles of elevation and direction;

Comes innocent from tools children might
Love, retaining under pillows,
Innocently impales on any flesh.

And with flesh falls apart the mind
That trails thought from the mind that cuts
Thought clearly for a waiting purpose.

Progress of poison in the nerves and
Discipline's collapse is halted.
Body awaits the tolerance of crows.

POEM

Between rebellion as a private study and the public
Defiance, is simple action only on which will flickers
Catlike, for spring. Whether at nerve-roots is secret
Iron, there's no diviner can tell, only the moment can show.
Simple and unclear moment, on a morning utterly different
And under circumstances different from what you'd expected.

Your flag is public over granite. Gulls fly above it.
Whatever the issue of the battle is, your memory
Is public, for them to pull awry with crooked hands,
Moist eyes. And village reputations will be built on
Inaccurate accounts of your campaign. Your name for orators,
Figure stone-struck beneath damp Dublin sky.

In a delaying action, perhaps, on hillside in remote parish,
Outposts correctly placed, retreat secured to wood, bridge mined
Against pursuit, sniper may sight you carelessly contoured.
Or death may follow years in strait confinement, where diet
Is uniform as ceremony, lacking only fruit.
Or on the barrack square before the sun casts shadow.

Name, subject of all-considered words, praise and blame
Irrelevant, the public talk which sounds the same on hollow
Tongue as true, you'll be with Parnell and with Pearse.
Name aldermen will raise a cheer with, teachers make reference
Oblique in class, and boys and women spin gum of sentiment
On qualities attributed in error.

Man, dweller in mountain huts, possessor of coloured mice,
Skilful in minor manual turns, patron of obscure subjects, of
Gaelic swordsmanship and mediaeval armoury.
The technique of the public man, the masked servilities are
Not for you. Master of military trade, you give
Like Raleigh, Lawrence, Childers, your services but not yourself.

HEROIC HEART

Ice of heroic heart seals plasmic soil
Where things ludicrously take root
To show in leaf kindess time had buried
And cry music under a storm of 'planes,
Making thrust head to slacken, muscle waver
And intent mouth recall old tender tricks.
Ice of heroic heart seals steel-bound brain.

There newer organs built for friendship's grappling
Waste down like wax. There only leafless plants
And earth retain disinterestedness.
Thought, magnetised to lie of the land, moves
Heartily over the map wrapped in its iron
Storm. Battering the roads, armoured columns
Break walls of stone or bone without receipt.
Jawbones find new ways with meat, loins
Raking and blind, new ways with women.

THOMAS O'BRIEN
1914–1974

Born in Dublin, O'Brien was a Republican socialist, joining the labour movement which included writers like Brendan Behan and Leslie Daiken. In 1938 he joined the International Brigade and fought in the Spanish Civil War. The author of several plays, he helped to set up the New Theatre Group and co-founded The O'Brien Press shortly before his death.

CONNOLLY

We shall not gather like banshees around his grave
And wail a sentimental dirge,
As if his Death were all his life;
Far better leave him quiet in the shade
Than remember only that he died,
He lived, lest smothered in an earthy avalanche you forget.
He was the Man who stood with clenched fist
Under the workers Red;
He who like a miner went below
And brought forbidden objects to the light –
Slimy things that crawled across the earth
And looked with bulbous eyes at their creators.
He was a demolisher of capitalism,
He was the breath of the Revolution,
He was the Red Terror –
Connolly, lest you forget.

1936

BEAUTY WE HAVE HEARD YOUR VOICE

Beauty we have heard your voice
And we have dared to answer
And we have dared to follow close behind
Trembling and faltering, but ever coming closer
Until, with a dint of sparks
Have we not passed you
Gone far ahead

And sat calmly awaiting you
That way a man waits for his wife
O, to be sure of you beauty
And not to tremble
Is an old man's feeling, he with an eye for wine
And no thirst.

1936

ALWAYS BATTLING

There is an exquisite torture in living with dull people,
Look with eyes of hate and fear
At a fine man or woman:
And the brutality of not caring,
Not feeling, not seeing, not hearing –
Not realising at all
Things that cry aloud for vengeance.

Exterminate!
O, to have the power to exterminate
All the cruel, stupid things about.

Do you wonder that people kill themselves?
Do you wonder that people run amok and kill others?
Do you wonder that men and women fling their bodies
    across the livid mouths of guns?
Mad with fury …

227

Weep not over the shot body of a young Communist
Lying face down in the gutter.
Had you known the wild delirium of his spirit,
The accumulated hate and bitterness compressed into
    his brain
Until he was mad with sanity –
Had you known the fever in him,
You would laugh at the poor torn body;
The least harm they could do him –
They had done their worst before.

One and one and one and still they come,
Men and women in revolt;
Out of one dead body leaps another living.
They killed one that I might be born,
Another that you might be born.
So on and on,
Until one day they'll smother in their own creations
With all they held and had,
Leaving nothing but a book of curious stories
For some small child to criticise with smiling eyes:
'I don't believe that ALL of it is true!'

1936

MARCHING FEET

Nowadays, is there an hour when workers are not on the march,
Somewhere in the world, in unified ranks,
For a dead or suffering comrade?
In defiance of those who cause the death and suffering,
And pollute the very vision of the future
By heaping their stinking corpses across the road of progress.

This time in memory of Rory, Liam, Dick, and Joe.
This marching is a lesser thing than their dying;
They did lesser things before they died,
Such as marching like this in the ranks;
But the flame that led to the consummation burned white in them
As they marched in the ranks.
You could not see the flame
But you could hear the tramping of the feet
Then as now.

And there are Rory, Liam, Dick, and Joe marching in the ranks,
And the hidden white flame which will lead to another
    consummation.
Poor ways we have of expressing the things we feel.
The spirit of a class-conscious worker
Is a clean, bright thing striving on the surface of their spew,
Striving to be free.
Struggling against the loathsome sucking which is the essence of it.

They want us all to be sucked down into the abyss,
But here we are marching over it,
Marching, always marching.

Under our feet, hypocrisy;
Under our feet, their decorated bellies;
Under our feet, the revolting mash of their brains.
We are destroying them.
There is a great mockery in the marching feet of the working-class
For them and their foolish antics,
As with long, solemn faces they try to resurrect the corpses,
And tell us life will return after all,
If only we stop marching on the entrails.

The working class is always on the march,
All over the world, in unified ranks.
Come suffering and death,
Lies and vilifications,
Treachery, vacillation, and a million compromises,
We will march to the head of things,
We will seize power,
WE WILL MAINTAIN IT.

1936

INTERNATIONAL BRIGADE DEAD

A lonely student in a silent room
Quits his lagging pen to dream
Of thundering mountains;
Crouches, tight-faced, where the vine-stump
Spreads its silent singing leaves,
Still eyes where the lifting dust
Speaks of death;
Leaps from vine to covering vine
To the mound of safety;
Dies, as fancy has it,
Gladly as the sun's bright theatre.

An old man lifts his misty eye
To the brown ceiling of his life,
Regrets the nearness of his papered walls,
Wonders why he dared not dare
The sun to cast his leaning shadow
Forward on a page of time
Unticked by clocks on tidy mantels.

A poet takes the sudden bayonet gleam to paper,
Waking hurried echoes in the huddled hills,
Not for any prideful lust or wing-clipped cause –
But for their beauty, those children of the wonder-moment,
Who dared to die in youth that youth might live.

Where the rising sun is,
Where the setting sun is,
Where the wind is
And the rain,
Where the striding spirit is
They go in their battalions,
Eager as the elements they conquered.

With you, O youth, forever,
They shall never rest in peace.

1939

TERROR

I lay and speculated on the impact of a bullet;
Had sight of a body spurting blood,
Sprawled helpless dying;
Clearly I saw myself erect and then
Staggered in the shock of bullets.
I saw the cold eye of the gunner,
I saw the black rim of the gun's muzzle;
I said, chewing breadcrumbs:
'In a few moments I may be dead.'
Terror is kept under a steel spring;
It is the octopus in every soldier's eye
In still deep waters calm, O calm.

1941

GEORGE HETHERINGTON
1916–2001

Hetherington was born in Dublin and educated in England. He worked as a printer in Dublin for forty years and in 1954 he became a director of the *Irish Times*. He published a collection of poetry, *Delphi and Other Poems*, in 1986 and was a gifted painter.

SONNET

Now keep that long revolver at your side
The chambers full, dry-clean, the action cocked;
Sandbag the windows, see the doors are locked,
Set all the fuses, time them and decide
The minute and the hour. Be patient; pride
Demands a shattered wall, a ruined keep,
A trinket for posterity, a cheap
Excursion to the mudheap where you died.

Cut out the loopholes, test their fields of fire,
Survey the ground, select your last retreat:
Somewhere between the earthwork and the wire
There is a foxhole where the meadowsweet
Will fold your anguish in a flowery net
And when you sleep be your sad coverlet.

LAS RAICES

(Franco on Tenerife: July 1936)

The treacherous officers stroll under the trees,
Breakfast, write their despatches, inspect the lines:
A blue sky, seen through this tent of pines,
Promises heat. From the north-east a breeze
Hisses through the forest – all else is still.
From somewhere near at hand a bugle calls,
Echoes along the woodland's open walls,
Dies in a craggy valley up the hill.

A young man checks his watch; time to set forth.
The camp is broken and the columns move
Like long green insects from the silent grove,
Spain and the future waiting in the north.
Their destination only time will tell –
Toledo's walls or slopes of Teruel
Or Ronda's bridge or Ebro's bloody shore –
But this green wood will shelter them no more.

GEORGE M. BRADY
1917–*n.d.*

Brady was born in County Clare and lived in Dublin and England. His poems were published in newspapers, literary journals and anthologies, including *Poems from Ireland* (1944).

THE HOSTS

Who shall welcome home
The soldier or the gray
Exile from shelterless seas?
Who shall hold out hands
To the late arrivals
Stumbling without a light?
Who shall hold the keys
To this shuttered house,
You, the ghost, or I, the living man?

For the days are short, the hours
Numbered upon the clock,
The guests will soon arrive,
The honoured one be back,
But who will stand within
The deep shadow of this door,
Who will light the lamps,
Dust of the hidden air,
You, the ghost, or I, the living man?

THE CONQUERORS

O, then, the bright day hung
Banners of sunlight from high balconies,
The helmets and the drumming music
Deafened and dazzled us, the soldier's sons,
Gaping between giant legs at men-of-war
Who strode through the gale of welcome,
    proud-backed, tall.

And at night, we lay in sleepless beds,
Their songs and laughter echoing through the streets,
Whispering deeds of wonder, feats of strength,
Of raging rivers crossed, fortresses taken,
Battles won on bloody hillsides,
Proud of these tall, strong-handed men.

To-day, they lie, sea-deep or settled clay, forgotten
By all but the very old or us. And we, their sons,
Walk the same pitted roads, the sun
Remote as any star, dust in our eyes,
Bloody the banners, and the women weeping
In darkened doorways under an evil sky.

Others, perhaps, shall recommend our deeds.
But the dying need neither words of praise nor
History's mention. This, only this is real,
This country of dry bones and vulture beaks,
O, and the terror striking like an angry God,
Heedless of friend or foe, where murder walks.

Now, we lie down to sleep, but uneasily.
The music dies along the unlit streets.
And the towns are derelict, the quays
Guarded by vizored men, the women
Lonely as ours, and the flags
Faded and listless in a stagnant wind.

HAVE YOU WALKED

Have you walked by the tide
And listened to the wind's
Anger, and the rocks
Chiming the water's tune;
Have you prayed for the dead
Close to your living side,
The dead below decks,
Who will not feel again
The shock of wave and gale;
Have you walked on the wall
Between the sea and the stricken town,
Have you walked alive and known,
As the sea rises, as the sea falls,
As the light narrows, and the wind moans,
That the ghost staring
With a ghost's eyes is your own?

VALENTIN IREMONGER
1918–1991

Iremonger was born in Sandymount, Dublin, and trained at the Abbey School of Acting. He served as Irish Ambassador to Sweden, Norway and Finland, Luxembourg and then Portugal. His poetry collections include *Reservations* (1950) and *Sandymount, Dublin* (1988). He also edited *Contemporary Irish Poetry* (1949) with Robert Greacen.

SOLDIER FROM THE WARS

Somebody, I gather, is fishing in Galway,
In afternoon drift on the Corrib's lower reaches,
Hooking deftly the wet fish, returning
Easily to tea at sundown.

He is, I think, a young man with girls in his eyes –
Afternoon tennis and romantic late-night dances,
Hoping to meet later the gallant girl, marry,
Have two children, live comfortably in the country.

He has survived Dunkirk and the Grecian islands,
Coming unscathed to fight on the cliffs of Crete
And after in Africa, to and fro across the desert,
Seeking the promised land of his happiness.

And he has known also his private danger,
The ugly nip in the night from the crab-like claws
Of *Why didn't I do it* and *What should I say*,
Through the strait hours and no answer.

And now, eluding London and the swinging girls,
He comes to this backwater to attempt to hook
The five-foot-ten of happiness which is his birthright
Before his blood trumpets a more insidious war.

Whom I heard of casually in a Dublin bus, to this
Unknown young man my hand reaches, to answer
The wishes in his sinews and behind his eyes,
Unspoken in the gardens of his longing.

I pray that this unknown young man who has known
The lightning's strict hour, the time of anger
And the thunder within, may know also
The peace following always the days of action.

May he survive unscathed the Dunkirk of middle-age
And cardiac decay, the Crete of married life,
The Peloponnese-like archipelagoes of children, to fish lazily
In the reaches of a quiet old age.

L.J. FENNESSY
1919–1941

Fennessy entered the defence forces in 1939 and was made lieutenant in 1940. On 16 September 1941 he was one of fifteen members of the County Kildare Anti-aircraft Battalion killed in an accidental training mine explosion in Glen Imaal, County Wicklow.

TWENTY-FOUR

A thousand mad, wild thoughts packed into a day,
with a lovable, laughable, wild unruly crew,
a moment's sadness or a moment's gladness,
and yet no sound or hint of dread.

They placed us there together,
twenty-four
Brady and Ryan and Dillon close to the door,
O'Loughlin and the black-haired mad O'Shea.
And so time fled like a single day.

Will we still be together when it ends?
How many dead?
How many no longer friends?
How shall we gather
In the Nation's need?
How many will tell the tale of glorious deeds
Performed by one we knew,
One of the twenty-four;
By Eager or Heron or Dillon by the door?
Perhaps in a week, perhaps this very night or next
Comes the dread call
A raid in the half dead light
A silver twinkling speck in a searchlight's ray;
A bomb on its way to earth hunting a prey.

Will it be one of the twenty-four,
One of the lads I knew,
Who falls in the night
Shorn of his radiant life, one of the gallant crew,
Struck in his prime?
There lay his broken gun
And will they be there to tell,
The rest of the twenty-four
How willingly he fell?
When at last the fight is over
Will there be more perchance
Than one to shed his blood
Dying beside his gun
Smilingly, even as he fell
Knowing the fight was good,
Knowing that someone will tell
Some of the lads he knew,
Some of the laughing twenty-four
How even in death were true.

MAURICE J. CRAIG
b. 1919

Craig was born in Belfast and educated at Cambridge University and TCD. He has published books on the history of Dublin and Irish architecture. His poetry collections include *Twelve Poems* (1942) and *Some Way for Reason* (1948).

SPRING, 1943

The crackling laughter of malignant gods
Disturbed our sleep all winter, yet we allowed
The smoke that lent a sharpness to the air
To stand for the resurrection of the dead.
And now the brighter bonfires of the spring
Are burning, and for a time we must admire
The flaring tongues of flame that lap and lick
Around the resinous twigs, the rivulets
Of sap, that hissing load the air with scent.
And for a time, like children, we delight
In finery of destruction, we who know
The same pot boils, however fresh the thorns.

KILCARTY TO DUBLIN

The paraffin-lamps and the home-cured bacon
The whitewash misty behind the trees
Are taken apart and sorted and shaken
By a war that rages beyond two seas

The sweets in the dim shop-window glitter
The idiot girl still sniffs in the bus
The literal meaning of all grows bitter
If not for her, then at least for us

But life goes on in the last lit city
Just in the way it has always done
And pity is lost on the tongues of the witty
And the wolf at the door is a figure of fun

1943

EOGHAN Ó TUAIRISC
1919–1982

Born in Ballinasloe, County Galway, Ó Tuairisc served with the Irish army during the Second World War. Writing also as Eugene Watters, he is the author of several poetry collections, plays and novels, in Irish and English. These include translations of the work of Mairtín Ó Cadhain, the experimental poem *The Weekend of Dermot and Grace* (1964) and *Lux Aeterna* (1964).

as AIFREANN NA MARBH

Fuair Bás ag Hiroshima
Dé Luain, 6ú Lúnasa, 1945

Transumanar significar per verba
non si poria; però l'esemplo basti
a cui esperïenza Grazia serba
DANTE, *Paradiso*, I, 70–72

1

INTROITUS

Músclaíonn an mhaidin ár míshuaimhneas síoraí.
Breathnaím trí phána gloine
Clogthithe na hÁdhamhchlainne
Ár gcuid slinn, ár gCré, ár gcúirteanna
Ar snámh san fhionnuaire.
Nochtann as an rosamh chugam
An ghlanchathair mhaighdeanúil
Ag fearadh a haiséirí:
Músclaíonn an mhaidin ár míshuaimhneas síoraí.

Broinnean an ceatal binnuaigneach i mo chroí
Ar fheiscint dom a háilleachta,
Géagshíneadh a gealsráideanna
Le hais na habhann, na coillte,
Líne na gcnoc pinnsilteach
Á háitiú ina céad riocht –
Mo chailín cathrach fornocht
Ina codladh ag áth na gcliath:
Músclaíonn an mhaidin ár míshuaimhneas síoraí.

244

from THE MASS OF THE DEAD

Died in Hiroshima
Monday, 6th June, 1945

Transumanar significar per verba
non si poria; però l'esemplo basti
a cui esperïenza Grazia serba
DANTE, *Paradiso*, I, 70–72

1

INTROIT

The morning arouses our unceasing unease.
From behind a pane of glass I look out
At the bell towers of the Adam-clan:
Our slates, our creed, our lawcourts
Floating in the freshness.
Out of the haze
The virginal bright city
Unveils herself for me,
Offering resurrection.
The morning arouses our unceasing unease.

The lonely-sweet pang in my heart
Stirs at the sight of her beauty,
Stretching her limbs, her bright streets,
Beside the river. And the woods
And the line of the trickling hill-peaks
Establish her in her hundred guises,
My girl-city stark naked
Sleeping by the wattle-ford.
The morning arouses our unceasing unease.

Tagann an aisling rinnuaibhreach anoir,
Scaipeann rós is airgead
Trí smúit a calafoirt
Ina lá léaspairte, súnas
Ag éigniú a maighdeanais
Nó go bhfágtar gach creat
Gach simléar, gach seolchrann
Ina chnámh dhubh, ina ghrianghraf
Ag léiriú inmhíniú mo laoi:
Músclaíonn an mhaidin ár míshuaimhneas síoraí.

2

KYRIE

*Siú Íosasú, amhaireimí tama-i!**

Déan trócaire orainn atá gan trócaire
Dár n-ainmhian eolaíochta déan trua,
Foilsigh trí shalachar na haimsire
A chruthaíomar dúinn féin, an ghrian nua.
D'aimsíomar an t-úll
D'fhág an tseanghrian faoi smál, *Siú Íosasú.*

Amhaireimí. Orainne ar na sráideanna
Chuireas cos thar chois amach ar maidin Luain
Gan aird againn ar ár gcuid scáileanna
Ag gliúchadh orainn ón ngloine, an dara slua
Ar choiscéim linn go ciúin
Mílítheach marbh múinte. *Siú Íosasú.*

* *'A Thiarna Íosa, déan trócaire orainn!' (Chualathas an phaidir sin
ar shráideanna Hiroshima maidin na tragóide.)*

The dream-vision out of the east, planet-proud,
Comes and scatters roseate-silver light
Among the grime of her harbour;
Comes as sparkling day, blinding,
And violates her virginity
Till each chimney, each beam
And ship's mast
Is reduced to black bone,
To photographic negative,
Bringing out the meaning of my verse:
The morning arouses our unceasing unease.

2

KYRIE
Siú Íosasú, amhaireimí tama-i!*

Have mercy on us who are without mercy,
Have pity on our lust for science.
Through the grime of the era
That we ourselves created
Show the new sun.
We split the apple
And left the old sun ash-coated. *Siú Íosasú.*

Amhaireimí, mercy on us who step out briskly
On the streets on a Monday morning,
Blind to the company of our bright shadows
Who peer at us from window-glass:
A second crowd of walkers
Quietly walking in step with our step,
Pale. Dead. Tamed. *Siú Íosasú.*

**Lord Jesus, have mercy on us! (This prayer was heard on the streets
of Hiroshima on the morning of the tragedy.)*

Siú. Siúlaim. Trí thionóisc na dteangacha
Gluaisim ar aghaidh ag machnamh ar an mbua
A bhaineamar amach, eolas na maitheasa
Agus an oilc i dtoil an té gan stiúir
Ina dhia beag ar siúl –
Amhaireimí. Amhaireimí. Siú Íosasú.

Siúd liom isteach tri áirse ollscoile
Ag snámh ina n-aghaidh, an t-aos óg gealsnua
A bhrúchtann chun solais lena málaí ascaille
Ag trácht ar an spás, an teoragán is nua,
An fhinnbheannach, an mhongrua
Is a dtálchuid faoi chuing na matamaitice. *Siú.*

Fanann a gcumhracht liom ar ghaoth a n-imeachta
Fanann seal nóiméid sa phasáiste cúng
Niamhracht agus naí-gháire na n-aoiseanna
A cnuasaíodh i bhfriotal binn nach buan,
D'éalaigh na nimfeacha uainn
Ach maireann mil a nginiúna faoin áirse againn. *Siú.*

Dearcaim arís trí shúile freacnairce
An chloch dhiúltach, an chearnóg mhanachúil,
Suaimhneas an chlabhstair ar a chearchall aislinge
Nach músclaítear ag clogdhán ná ag an uaill
Bhalbh phianstairiúil
I gcroílár an róis crochta chois balla. *Siú.*

Luaitear na dátaí, ainmneacha ailtirí,
Comhrá cneasta cinnte coillte acadúil,
Ní ligtear le fios i bhfocal paiseanta
Ainm an ailtire a dhearaigh an bunstua
Ní luaitear lá an Luain
Nó go labhraíonn an gairbhéal gáirsiúil faoinár sala. *Siú.*

248

Siú. I walk. Through the accident of languages
I move on, reflecting on our triumph –
The knowledge of good and evil
Under the control of the uncontrolled one
Like a little god in its progress.
Amhaireimí. Amhaireimí. Siú Íosasú.

In through a university archway,
Breasting the stream of bright young faces,
Bags on shoulders, pushing toward the light,
Discussing space, the latest theorem –
The blonde heads and the red –
Their contribution under mathematics' yoke. *Siú.*

Their freshness stays in the draught their passing makes:
Pausing a moment in the narrow passageway,
The shine and young laughter of the ages
That was stored in fragile sweet speech.
The nymphs stole away from us,
But the honey of their begetting stays
Under this arch of ours. *Siú.*

Through contemporary eyes I look again
At the stubborn stone, the monastic square,
The quiet of the cloister, the circle of its dream-vision
That will not be aroused by the bell,
Nor the mute pain-filled howl of history
That's deep in the heart of the rose that hangs by the wall. *Siú.*

Dates are cited, the names of architects,
The confident discourse of mild-mannered gelded academics.
Not conveyed in passionate words,
The name of the architect of the original arch.
The fatal Monday goes unmentioned
Till the bawdy gravel's voice is heard under our heels. *Siú.*

Tagann tollbhlosc ón bhfaiche imeartha
Ag méadú an chiúnais is ag cur in iúl
Dhíomhaointeas an dísirt ina bhfuilimid
Faoi aghaidheanna fidil leanbaí ag súil
Nach dtitfidh an tromchúis
Orainne, cé go screadann na rósanna as
croí a gcumhrachta. *Siú.*

Fiosraím an fál in uaigneas leabharlainne,
An litir ársa is an dobharchú
Ag breith ar an iasc i gcoidéacs Cheannannais
Idir an crot is a chéasadh, an dá rún,
Ag ceangal an chlabhsúir
San ainm seang a mharaigh mé. *Siú Íosasú.*

Siú. Siúl. Siúlaim. Siúlaimid
Trí rélmniú briathar, faí mharfach, ar aghaidh
Ó Luan go Luan ag ceapadh suaitheantais
In eibhearchloch na cathrach seo gan aidhm,
Tá an cailín ina haghaidh.
Siú Íosasú, amhaireimí tama-i.

3

GRADUALE

Ná tóg orm a Chríost
Go ndearnas an ghadaíocht
Is foirm do cheatail ghlinn
A dhealbhú dom aisling,

Buairt m'anama nach beag
I mo sheasamh ar chéimeanna
Na cathrach céasta, ceannocht,
Is cúis dom an ghadaíocht.

A piercing roar comes from the playing-field,
Deepening the quiet and bringing home
The sterility of the desert where we are,
Behind our childish masks, hoping
The heavy consequences don't fall on us
Even though the roses are screaming from
      their fragrant core. *Siú.*

In the solitude of the library I seek answers –
The noble lettering and the otter
Seizing the fish in the codex of Kells.
Between the conception and its crucifixion,
The two secrets binding the conclusion of the work,
The emaciated name of the one I killed. *Siú Íosasú.*

Siú. Walk. I am walking. We are walking
Through conjugations of verbs, the fatal whine,
Onward from Monday to Monday inventing emblems
In the granite blocks of this purposeless city:
The girl-woman stands against it.
Siú Íosasú, amhaireimí tama-i.

3

GRADUAL

    Don't hold it against me O Christ,
    That I stole
    The form of your bright passion
    To fashion my dream-vision

    My soul's anguish,
    Standing head uncovered
    On the steps of the crucified city,
    Is the reason for my thieving.

Sinne na mairbh fuair bás
In Áth Cliath is in antráth
Lá gréine na blasféime
Shéideamar Hiroshima.

Ní Gaeil sinn a thuilleadh de shloinneadh Ír is Éibhir,
Ní hoíche linn an spéirling a fuineadh do bhláth Dhéirdre,
An tráth seo chois Life an loingis i gcríon mo laetha
Is léir dom ár ngin is ár ngoineadh, síol Éabha.

We are the dead who died
In Dublin and out of season,
On blasphemy's sunny day
We blew away Hiroshima.

We are no longer Gaels from the line of Ir and Éibhir,
The slaughter done in pursuit of Deirdre is no news to us.
Now, by the ship-crowded Liffey in the time of my decline
I see our beginning clear, our ending – we, children of Eve.

Translated by Aidan Hayes with Anna Ní Dhomhnaill

ROBERT GREACEN
1920–2008

Greacen was born in Derry and educated at TCD. He worked for the United Nations in London and later lectured in adult education. The author of several volumes of poetry and criticism, his *Collected Poems* was published in 1995.

BELFAST

30 January 1942

Stranded here on this archipelago of winter
The evil wind swirls in the sail, and the bitter soil
Is hot and heavy to the hand that fondles.
Guard from fever, fret, infection the fervent fire
That streams its whiteness, like a maddened headlight tossing
On a copper sea, locked fast as mercury in palm.

SPRING 1943

And now the prisoned year has burst
The relentless circle of the seasons' spin:
And life is warm on lips in hedgerows,
Warm with the year's accumulated lust.

Spring's over there! And the frigid grate
No longer hungers for the crackling earth's decay;
Spring of the daffodils, offensives, chills –
And a girl in Sunday's park to greet.

Raids on Munich and Essen, we read,
Hearing the heavy pound and punch of bombs
Falling in parabolas like tipsy boulders ...
Revenge is audible but left unsaid.

Raid on the heart, *putsch* of spring,
The sand is falling and the dizzy mind
Registers its dumb protest – O sweet, mad life
The fertile mountains and the free birds sing!

POEM WRITTEN IN SEPTEMBER

Now in September, while trees are continent though tired
From summer's steam and the storm-wet days of last August,
Now in the soiled end-paper of the season's book
It is opportune to add the double-column entries,
Balance the accounts of reason, faith and sentiment.
Tot up the afternoons of warmth and moisture,
The chance meeting with the beautiful and plain,
To eye in retrospect the talk in railway carriages,
The tennis elbow and the pilgrimage for chocolates,
To view the ragged peaks of loveliness,
The fevered graph of fervid sirens.
Perhaps one too should speak of love?
But love is too magic and too precious,
Too intangible, too difficult, too easily lost ...
Rather, the khaki strokes of lorries in the streets,
That run into the tapestry of total war,
And the search for individual responsibility,
And the conscious lack of integration.
Where has leaped the faith of that September,
When black-outs were expensive novelties,
When resolution flowed in flowering cascades?

Still, in the last curve of faith's circle,
There is little tarnished brightness,
There springs a sullen spark to fire.
Now in September, while trees are clothed and continent,
Before they strip for winter's bitterness,
In the crushed end-paper of this season's book,
Write off the score, revise the notes, correct the proofs,
For now it is opportune to add the double-column entries.

POEM TO K.D.

I send you greetings, Kay, now in this exiled time
From this careless Augustan city of grace and slums,
Where in Merrion Square the whispers of death
Gauze over the rhododendrons and the parched grass.
I greet you from a neutral country in a neutral hour
When the blood pace slows and nothing stirs
But the leaves in the parks, so gently:
So gently that not even the newspaper headlines
Can fluster the plumes of swans, gliding, gliding,
As on a lake of fire, fringed by pink water.
The pulse of life is faint, as in a trance,
As we await the backwash of hate's last outrage.
All Europe's continent pivots, for me, in Stephen's Green:
Your Warsaw and Normandy fester in happy Hampstead,
Cupped in a shell of gentleness, withdrawn from the terror
That, fevered with swift desire, strides beyond our barricades ...
But everywhere we see the uncharted darkness melt,
We see the sun pour on the sap-drained faces,
The oil of joy press motion in the wheels of love,
The masks fall off, the undying day return!

THE GLORIOUS TWELFTH
12 July 1943

You will remember that the Twelfth was always dry,
That rain followed the day after, some said as Judgement,
While others argued that drums of Ulster stirring
Pulled out the corded wetness from our local skies.
Four years ago we heard them last, heard the thunder
Smouldering through the ribboned streets towards the battle
In the fields of Finaghy. There was fire then,
Fire in our throats, fire beaten out from our cities,
Cold, distant, strongly arid in the normal weather:
Four years ago since last we heard the drums' thunder,
Since the Orange banners looped in gay procession
And bands of flute and fife, of brass and silver
Played hell to the Pope and immortality to William –
To William, Prince of Orange, defender and avenger,
To William, the stiff Dutch Protestant who saved us
From villainous James, the tyrant Stuart King.

Remember 1690, remember the ancient wrongs of Rome,
Remember Derry, Aughrim, Enniskillen and the Boyne,
The Glorious Boyne in Ireland, where the Pope was overcome,
Remember the Maiden City and the breaking of her boom.

These were my people marching on the streets,
Released from inhibition and resolved to keep the faith.
Four years have passed since Ulster opened up her heart,
And toasted her deliverance from the Seven Hills,

Four years since fire has run swift rivers into Europe
From Dunkirk to Briansk, from Naples to Novgorod,
From Caucasus to Clyde, from Warsaw to Belfast.

And now, in Derry and Downpatrick, no Ulstermen
    are marching
To the rustle of their banners and the flogging of their drums.
Our red-brick cities have their blackened skeletons,
Our people carry the public and the personal wound.

Forgotten 1690, forgotten the ancient wrongs of Rome,
Forgotten Derry, Aughrim, Enniskillen and the Boyne,
The Glorious Boyne in Ireland where the Pope was overcome,
Forgotten the Maiden City and the breaking of her boom.

You will remember that the Twelfth was always dry,
While now in Italy the bloods of Continents are joined,
While now the Russian plains are stacked with corpses,
Rotting in the Red sun, feeding plagues to common rats ...
But after carnage there will be music, after death will be hope,
After the horror of the day will come the evening dream,
After hatred's harvest joy will march, shrouded, to Finaghy.

LAMENT FOR FRANCE

All, all is fallen now, fallen and flouted.
All the bridges are mined, all the flags are withered,
All the frontiers are twisted back, all the faces
Have become the one face, the gigantic face of terror.
('Nothing will stop us now', say the feet,
'Down are the barriers. Nothing stands in the way!
What do they say – do they say "Liberty"?
My truncheon, Hans, that's the answer to freedom!')

On the boulevards there are only the dead leaves,
Falling, falling, before the appointed season:
In the heart there is only the black knock of fear
That thumps unceasing sordid thunder,
('What do they say, Fritz? – what's this equality?
So men are equal! The equality we respect
Is that of the steel arm, the knuckleduster fist ...
That's our equality! Death to the Jews!')
Everywhere they are taking down the symbols of France!
The people speak in the whisper and gesture of death,
Eyes drained of meaning, tongues dry with despair.
O what have we done, O what is our crime?
('They say that men are brothers! They'll be brothers all right.
Brothers at the abattoir! You like my joke, Friedrich?
We'll teach them a new humour ... Where's my whip?')
They will take everything – yes, everything
That can be assessed, all that will be taken.
They will smash down pity and loveliness, trample them down.

They will kill and plunder, break and ravish,
They will do these things: nothing can stop them now.
On the boulevards the crisp leaves are mourning,
Weeping for all that is fallen before its due season.
In the heart, the only flow is the trickle of hope
Which cannot be commandeered like the lorries or cattle.
In the heart, the Republic lives beyond her death
Till grave-faced men shall bring the phoenix-birth.
Where brothers shall be equal, proudly free,
They will remember France, salute her memory.

SUNDAY IN COUNTY MONAGHAN, 1935

Dewy rose-bud in buttonhole
Hair slicked, violet-scented.
The minister prays for farmers' weather.
The harmonium swells in reedy praise.
I daydream beside still waters.
Outside the crumbling church they gather,
A dwindling clan, greying:
Adairs, Gillespies, Wilsons, Smyths –
King's men without a King.
Chat of government and crops,
Taxes, swine fever, price of land,
Sons prospering 'across the water'.
A drive back over powdery roads
And up the hunchback lane to chicken,
Uncle George's talk of Armageddon
And why the Kaiser lost the war.
A stroll across the townland.
Brontë pages skimmed under the elm,
Tea in Belleek china, ginger snaps,
'Throw Out the Lifeline' baritoned
On the wind-up gramophone.
A spin on the gleaming sports bike
A burnt-out house, thatched cottages,
'Up Dev!' chalked on a wall.
'Brave day', cries Pat O'Byrne,
Jetting an arc of tobacco juice.
The twilit fields with cousin Jane,
A collie bark from Kelly's yard.

I.M. LESLIE OWEN BAXTER
1919–1995

Above the crackle of our Philco Five
I listened to the scream from Nuremberg:
Ein Volk, Ein Reich, Ein Führer!

In Hitler's year of '33 I went to grammar school,
Proud in my uniform with its blue monogram,
Eager for Latin and the Rugby field.

First day I chanced upon a tall, shy boy
Who lugged around a case of books,
An earnest scholar but unlikely friend.

Friendship's bud exploded into flower
When in the locker room a boy who jostled him
Felt my clenched fist hard upon his nose.

We walked together through the cosy dusk
Years on, engrossed in dreams, anxieties,
The future stretching out in black or rose.

Since he has left me, the familiar streets
Stare back into a stranger's eye.
The city's foreign now, not his and mine.

The old and easy tag maintains
That time can heal the wound of loss.
Not so, not so, not so.

ROY McFADDEN
1921–1999

McFadden was born in Belfast and educated at Queen's University, where he contributed to *The Northman*, edited by Robert Greacen. He practised law in Belfast and was a pacifist during the Second World War. The founder and co-editor of the journal *Rann*, he wrote reviews, short stories and essays, and broadcast regularly on BBC radio. His *Collected Poems* was published in 1996.

2 SEPTEMBER 1939

At ease, basking in talk, as if
Respectful distances deferred,
Giving him time, the dandelion light
Already sentimental on the wall,
He stands forever graced by that afternoon:
Which I, looking for something else,
Thoughtlessly stumble on, as if
All the dead-and-gone had still to arrive
With ribbons and flowers, or wreaths under their arms.

POST-WAR

Cold and clear are the words
That belong to bright March days,
If you think of mornings
When sky is gunmetal blue
And a terse breeze flexes its strength in
        the raw trees.

The hard years after the war
When life, in a word, was spare,
Were like March mornings
Cold-shouldered or cut by spring,
Yet with promise, in spite of the promises,
    sharpening the air.

Remembered merchandise –
Shelved childhood's packets and tins –
Trailed back from limbo,
Nostalgically labelled, and we
Reflected on pots and pans, matched
    saucers and spoons.

Under the cenotaphs
The poppies foundered on stone;
And over the bomb-holes
Pert window-boxes presumed.
They restored the excursion train and
    the ice-cream cone.

Then we dallied with summer again,
Making light of the rusting guns,
The snarled wire's venom,
The abandoned towers on the dunes;
And salvaged stray bullets for girls to give
    to their sons.

ARMISTICE DAY 1938

Every year in the Assembly Hall
We would exhume the dead
Protagonists of the Great War.
With marbled eyes McKelvey prayed
For unknown uncles killed at Passchendaele.

The blood-roll of the drums, the bugle's cry,
The curt succeeding hush
For masochistic memory,
Insinuated a death-wish;
And history sugared to mythology.

In my last year, the radio relayed
A nation's fading grief
Live from the London Cenotaph;
But my suspended disbelief
Was shattered with the silence when a loud

Dissident voice charged puppet-masters with
Rigging another war.
McKelvey broke ranks also, and
Came out against more murder for
Conflicting emblems cut from the same cloth.

A SONG FOR VICTORY NIGHT

The bonfire lights the foolish faces; sky-
Rockets reel and plunge with dripping fins;
Patriotic music floats and falls:
The small bomb loses and the big bomb wins.

Listen, trees, stern in the star-lost light,
As rich wood crackles in the victory fire.
The catherine-wheel goes crazy with delight.

There was a victory. How much was lost
Under the rubble of the rabble's slum.
(O past, avenge through me the blasted heart.)
The drunken citizen bangs on his drum,
The draught-board mind square-patched with
        black and white.
Burning wood, o past: churchillianly
The catherine-wheel turns circles in the night.

I watch the scarlet fire consume the sky,
The branches writhing in the murderous flame.
(Hamburg, Rotterdam and Coventry,
People and cities, named, without a name,
Replenish pity in us that will fight
With white, white waters continents of fire.)
The catherine-wheel drops suddenly in flight.

DUBLIN TO BELFAST
WARTIME

Dublin left, with its uncensored lights
Careless of retribution from the skies,
Unreprimanded and insouciant streets,
A goodnight's sleep and morning unimpaired:

You tunnel back to war, where licit light's
A swinging arm redeeming the night sky,
Grabbing for midges dancing in the dark
Over the braced and vulnerable town:

Sobered from extravagance of lights,
Adjusting to the place's temperament,
The brazen gantries and the querulous gulls
Harsh from the islands occupied by storm.

PORTRUSH

I came to you first as a solitary child,
And built a castle with a seaweed lawn,
And then created continents and seas.
Across where Donegal extends an arm
I thought of shipwrecked Spanish mariners
And galleon-treasure glowing in the depths.

Yes; I have given and received in marriage.
My past is laid quiet on a lap of sand.
You who survive the Atlantic storms and smuggle
Sun yearly from Europe, crowned with gulls,
You hold my sighing tides chained to your shores,
Where seas lay down and stretched out paws to play.

Now at the season's end, when clouds become
Barrage balloons alerted by the wind,
And sun deserts the sea, and the slow march
Of death quickens in Europe and beyond,
I put away my bucket and my spade,
And store my shells and pebbles in a jar.

Reg : 003   18:09 11/11/08

Dk.No. : 0511118Q758

Description   Price

EARTH VOICES AND SPEAKING   1   21.99
9780856408229

Euro Total Due :.   23.60
Visa   23.00

Salesperson: PHIL

Punt Value = 18.59 @ .787564

VISIT www.museum.ie

BRUCE WILLIAMSON
1922–1991

Williamson was born in Belfast and educated at TCD. He joined
the *Irish Times* in 1965, working as literary editor and later as
senior deputy editor. His poems were included in several
anthologies and in 1944 he collaborated with Robert Greacen
and Valentin Iremonger on *On the Barricades*.

HOMAGE OF WAR

Across the barrage, the cities of Europe remember
The lovers that paced in their parks, that in spring
To walk was to waltz like the flowers in a border
With the soft caracole of the breeze, and they sing
To the shells and the bombers intent on their murder.

Impatient and lovely, some trees still have their leaves
In green shawls about them. The undershot jaw of the sky
Will menace their magic and rinse them
With words that are bullets and fire, with hate that's a lie
Turned in on itself, an ignoble ransom.

The young are apart and their love has become
A strained girl in the house, a man with no thought of her
That war can't suppress. And the roses he sees
Have petals that grow round a wound, a flower no wind can stir,
These cannot be dressed into bouquets. They are not for praise.

When the smoke drifts away like a drunkard
The crazy harangue of the guns is better than silence.
Death is a better end than to be accused
By the unpeopled streets, or by the cool, tense
Shadow of courage from those whom the battle erased.

The conquered are always at fault. The white throat
Slipped under a knife, a soul that breathes through its bruises
Is only temptation, man's wicked thought in the night.
After its falcon dive, the soul gently cruises,
Lost in voluted space without compass or light.

There's no escape to the future, no rest in the present.
A terrible homage this is, on broken knees, in death's hall,
And the inward man contentedly breathing
As if admiring the murals on the execution wall,
As if grateful for his stark historic fading.

PADRAIC FIACC
b. 1924

Born in Belfast, Fiacc was brought up in New York and returned to Belfast in 1946. He is the author of several poetry collections, including *Woe to the Boy* (1957) and *Nights in the Bad Place* (1977). He also edited the controversial anthology, *The Wearing of the Black* (1974).

DER BOMBEN POET

Spring song 1941

Today is my birth
-day. I am seventeen.

My home town
Has just bin
Blown up:

Dead feet in dead faces,
Corpses still alight,
Students helping kids
And old people out of

Still burning houses.

I have nothing to write
Poems about.

This is my twentieth-century

Night-life.

THE OTHER MAN'S WOUND

In the communal shower after the drowning
We felt like Jews in Nazi Germany:

The water, flagellating down, took on
Something of the hostility in that
                                    dooms
-day for all who are born ...

Soaping our sweat to goose pimples, we
Kept thinking about us, not him.

SON OF A GUN

*Woe to the boy for whom the nails, the crown of thorns,
the sponge of gall were the first toy.*

FRANÇOIS MAURIAC

Between the year of the slump and the sell out, I
The third child, am the first born alive ...

My father is a Free Stater 'Cavan Buck'.
My mother is a Belfast factory worker. Both

Carry guns, and the grandmother with a gun
In her apron, making the Military wipe

Their boots before they rape the house. (These
Civil wars are only ever over on paper!)

Armed police are still raping my dreams
Thump-thud. Thump-thud. I go on nightmaring

270

Dead father running. There is a bull
In the field. Is Father, am I, running away

From the bull to it? Is this the reason why
I steal
      time, things, places, people?

Barman father, sleeping with a gun under
Your pillow, does the gun help you that much?
                                I wonder

For the gun has made you all only the one
In of sex with me the two sexed son (or three

Or none?) you bequeathed the gun to
Still cannot make it so. I can

Never become your he-man: shot
Down born as I was, sure, I thought

And thought and thought but blood ran ...

SOLDIERS

The altar boy marches up the altar steps.
The priest marches down. 'Get up now
And be a soldier!' says the nun
To the woman after giving birth. 'Get up now
And march, march: Be a man!'

And the men are men and the women are men
And the children are men!

Mother carried a knife to work.
It was the thorn to her rose ...

They say she died with her eyes open
In the French Hospital in New York.
I remember those eyes shining in the dark

Slum hallway the day after
I left the monastery: Eyes that were
A feast of welcome that said 'Yes
I'm glad you didn't stay stuck there!'

'Would you mind if I went to prison
Rather than war?'
'No, for Ireland's men all went to prison!'

At the bottom of a canyon of brick
She cursed and swore
'You never see the sky!'

A lifetime after,
                    just before
I go to sleep at night, I hear
That Anna Magnani voice screaming
Me deaf 'No! No, you're not
To heed the world!' In one swift
Sentence she tells me not to yield
But to *forbear*:
                    'Go to prison but never
Never stop fighting. We are the poor
And the poor have to be "soldiers".

'You're still a soldier, it's only that
You're losing the war

'And all the wars are lost anyway!'

THE BRITISH CONNECTION

In Belfast, Europe, your man
Met the Military come to raid
The house:
      'Over my dead body
Sir,' he said, brandishing
A real-life sword from some
Old half-forgotten war …

And youths with real bows and arrows
And coppers and marbles good as bullets
And oldtime thrupenny bits and stones
Screws, bolts, nuts (Belfast confetti),

And kitchen knives, pokers, Guinness tins
And nail-bombs down by the Shore Road

And guns under the harbour wharf
And bullets in the docker's tea tin
And gelignite in the tool shed
And grenades in the scullery larder
And weedkiller and sugar
And acid in the french letter

And sodium chlorate and nitrates
In the suburban garage
In the boot of the car

And guns in the oven grill
And guns in the spinster's shift

And ammunition and more more
Guns in the broken-down rusted
Merry-Go-Round in the Scrap Yard

Almost as many hard-on
Guns as there are union jacks.

PATRICK GALVIN
b. 1927

Born in inner city Cork, Galvin joined the RAF in 1943, serving in Bomber Command in the UK, Middle East and Africa. He began writing poetry in the 1950s and his collections include *Heart of Grace* (1957) and *The Wood Burners* (1973). He is also a playwright and director, and has written for radio. His memoir, *The Raggy Boy Trilogy*, was made into a film in 2003.

MY FATHER SPOKE WITH SWANS

1

Leaning on the parapet
Of the South Gate Bridge
My father spoke with swans
Remembering his days
With the Royal Munster Fusiliers.

India was dawn
The women cool
The sun cradled in his arms.
Sometimes,
When the clouds were wine
He washed his face in the Ganges.

The swans rose from the Lee
And held their wings.

Leaning on the mysteries
Of her twilight room
My mother spoke with God
Remembering Pearse
And the breath of Connolly.

Ireland was new
The men tall
The land mirrored their brightness.
Sometimes,
When the eagles called
She walked the roads to Bethlehem.

God opened his eyes
A loss for miracles

From these two I was born
The Ganges swaying with the Lee
And gunfire rising to a fall.
My mother wore green till she died
My father died with swans.

Only the rivers remain
Slow bleeding.

A DAY OF REBELLION

Softly
As if the world might break with moving
This little army rested on the city.
Rifles and green jackets
Bullets for empty pockets
Careful of the British soldier
Standing sentry against the sun.

And so we took the tram from Donnybrook
And wondered if we had to pay
For this was Revolution Day
When all the soldiers play:
This is the nation of the free,
Drown all the others in the sea.

And at high noon
The eagles of this ancient race
Gathered together on High Rock.
The blood groaned heavy on the pavements
The windows opened and the rifles cracked
Fire and gold rode through the streets

For Liberty, Equality and Death.

And we maintain
The right of the Irish people
To the unfettered control ...

Of Liberty, Equality and Death.

All but the beating of wings!
Think of the death it brings
The bodies falling from the roof
And then where's the proof?
The nettles growing in Parnell's mouth
The blood raining from the stars.

O'Leary's ghost in Sackville Street
Where all young heroes meet
Fionn and Cuchulain of the Ford
Pearse with his pamphlet of the free –
They died for liberty
Sagart Aroon.

Don't let this Easter pass
All the gentry trotting off to Mass
Snipers lying on the roof
On the Four Courts, on Boland's Mill
This day we'll drink our fill
Of Liberty, Equality and Death.

And we place this cause
Under the protection of the most high God
Whose blessing we invoke
Upon our arms
And we pray
Never to relent
Signed on behalf of the Provisional Government.

O Leinster's wound is wide
With every shot that sings
Over the swollen river.
The blood is hard upon the walls
And no one shall deface
The glory of this ancient race.

O Leinster's wound is blowing wide
And April cuts the root.

* * *

Sweet young girl from Evergreen
Dressed to kill in Irish green
Finest girl ever seen
Dead with a bullet through her head
Stone dead with a bullet through her head
Round and round we go …

And Logan standing on the bridge
Dreamed an evening with Maloney's mott
While Maloney played soldiers in the street
To the tramp tramp of marching feet
Till he was shot dead
With a bullet through the head.

And she with a boxcar full of loot
Sang 'Down with the English and the Jews
Three cheers for the Rebels and the Blues'
(O the right of the people to wear shoes!)
Till a bullet from a German gun
Stopped her dead.

Christ! Me heart's blood is pouring away
Like a great river
Me new shawl is drenched with blood
And some bastard has pinched me purse –
O no one gives a tinker's curse
For Maloney's mott

Stone dead
With a bullet through her head.

An English pound wrapped round her yellow garter
(Go on, Mick! I know what you're after)
Katie played the fiddle in a Dublin snug
Wept for the English and the Irish dead
Drowned her sorrows in a jar of stout –
Business should pick up before the night is out

But she was dead
With a bullet through her head.
Smashing windows, blinding glass,
A bullet through the open door
And now the fiddle on the sawdust floor
Playing music no more.

All dead
With a bullet through the head
Stone dead.

Liberty, Equality and Death.

* * *

Softly
As if the world might break with moving
They walked over the bodies of the dead
The flag is burning on the GPO
Now tell me where all good Christians go?
Christ with his side pierced through
Is terrified of English cannon.

All for a twilight of history!
The red horses rearing at the sun
The children playing among the lilies
Dry skulls turning in the dust
Where are the preachers and the just?
My Johnny has gone for a soldier
Och anee!

Burning buildings
Pavements cracked
Yellow frost
And windows smashed

Women screaming
Green and red
Children thieving
Loaves of bread

Iron guards
With skulls of brass
Fingers filled
With a fountain of knives.

*　*　*

And nowhere
Have our lines been broken through
An Ireland glorious and new
Worthy of her place
Heroes of this noble race ...

Who looked at Connolly's face?

The eagles whispered on High Rock
The arrows pierced Cuchulain's feet
The Irish rebel with his sword of glass
Swore he would never go to Mass:
Put all the clergy in their place!

Who looked at Connolly's face?

Old news to the generations
Riding through the green sky
Wearing their glittering swords
Sounding their hollow trumpets
Till the heavens burst open
And it was blight of day.

Old news
Dead and buried deep.

* * *

And Pearse was demented
No denying that!
Standing there with his pamphlet
And his cocked hat
What do you think of that?

And who were they all
I'd like to know?
Freedom in the GPO
That lot will have to go!
Death.

And as for the rest
Who cares
Twopence a pound the apples and pears
Wait till I get you upstairs
Stopping out all night.

Round and round we go.

* * *

When Albion's demon rolled the tide
Slinging her blazing irons at the stars
There was death.

Lying over the broken rifles
Over the bugles
Nailed to the stakes of history
A bellowing rage of agony

The Earth heaves
The prisoners are dead
The rain falls eternally
And down
Over this sickening fuchsia.

Who'll sing 'Sixteen Dead Men'
Never to rise again
In the Western World?

Softly – lightly
As if the world might break with moving
We scrawled their names upon the glass
And saw forever
Through the burning world.

PEARSE HUTCHINSON
b. 1927

Hutchinson was born in Glasgow to a family of Irish extraction and studied languages at UCD. He worked as a journalist and radio presenter, and is the author of several poetry collections written in Irish and English, as well as translations from Catalan and Galaico-Portuguese.

THE DEFEATED
from the Catalan of Francesc Parcerisas

Those who invade the streets, in their sheepskin coats,
their medals and their uniforms, are a different race.

FELICIDAD BLANC, *Espejo de Sombras*

What is gained in losing

ROBERT LOWELL

They are Franco's troops and they have won the battles.
For you there's nothing left but the grave or beyond,
the luckless marvel of waking up among the ashes.
You hear a shout: 'It's them! They're coming!'
and feel like cowards, afraid, offended.
You were done down by an abject shadow of life.
And now, fifty years later – too young
to look for reparation – I can still see you,
silent with a trembling finger at your lips,
and I love you submitting to an order of great fear,
with the dignity of being in the right
or under nocturnal headlights of defeat.
Your silence has been a tangled wire,
showing us what is gained in losing.

OSTFRIESLAND
for Theo Schuster

1

I'm eating with four Germans
in a small East-Friesian town
magnificent Italian food.
Our host, a gallant man
who keeps on bringing out
books and records in the Nahsprachen –
tongues near to German –
for example: Plattdütsch.
And,
     for example,
          Yiddish.

He tells us, over
the sumptuous food,
there lives here now
only one Jew.
For a wild second I wonder
is it him?

Earlier, in his bookshop, leafing through
a history of this town,
I found a synagogue-photo.

Built in the 1880s. Burnt down,
like so many,
on Kristallnacht.

Now at the Italian table
I remember that small picture,
   and wonder.

                    But imagine it,
that one Jewish man
going back there, after the war –
after that war –
coming back (from where?)
coming back to what had been
his town too,
to make it, perhaps, his town again,
to be, in a way, alone there.

I fall silent, we all do
for a minute.
What right have I to wonder
or imagine?
Common humanity?
What right to assume it was ever
his town? Or doubt it?

                    2

One of these four I'm eating with
is the friend who brought me here,
a poet who has railed against and mocked
all hatred and savagery.
Two are sisters,
charming and beautiful,
who fed me as well as Italians could
on a balcony under the warm night
a week ago in Bremen.

I remember Elie Cohen the Dutch rabbi
telling the Dutch, after that war:
Don't think it couldn't happen here,
it could happen anywhere,
even in Holland.

3

Isroel
not ah but oh
not Israel but Isroel – that so
surprising vowel that unexpected *o*
sounding out clear on the LP sent – as good as his word –
to me in Bloom's town (whether his, or mine)
from a small East-Friesian town
sounding out in the rich prose
of a great storyteller Itschak Leib Peretz
in the rich voice
of Zvi Hofer
of the Institutum Judaicum
of Münster – Leib Peretz
who spoke with passion for Yiddish to be
the national tongue of the nation-to-be
                                        Isroel

Peretz
lost out to Hebrew, but on this record
made in Germany, not anywhere else,
his passion speaks again, his vivid zest,
all that humour and variety
which even goyim can tell (with the aid
of certain famous books) all that life
defying oppression, prejudice, all the narrowing forces,
abounds again, speaks Yiddish again, in Zvi
Hofer's abundant voice
as rich as Hebrew itself.

JUDENGASSE

Over lunch at the long table in the lakeside castle
    someone names
        a Judengasse.
To which another says:
'It's an empty lane.'

Four of us by dusk we're in the city
    pub-crawling our way
        to the Jewish lane.
At midnight we've got to the mouth of it,
Lars and Folke and I, all in our early twenties,
and the novelist William Sansom,
an older man.

We're standing looking down the deserted, narrow,
longish, nearly-but-not-quite-straight
once Jewish lane.

No human light there now,
no sign of houses or workshops,
alive or empty.
Seven years after the war,
only the moon to glisten
the wet ground
of an empty lane.

Sansom is dark-haired, portly, a little flushed.
He's tightly encased in a dark suit, with a dark tie and
    a white shirt.
Impeccable. Handsome. Not undebonair.

Suddenly without a word
he up-ends himself, launches, flailing,
into a series of cartwheels along the wet lane to
    its empty end,
then barely pausing repeats the performance all the
    way back again
to land at our feet, exhausted.

We help him up, and back to the dead bishop's castle.

He spends the next day in bed.
I want to tell him I never admired him more.
But that were too banal an infringement
of friendliness so tightly encased.

A year or so later, Swiss Cottage,
he gave me a Jewish lunch.
Chicken livers with lemon I'd never eaten before.
They positively melted in the mouth.

RICHARD MURPHY
b. 1927

Born in County Mayo, Murphy spent his early years in Sri
Lanka where his father was the last British Mayor of Colombo.
He studied English at Oxford and then moved to County
Galway, where he lived and worked for many years. He has
been poet in residence at many leading American universities
and is the author of several poetry collections, including
Collected Poems (2000) and a memoir, *The Kick* (2003).

OXFORD STAIRCASE

Going up a flight of stone at seventeen
In wartime, wearing thin your plodding soles
On coupons by degrees, you pass between
Dons' billowing gowns and chapel aureoles.

Brought to your knees by genuflectory prose –
C.S. Lewis, stoking the clinkered grate
Of lost causes, keeps you on your toes –
You're taught to criticise, but not create.

That numinous cloud of jovial pipe-smoke round
His Tudor head, wraps you tongue-tied as bells
Before VE Day, taking steps to sound
The blissful city fraught with private hells.

A fellowship of bowls on the cloister lawn
Do you miss, old man? You slipped up, going down.

CARLYON BAY HOTEL

Designed for luxury, commandeered to house
Your bombed out school, under Spartan rule I live
In a Cornish idyll, with high and mighty views:
Royal blue channel, Phoenician tin-veined cliff.

Don't you know there's a war? It's why you're here
Debarred from girls, a pup among top dogs.
Home is ninety days off, and you've no future
Hunting hares over treacherous Irish bogs.

Wing-collared Milner scholar, don't forget
Your gas-mask, ration book, identity card.
My buckthorn wood hears inklings in the black-out.
Uncle Jack's killed in Africa. Work hard!

Your voice is breaking. Kneel, and be confirmed
By Truro's hands of clay. Do you feel transformed?

WELLINGTON COLLEGE

Fear makes you lock out more than you include
By tackling my red brick with Shakespeare's form
Of love poem, barracked here and ridiculed
By hearty boys, drilled to my square-toed norm.

Yet ushered in, through my roll of honour voice,
Cold baths in winter, field days on Bagshot Heath,
Poetry gives you unconscripted choice
Of strategies, renaissance air to breathe.

Your father's brother fell in the Great War,
Your mother's fell in this. You ate our salt.
Should you plead conscience when called up next year
Their greater love would find the gravest fault.

Weren't you born to command a regiment?
How selfishly you serve your own heart's bent.

SUNTRAP

One year at home, under our flagging roof
During the war, learning and love made peace.
As with a cottage weaver's warp and woof
Your heart and mind were shuttled into place.

Verbs conjugating in our pleasure ground
Held the past present in contiguous time.
Here was the Bower of Bliss, painlessly scanned.
You found the oldest trees were best to climb.

In neutral Ireland, our walled demesne,
While tilting you towards knight-errant books,
Groomed you to mount war-horses to gain
Rewards beyond our laurels and our oaks.

A peeled rush, dipped in tallow, carried light
From the dark ages, kissing you good night.

ANTHONY CRONIN
b. 1928

Cronin was born in Enniscorthy, County Wexford, and educated at UCD and the King's Inns. Editor of *The Bell*, he was Cultural and Artistic advisor to Taoiseach Charles Haughey. A founding member of Aosdána, Cronin is a novelist, poet, critic, broadcaster, essayist and biographer. His *Collected Poems* was published in 2004.

WAR POEM

Valerian, a local flower,
Likes Wellington and Waterloo.
The Irish marched to any drum
From Spion Kop to Fontenoy.
When Collins' bullets pocked the dome
I wasn't in a State to know.
In thirty-two as well as Dev
Came large campaigns in Manchukuo,
We fought it out in slush beside
The asylum where the Slaney flows.
Jim Lynch and I were Japanese
When not swamped in the Gran Chaco.
The age of lead and cut-outs passed
And Baillie-Stuart marched no more
(What Sandhurst bugles in our blood
And what blood-thirsty mites we were).
Ras Kassa though as tall as spears
Was no match for Badoglio.
Came Spain and Jim, a restive spirit,
Wrote to Quiepo de Llano,
He wanted in on any side
In any sort of real war.
He joined the blue-shirts, then, being baulked,
The IRA, he had a go

At length high in the German skies.
I heaved a neutralist heigh-ho
And dithered where Valerian
Commanded heights round Waterloo.
There's something in what Johnson said
And no reportage of the bo-
Ring aspects of it quite suffice
To compensate for a lost war.
Whatever reason said because
I won no wounds I bore a scar.
Nor could the staring facts root out
Such strange ambitions, even girls'
Indifference to uniforms,
Remove the masochistic, ro-
Mantic censored rubbish from
My screens and make them fit to view
Until much hoarier than I was
In Autumn nineteen forty-four.
And this applies to other things,
Like Scott I pined for ever more
Evidence from other worlds,
Enjoyed my own scenario
Of courtship and of self-escape,
The rescues and the racing cars,
Although I'm rescueless to date
And never hammered round Le Mans,
Nor ever either won the fight,
Having climbed up off the floor,
Alas, alack! This sedentary
Trade it's not only Yeats it broke.
But yet compared to most it's not
All that much lacking in rough sport,
And what the hell, intensity
Has not been wanting, danger nor
A casualty rate among
My lot of about one in four,

Whatever about self-esteem.
Or in some darling's eyes a glow.
Of course it's said all round today
The civilized don't hanker for
The epaulettes, the smart salutes,
The laurels round the soldier's brow,
Jabbing with bayonets, dropping bombs
On children, women and the old.
Militarist is a dirty word.
If bombing babies is supposed
This last time to have been quite just
In part at least that is because
No one could otherwise have had
That great experience, a good war;
And those who had one couldn't come
On TV or the radio
And in the tones of warriors say
That war is frightful don't you know.
In fact now that I think of it
It's so unfashionable to
Confess to ever having had
Such military hankerings or
Confusions about proving one's
Manhood in the sphere of mars
(Though I think much of what I felt
In the aforesaid forty-four
Was probably the product of
Unceasing propaganda for
Provence's propertied ethos shrunk
Transformed to Hollywood machismo)
I'd better cut it out and give
Myself more marks for moral fore-
Sight, thinking warlike thoughts but watching,
On sunny afternoons of woe,
Valerian, that local flower,
Take root on walls round Waterloo.

64

These were the modern things. One spoke of Schoenberg,
Hofmannsthal, Rilke, Kaiser, Stefan George.
The Secession was, as you might say, well-established.
One argued about Freud and knew that Mach
Had at last rid science of metaphysical ghosts.
It was really only ill-bred schoolmasters,
Post office clerks, Slavonic mysticists,
Those ill at ease in our great German culture
And politicians on the make who spoke
At boring length about what they would call
The problem of the nationalities.
And yet you know they made this jejune topic
Somehow the burning issue, though even the Marxists
Laughed at them. They did. They really did.

66

In 1901 Marconi sent
Across the wastes a more ethereal message.
While Chesterton on the 9.15 regretted
Dying romance and blamed Lloyd George, the jews,
Moustaches tickled thighs as white as ivory
And gents and mashers hunted the same game.
The ether grew more bodeful, fleets assembled
Off stormy headlands hissed the stokers' fires.
The Boys Own Paper went to bed to taps.
Romance persisted, even on the Somme.
One morning as old Europe's sun brought dawn
A quarryman who was placing charges would
Look at the vibrant sky and see come in
A monoplane irradiate with rain.

75

How sad the bugle in the wood's green depths
Aching for what is lost now to the world,
Least told of all tales now, least sung of songs
Since on those summer roads the marching boys
Sang out between the poplars in their dream
Of death in some great circumstance of friends,
Some proof of love beyond the dull demands
They never had expected, made each dawning
Among the little houses, little streets,
Between the window and the door of bedrooms,
In offices where courage was submission,
Where duty was a dragging chain and sacrifice
A grim sad burden carried to the end,
No bugle sounding, even for the brave.

Hate was in short supply as were munitions,
And needed to be mass-produced like them.
'I hate not Germans,' Edward Thomas wrote,
And he was typical in that of many.
Until Lord Northcliffe found the right imago.
Self-images were stronger. In imagination
A valorous self had waited which could be
Ardent, magnanimous and chivalrous,
Could prove itself at last a schoolboy's hero.
And it was strange how as the nations parted,
Their promontories reaching for each other,
Their shore lights vanishing beneath dark seas,
They were united in their knightly yearnings
As they had never been by saner visions.

When I took the train my work was thoroughly abstract.
In the years before I had been, as I thought, liberated,
But at the front, without any break at all
I found myself among real, intractable things
And the men who worked with them every day of their lives.
My companions in the engineering corps
Were miners, drivers, workers in metal and wood.
On my first day there I was dazzled by the breech
Of a seventy-five, a gun which was standing uncovered
In the August sun, the magic of light on white metal.
This was enough to make me forget abstraction,
The art of nineteen twelve was dead for me.
Once I had fallen in love with that kind of reality
I was never again released from actual objects.

78

In those first months of the war he grew quite thin.
The skull, which has always been near, showed clearly through.
Although at Cracow after Krasnin he
Had seen the stretchers jostled through the crowds,
The dead laid out in rows, the women wailing,
He never spoke of war as suffering.
He would open newspapers eagerly and read
As if he were burning a hole in every page.
The gruff good nature those who knew him best
Had noted as his mode of intercourse
Vanished. He was quite impersonal.
Worse, when he read of some atrocious happening
He would burst out laughing. His amusement then
Seemed genuinely uncontrollable.

We went to Brighton in our Little Nine,
The open touring model Leslie bought
On what was called H.P. A gorgeous day,
The sky was somehow deep, you know, like heaven,
I thought the bubbling tar might melt the tyres
And Leslie laughed, called me a silly juggins.
He was a lovely driver, doing forty
Once we were free of Staines. Its tommy rot
To tell us now that people weren't happy.
We had our own nice house, a tudor villa,
Which was the new thing then, a vacuum cleaner,
Dance music on the wireless, lovely murders.
Of course the war was still to come, that Hitler,
But it all seemed somehow new then, somehow modern.

97

And we have sat, intent, in scuffed red plush
In scented darkness, watching Gable go
While someone else stayed home, back at the ranch
Perhaps, or at the base, neat, zipped or starched,
But hot for his returning underneath.
So many ages lasted the male dream,
Coming to us in tattered form while war
Ripped skies apart and Papa Hem rejoiced.
The scripts all said the girls were sweet on Clark,
But whether for his martial prowess or
His moustache … ? Know the heart of maid
We may not, but the heart of man we know,
Mankind that is, both sexes interlocked
In senile dreams and conflicts, both as one.

ENCOUNTER

When I was looking for a place to kip
In a bombed-out house
Which smelled of fog and burnt wood
Just above Lord's cricket ground
One night in the late forties,
On the landing where the stairs turned
I almost stepped on an old woman.
There was a fierce practicality about her going.
Gathering her bundle,
Rushing past me into the fog.
She had made a sort of nest for herself
Out of old newspapers.
There was no use calling her back.
She knew what men were like.

THOMAS KINSELLA
b. 1928

Kinsella was born in Inchicore, Dublin, studied at UCD, and joined the civil service in 1946. The founder of Peppercanister Press, he is the author of several poetry collections and has also published translations of Irish poetry, notably *The Táin* (1969) and the anthology *An Duanaire: Poems of the Dispossessed* (1981). His *Collected Poems* appeared in 2001.

THE LAUNDRESS

Her chair drawn to the door,
A basket at her feet,
She sat against the sun
And stitched a linen sheet.
Over harrowed Flanders
August moved the wheat.

Poplars sharing the wind
With Saxony and France
Dreamed at her gate,
Soared in a Summer trance.
A cluck in the cobbled yard:
A shadow changed its stance.

As a fish disturbs the pond
And sinks without a stain
The heels of ripeness fluttered
Under her apron. Then
Her heart grew strained and light
As the shell that shields the grain.

Bluntly through the doorway
She stared at shed and farm,
At yellow fields unstitching
About the hoarded germ,
At land that would spread white
When she had reached her term.

The sower plumps his acre,
Flanders turns to the heat,
The winds of Heaven winnow
And the wheels grind the wheat.
She searched in her basket
And fixed her ruffled sheet.

DOWNSTREAM

The West a fiery complex, the East a pearl,
We gave our frail skiff to the slow-moving stream,
Ruffling the waters. And steadied on a seam
Of calm and current.

                        Together, both as one,
We lifted our dripping blades in the dying light
And thrust ourselves forward, thrusting behind
Old willows with their shadows half undone
And groves of alder mowing like the blind.

A swan woke shapelessly in muffled stress
And thrust on ploughing wings, diminishing
Downstream.
            Ghost of whiteness.

We drifted in peace, and talked of poetry.
I opened the Cantos; and chose the silken kings,
Luminous with crisis, waging war
Among the primal clarities.
Their names dying
Behind us in the dusk.

* * *

I closed the book,
The gathering shades beginning to deceive,
And wiped the dewy cover on my sleeve.

We halted by a thorn, against the bank
Of a tributary stream. He clambered out;
I held on by a branch.

Night voices: soft
Lips of liquid, while the river swept
Its spectral surface by.

He coughed,
Standing against the sky. I took my turn,
Standing on the earth, staring aloft

At fields of light sprinkled in countless silence;
I named their shapes, above the Central Plain,
With primal thumb.

Low on the horizon
A shape of cloud answered with a soft flash
And a low word of thunder.

* * *

Toward Durrow Wood.

Thick slopes from shore to shore
Lowered a matted arch and moved out roots,
Full of slant pike, over the river floor.

The black cage closed about us:
                                    furred night-brutes
Stopped and listened, twitching their tiny brushes.

And I remembered how, among those bushes,
A man one night fell sick and left his shell
Collapsed, half eaten, like a rotted thrush's

To frighten stumbling children. 'You could tell',
My co-shadow murmured, 'by the hands
He died in trouble.' And the cold of hell,

A limb-lightness, a terror in the glands,
Pierced again as when that story first
Stopped my blood. The soil of other lands

Drank lives that summer with a body thirst.
Nerveless by the European pit,
Ourselves through seven hundred years accurst,

We saw the barren world obscurely lit
By tall chimneys flickering in their pall,
The haunt of swinish man. Each day a spit

That, turning, sweated war. Each night a fall
Back to the evil dream where rodents ply,
Man-rumped, sow-headed, busy with whip and maul

Among nude herds of the damned. It seemed that I,
Coming to conscience on that edge of dread,
Still dreamed, impervious to calamity,

Imagining a formal drift of the dead
Stretched calm as effigies on velvet dust,
Scattered on starlit slopes with arms outspread

And eyes of silver ... When that story thrust
Pungent horror and an actual mess
Into my very face, and taste I must.

* * *

Like mortal jaws, the alleys of the wood
Fell-to behind us. At their heart, a ghost
That glimmered briefly with my gift of blood,

Spreadeagled on a rack of leaves, almost
Remembering, facing the crowded sky,
Calmly encountering the starry host,

Meeting their silver eyes with silver eye,
An X of wavering flesh, a skull of light,
Fading in our wake without a sigh.

* * *

Soon the current shuddered in its flight
And swerved on pliant muscle. We were sped
Through sudden quiet into a pit of night

– The Mill Hole, its rocky fathoms fed
On moss and pure depth and the cold fin
Turning in its heart. The river bed

Called to our flesh, under the watery skin.
Our shell trembled in answer.
                              A quiet hiss;

Something shifted in sleep; a milk-white breast.
A shift of wings betrayed with feathery kiss
A soul of white with darkness for a nest.

The creature bore the night so tranquilly
I lifted up my eyes. There without rest
The phantoms of the overhanging sky

Occupied their stations and descended.
Another moment, to the starlit eye,
The slow, downstreaming dead, it seemed, were blended

One with those silver hordes, and briefly shared
Their order, glittering. And then impended
A barrier of rock that turned and bared

A varied barrenness as toward its base
We glided – blotting heaven as it towered –
Searching the darkness for a landing place.

38 PHOENIX STREET

Look.
    I was lifted up
past rotten bricks weeds
to look over the wall.
A mammy lifted up a baby on the other side.
Dusty smells. Cat. Flower bells
hanging down purple red.

Look.
       The other. Looking.
My finger picked at a bit of dirt
on top of the wall and a quick
wiry redgolden thing
ran back down a little hole.

* * *

We knelt up on our chairs in the lamplight
and leaned on the brown plush, watching the gramophone.
The turning record shone and hissed
under the needle, liftfalling, liftfalling.
John McCormack chattered in his box.

Two little tongues of flame burned
in the lamp chimney, wavering
their tips. On the glass belly
little drawnout images quivered.
Jimmy's mammy was drying the delph in the shadows.

* * *

Mister Cummins always hunched down
sad and still beside the stove,
with his face turned away toward the bars.
His mouth so calm, and always set so sadly.
A black rubbery scar stuck on his white forehead.
Sealed in his sad cave. Hisshorror erecting
slowly out of its rock nests, nosing the air.
He was buried for three days under a hill of dead,
the faces congested down all round him
grinning *Dardanelles!* in the dark.

They noticed him by a thread of blood
glistening among the black crusts on his forehead.
His heart gathered all its weakness, to beat.

A worm hanging down, its little round
black mouth open. Sad father.

* * *

I spent the night there once
in a strange room, tucked in against the wallpaper
on the other side of our own bedroom wall.

Up in the corner of the darkness the Sacred Heart
leaned down in his long clothes over a red oil lamp
with his women's black hair and his eyes lit up in red,
hurt and blaming. He held out the Heart
with his women's fingers, like a toy.

The lamp-wick, with a tiny head
of red fire, wriggled in its pool.
The shadows flickered: the Heart beat!

JOHN MONTAGUE
b. 1929

Born in Brooklyn, New York, and brought up on a farm in County Tyrone, Montague was educated at UCD and Yale University. He is the author of several poetry collections, including *A New Siege* (1970), *Time in Armagh* (1993) and *The Drunken Sailor* (2004). He became the first Ireland Chair of Poetry in 1998.

THIS NEUTRAL REALM

The great achievement of the South of Ireland
was to stand aside.

LOUIS MacNEICE

Here, too, they defied Adolf.
A platoon of the L.D.F.
drilled in the parochial hall,
shouldering Lee Enfields.
A war intimate as a game,
miles better than Indians,
like the splendid manoeuvres
when the regular army came.

We defended Abbeylara
watching the Northern road –
signposts all gone –
from a girdered haybarn,
rifles at the ready,
with dummy cartridges,
until Southern Command
came behind our backs:
took over the town.

So I and my cousin
were captured, condemned
to spend a warm afternoon
incubating in an armoured car,
peering through slits,
fingering the intricacy
of a mounted Bren gun.

So we learnt to defend
this neutral realm,
each holiday summer,
against all comers,
including the Allies
if they dared to cross over
(Hitler being frightened).
Eire's most somnolent time
while, at home, invasion
forces risked chilling seas
to assemble in Ulster.

Already seen through
the stereoscopic lens
of a solitary childhood,
our divided allegiances;
a mock and a real war:
Spitfire and Messerschmitt
twinned in fire, Shermans
lumbering through our hedges,
ungainly as dinosaurs, while
the South marched its toy
soldiers along the sideline.

A WELCOMING PARTY

Wie war das möglich?

That final newsreel of the war:
A welcoming party of almost shades
Met us at the cinema door
Clicking what remained of their heels.

From nests of bodies like hatching eggs
Flickered insectlike hands and legs
And rose an ululation, terrible, shy;
Children conjugating the verb 'to die'.

One clamoured mutely of love
From a mouth like a burnt glove;
Others upheld hands bleak as begging bowls
Claiming the small change of our souls.

Some smiled at us as protectors.
Can these bones live?
Our parochial brand of innocence
Was all we had to give.

To be always at the periphery of incident
Gave my childhood its Irish dimension;
Yet doves of mercy, as doves of air,
Can falter here as anywhere.

That long dead Sunday in Armagh
I learned one meaning of total war
And went home to my Christian school
To kick a football through the air.

WAITING

Halting in Dungannon between trains
We often wandered outside town
To see the camp where German
Prisoners were kept. A moist litter
Of woodshavings showed
Ground hastily cleared, and then –

The huge parallelogram
Of barbed wire, nakedly measured
And enclosed like a football field
With the guard towers rising, aloof
As goalposts, at either end.

Given length and breadth we knew
The surface area the prisoners paced
As one hung socks to dry outside
His Nissen hut, another tried
To hum and whistle *Lili Marlene*:
They seemed to us much the same

As other adults, except in their
Neutral dress, and finding it normal
To suffer our gaze, like animals,
As we squatted and pried, for an hour
Or more, about their human zoo

Before it was time for shopfronts,
Chugging train, Vincentian school.
A small incident, soon submerged
In our own brisk, bell-dominated rule;
Until, years later, I saw another camp –
Rudshofen in the fragrant Vosges –

Similar, but with local improvements:
The stockade where the difficult knelt,
The laboratory for minor experiments,
The crematorium for Jews and Gypsies
Under four elegant pine towers, like minarets.

This low-pitched style seeks exactness
Decided not to betray the event.
But as I write, the grid of barbed
Wire rises abruptly around me
The smell of woodshavings plugs
My nostrils, a carrion stench.

A BOMBER'S MOON

Then there were the terrible nights when Belfast was bombed
and planes of the Luftwaffe penetrated as far as Armagh. One
crossed low over the tossing trees at the end of the football
field: we could hear the engine's roar as it swooped. Crouched
in the dampness of the hastily constructed air-raid shelters
we awaited the shudder, the flash, the quick moment of
extinction.

'Oh, Lord,' I prayed, on my knees at the leaf-strewn entrance,
'let me not feel death, only die so suddenly that I will not know
what it is all about.'

The air seemed to quiver with the upward beat of wings as
the plane zoomed over the school buildings and away, leaving
the frightened boys staring at the sky, the silvered spires of the
Cathedral; moonlit nights were best for bombing raids. In that
moment he had known everything; the possibility of death, in
the shape of a dark angel, something apocalyptic and avenging
as the images conjured up in a Lenten sermon in the chapel.
Then the rising wail of the All Clear.

'It's gone ...'

In the candle- and torch-lit darkness of their concrete cave the boys turned frightened heads upwards, no longer in fear, but in thanksgiving.

'It's gone', they chorused.

Father Rafferty, their favourite priest, blessed himself again, and began to lead the Rosary, with relief, in the blessèd silence of the raid's aftermath.

'Come now, boys, let us kneel down and pray to the Blessed Virgin, in thanks for having been saved, this time.'

As he knelt, running the beads through his fingers with practised skill, he was aware of some menace, at the edge of his retina. From his vantage point he could see that, although they themselves were safe and sound, the stain on the Eastern sky was growing, like a bloodshot eye.

'Let us pray,' he said to himself, 'for all the poor people of Belfast.'

A FERTILE BALANCE

1

The ring of pure light
on the table, bread and wine,
under the roof of baked tiles,
rooms cool as a pantry.
Stiff dried flowers and herbs
spice the oak beam's
fertile balance: an interior garden.

2

Leaving, returning,
a round of ritual visits:
a tree creaks its slow greeting,
a windlass well, long deserted,
thickets of odorous lavender,
perfumed stone, a spade laid
in drills of aubergine, dense
and dark as hand grenades.

3

A half century ago, the poet
hides in the brush, rifle
butt cradled against shoulder,
as the German convoy grinds near:
before he orders 'Fire!'
a brief scent of wild thyme.

4

A warm day, the ochre earth
leaps before us: the khaki back,
bulging eye, of the cricket,
lofting away like a tiny helicopter
at an angle on its spindle legs.
The shrewd-eyed lizard sprawls,
then darts along a corbelled wall
in a continuous thrum of flies.

5

Now the tall poet greets us
under his lintel, speaking
of rare flowers, scarce birds,
pollution in the rivers great
and small, the muscled Seine,
his homely Sorgue, the sun
on those waters darkening
as the trout turns belly up.

6

'In the land of the day before
the thunder rang pure in the streams,
the vine fostered the bee,
the shoulder lifted the burden.'
Now rocket ranges in the Vaucluse,
the stink of Rhone Poulenc.
'Voters, students of your townland,
of its beasts and flowers, do not
falter in your duty. This is a call
to order, to halt the march of death.'

7

Starless night over the Luberon,
the drone of a friendly plane,
a blossoming of parachutes;
the watchdog lopes between
them, nuzzling their freight
of guns and grenades, but
making no sound, neither bark
nor whimper, before dropping
to sleep on the crumpled silk.

8

'I try not to go to Paris now,
source and centre of all this filth.'
Petrarch, fleeing southwards;
To redeem myself from that
pit of iniquity called Avignon
I fled to where a slate-blue
and white fountain pours,
while birds circle the cliff,
and drank till I felt restored.
Now when I make love
it is for the last time.

from WREATHS

CIVIL WAR VETERAN
i.m. C.S. (Todd) Andrews

At the cigar and brandy stage,
an old civil war veteran recalls
someone he killed – a half secret –
or someone he missed – a half regret.

Somehow, it now amounts to the same thing.
'Sure, he'd be dead, or –' (half-laughing,
blinking age-cowled saurian eyes)
' – half dying now, like myself.'

SPEECH LESSON

I

The chant of those carriage wheels
As we chug towards Belfast;
Clickety-click, lickety-split,
When will I learn again to speak?

A straggle of villages before Dungannon:
Beragh, Carrickmore, Sixmilecross,
(Forlorn stations, later bypassed)
Or *Will I never, ever speak again?*

II
The Flower

After hilly Dungannon, holy Donaghmore.
A cluster of convent girls clambers
Aboard the train, sweep and swirl
Past the place of the tongue-tied boy
Who huddles his head in his book
(which suddenly sheds all importance)
While they pile into the next compartment.
A chatter-and-clatter like starlings
As they settle. But one, bolder,
Tiptoes along the swaying corridor,
To risk a look where he sits, blushing.
Then another. A flurry of giggles.
Though as the troop leave, prodding one another,
The bold one turns, to throw him a flower.

III

Under the leather seats, the creak
Of iron wheels, as we steam towards Belfast:
When will I learn again to speak?
The Calvin Mills at Portadown,
Balmoral Show Grounds, and tethered
Above the wartime city, a silvery barrage balloon.
(Belfast's knell had not yet rung.)

IV

Near the bulky City Hall, 20 Wellington.
An ardent young Englishwoman,
Speaking of War and Poetry,
Places a hand on his tummy-tum-tum,
(The first stranger to have so done.)
'Young man, learn to speak from your diaphragm:
Many merry men marched many times.
And you should read Drummond Allison.
He was stationed here in Northern Ireland.'
She presses down, again and again:
'Consider our King: he broadcasts, stammering.
So let the wind whistle through your lungs.
And read poetry aloud, it can be such fun!
From how far away did you say you've come?'

Clickety-click, clickety-clack as
The Derry evening train ferries him back
All the way to County Tyrone and
Beragh Station, a lantern swaying
Along the platform. The parting whistle.
Then the long pull on his bicycle
Through the hay-scented countryside
To the turf-heavy hearth at home,
The Rosary and a mug of Ovaltine
In the Sacred Heart-flushed kitchen.
Candle in hand, he climbs to his room.
A scurry of giggles, the shock of that flower.
Many men marched many times:
Shall I begin to speak again?

I can still smell her perfume.

JAMES SIMMONS
1933–2001

Simmons was born in Derry and educated at the University of
Leeds. He taught in universities in Northern Ireland, England
and Africa and was a founder editor of *The Honest Ulsterman*.
His *Poems 1956–1986* was published in 1986. As well as
being a poet and critic, Simmons was also a singer-songwriter
who released a number of records.

IN THE DESERT WAR

Of four friends three survive. One is dead drunk,
another walked in darkness by the sea
and now lies, stiff with sorrow, in his bunk.
We, in our minds, and wild dogs really,
drag out that corpse from the shallow grave we made.
Four friends foresaw such resurrections
before the battle and laughed and were afraid.
I laugh, remembering, going into actions
he enjoyed, like this, glad to be human,
glad of my drinker's sway, my smoker's cough
that well might wake the husband of this woman
who giggles at me with my trousers off.
All his effects were sent off to his mother
except this contraceptive which I don
in memory. I wish his ghost could hover
over me, smiling, with a good hard-on.

UNCLE JACK

In the first Great War my Uncle Jack
fought and only just came back.
To Derry, to the old homestead,
he brought war with him in his head.
When governments closed down their hell
he still kept waiting for the shell
that ruined his mind and killed his mates.
He raced along the parapet
screaming as though he'd never stop.
His soldiers dragged him off the top
and patched him up, not lame, not blind;
but shell-shocked. Everyone was kind
and helpless. He was never still.
He went to church and steeled his will
to sit like other men, but sweat
dripped off his fingers' ends and wet
his boots. They led him home again,
but every turning of the lane
hid snipers. Any sudden sound
flicked him face-down on the ground.
My mother's glad the Asian Flu
killed him. 'He was so much like you,'
she often tells me. Jack and I,
bookish, intelligent and shy.

Years after you had been betrayed
I grew up innocent and played
in fields and haysheds round the farm
you knew before you came to harm.
I liked the odds and ends one hears
of a dead uncle through the years.
I touched and smelt your uniform
but never dared to put it on.

The sort of tricks you used to do
for cameras are my tricks too.
I have this feeling that I owe
something that you will never know
to you, Jack – *my* life lived with care.
I'm older than you ever were.

REMEMBRANCE DAY

I was working on old poems when the cock crew
and I saw myself and the rest as we once were,
our acts and feelings from which poems grew
to witness and to judge what happened there.

I help create the conscience of this nation,
a soldier-spokesman who's survived the wars
praised for his clarity and penetration
and wit in telling how he got his scars.

Soldiers are simple when they fight. I too
was simple, anxious, aimed by fierce desire.
Resigning seemed a clever thing to do,
for words came easier not under fire.

Now I'm dream-marching at some Cenotaph
which is my poems; the wounded veterans start
to break ranks, piss on it and me and laugh,
while others walk away and break my heart.

THE USE OF HISTORY

In their first action force-marched in the snow
For thirty miles, wiped out a large patrol
Of tough, experienced Regulars, and stole
Their armoured car. They had lain low
In ambush, soaked and cold, for an hour.
Their plan went badly wrong. Scared and confused,
They still obeyed young officers who used
No threats or bullying to assert their power.
That night these rebels slept on a stone floor.
Their brigadier came from headquarters, creeping
Five dangerous miles to guard them, sleeping.
He stood in silence at the stable door.
English and Irish women reared these sons,
But now the pride and shame is everyone's.

DEATH OF A POET IN BATTLE-DRESS

(for George Craig)

'I shall forget in 1920
You ever hurt a bit!'
RUPERT BROOKE

His body was broken. Blood, still pushing round,
Fulfilled no function, spilled out on the ground.
He prayed, 'Oh Jesus, please let me fulfil
My early promise, if it be Thy will.'
And I, embarrassed, said, 'What can he do?
Christ may be understood not spoken to.'

He said, 'To me war's crazy, it was the others
Brought me here.'
     I said, 'All men are brothers.'

His right hand held his tunic where he bled,
His left-hand fingers plucked up grass. He said,
'I couldn't lead, I couldn't leave them: trying,
I suffered with them, from them. Now I'm dying,
My good mind never used, and all you see
Is a soldier in a uniform, not me.
Help me unbutton this ...' and then he tried
To strip himself. Half dressed for war he died.

A MAN'S A SOLDIER

A man's a soldier, but the smoke won't clear,
So he shoots first, his questions come too late.
Misguided courage and unfounded fear,
Weapons too new or sadly out of date,
A man's a soldier, but the smoke won't clear.

What men would conquer seems to disappear
And leave Bluebeard or Eichmann within reach
Whose twisted bodies only death makes queer.
Is that the villain makes the victor's speech?
A man's a soldier, but the smoke won't clear.

But any soldier has a sad career.
If he has more success than Joan of Arc,
He finds the enemy not there but here.
Power makes the vulture, prison made the lark.
A man's a soldier, but the smoke won't clear.

BRENDAN KENNELLY
b. 1936

Kennelly was born in Ballylongford, County Kerry, and was Professor of Modern Literature at TCD until his retirement in 2005. A prolific writer and cultural commentator, his many poetry collections include *Cromwell* (1983) and *The Book of Judas* (1991). His *Familiar Strangers: New and Selected Poems* was published in 2004.

OLD SOLDIER

'I'm eighty-eight,' he said,
    trenchtwinkle in his eyes,
'and though I fought in the worst o' wars
    I'm barkin' lively.

Slogged in the Kimberley Diamond Mines,
    sang on Fiddler's Green
and never, never would accept
    the notion of a has-been.

The years are old, my heart is young,
    there's plenty left to do;
strings of a fiddle, words of a song
    keep me feelin' new.

Complainin' gets ya nowhere.
    Old eyes need a sparklin' sight.
Take me for a walk, young friend,
    to see the Shannon light.'

WALL

I surround the Big House
hundreds of years old.
Craggy, cracked, indigenous,

I'm close to the Shannon tides,
aware of what it means to be
the line between warring sides.

I saw the Civil War, I was there
the day Eddie Carmody was shot.
A quiet man, Eddie. He whispered a prayer.

Others shouted curses. They swore
they were doing a favour to those
they chose to murder.

One said it was the Civil War
made the Irish grow up, made
men of them. I stood there, undismayed.

Killers will justify whatever they do.
A man must face himself, know the world.
Killing one neighbour can be hard. It's easier to kill two.

In there at my back, among flowers and trees
a cultured man
owns everything anyone sees.

I lack nothing. I know the weathers. I know rage
and easy does it, moon, earth, clouds, stars,
sun, green mossy peace between wars.

I saw Angela Raine drown herself.
I might have saved her. If she'd turned her head
she might have climbed over me instead

of stepping naked into the Shannon.
She went down in no time at all.
The Shannon swallowed her, grateful.

The Shannon rejects nothing: darkness, light,
poison, bird, weed, flower, stone, bone. It tells me
what it means to be pure appetite:

make hunger your friend, watchful and calm,
innocent and clean, waiting and flowing.
Never complain.

Lovers scale me now and then
to find a bed in summer grass.
Only the grass might say what comes to pass.

My silence is my strength. The river talks.
The trees talk. Even the flowers whisper.
I draw the line and witness

changing tides, each dance of shame and glory,
rights of way, who pays the rent, who hoards
and spends. I see the nine sides of the story.

I'm sturdy, vigilant, dependable, old.
What happens, happens. I note the history
of what's never been told.

What's known is a tiny part of what is.
Night and day, year after year, sleepless, I stand
and listen to the river's heart.

Not a word has ever passed between us.
No need for truth or lies.
We are what we are, do what we do,

serving the cause of water and stone.
Killers and killed are deep in the earth,
a ceasefire of bones.

BOMB

Though I nestled in Adam's brain
he'd no time to think of me when
day and night he longed for Eve
and the inane birth of human love.
I wandered through the mind of Cain
and through the hearts of murderous men.
I was the alert, indifferent star
contemplating fields of war.
I was vigilant and relaxed,
the death-arc of a flashing axe,
the candid claymore, the sly sword
killed as they listened to my word:
In the beginning was the Bomb.
In the end will be the same.
The holy images I defiled
became for me a deformed child
unknown, unseen, grotesque, absurd.
In the beginning was his Word:
darkness cannot know the light,
why should darkness want to, since it
palls and shrouds each little mind?
I am what light can't comprehend.
I am the quarrel in the marriage bed
when he longs to choke her dead

and when their children face each other
in hate, I am each murdering brother.
Hatred I love, and still I hate
peacemongers out to pray and prate.
For centuries I strove to be
born but my children ignored me.
Children of hatred love to play
and pitch the world into disarray,
to hear the maimed and wounded scream.
I could have realised their dream
but still they couldn't make me exist
until one morning, hate be praised,
a gifted son made me come true
and down to earth to trouble you,
I'd waited centuries to become
the one and only ultimate bomb,
to turn the seas into seas of blood
to prove the stupidity of the good
to annihilate in one small hour
superb creations of man's power
to show that only fools create
while I'm content to devastate
this earth some potty god has given,
a lunatic substitute for his heaven.
I burn everything for I know well
men work hard to make their hell
to sweat their way from cradle to grave,
graceless, ageless, insatiate slaves.
So I offer myself, my explosive style,
to comfort and beguile you while
you prattle, argue, haggle, chide.
I'm waiting here, your invented god
hoping you find courage at last
to lay yourself and your world waste.
I rest assured you'll do your best.

Who knows? Another world may begin
mythologising grace and sin
and I'll go into the dark once more
till a chosen child will find me there
and his heart will hurt with joy
hearing my heart, Destroy! Destroy!
I rest my case until you find
me ready in your ticking mind.
When I go off, your world goes blind.
Bloodspattered stars can't hear a sound.

MICHAEL LONGLEY
b. 1939

Longley was born in Belfast and educated at TCD. He worked
as a teacher and later for the Arts Council of Northern Ireland.
Longley's poetry collections include *No Continuing City* (1969)
and *Gorse Fires* (1991). His *Collected Poems* was published in
2006 and he became the Ireland Chair of Poetry in 2007.

IN MEMORIAM

My father, let no similes eclipse
Where crosses like some forest simplified
Sink roots into my mind; the slow sands
Of your history delay till through your eyes
I read you like a book. Before you died,
Re-enlisting with all the broken soldiers
You bent beneath your rucksack, near collapse,
In anecdote rehearsed and summarised
These words I write in memory. Let yours
And other heartbreaks play into my hands.

Now I see in close-up, in my mind's eye,
The cracked and splintered dead for pity's sake
Each dismal evening predecease the sun,
You, looking death and nightmare in the face
With your kilt, harmonica and gun,
Grow older in a flash, but none the wiser
(Who, following the wrong queue at The Palace,
Have joined the London Scottish by mistake),
Your nineteen years uncertain if and why
Belgium put the kibosh on the Kaiser.

Between the corpses and the soup canteens
You swooned away, watching your future spill.
But, as it was, your proper funeral urn
Had mercifully smashed to smithereens,
To shrapnel shards that sliced your testicle.
That instant I, your most unlikely son,
In No Man's Land was surely left for dead,
Blotted out from your far horizon.
As your voice now is locked inside my head,
I yet was held secure, waiting my turn.

Finally, that lousy war was over.
Stranded in France and in need of proof
You hunted down experimental lovers,
Persuading chorus girls and countesses:
This, father, the last confidence you spoke.
In my twentieth year your old wounds woke
As cancer. Lodging under the same roof
Death was a visitor who hung about,
Strewing the house with pills and bandages,
Till he chose to put your spirit out.

Though they overslept the sequence of events
Which ended with the ambulance outside,
You lingering in the hall, your bowels on fire,
Tears in your eyes, and all your medals spent,
I summon girls who packed at last and went
Underground with you. Their souls again on hire,
Now those lost wives as recreated brides
Take shape before me, materialise.
On the verge of light and happy legend
They lift their skirts like blinds across your eyes.

WOUNDS

Here are two pictures from my father's head –
I have kept them like secrets until now:
First, the Ulster Division at the Somme
Going over the top with 'Fuck the Pope!'
'No Surrender!': a boy about to die,
Screaming 'Give 'em one for the Shankill!'
'Wilder than Gurkhas' were my father's words
Of admiration and bewilderment.
Next comes the London-Scottish padre
Resettling kilts with his swagger-stick,
With a stylish backhand and a prayer.
Over a landscape of dead buttocks
My father followed him for fifty years.
At last, a belated casualty,
He said – lead traces flaring till they hurt –
'I am dying for King and Country, slowly.'
I touched his hand, his thin head I touched.

Now, with military honours of a kind,
With his badges, his medals like rainbows,
His spinning compass, I bury beside him
Three teenage soldiers, bellies full of
Bullets and Irish beer, their flies undone.
A packet of Woodbines I throw in,
A lucifer, the Sacred Heart of Jesus
Paralysed as heavy guns put out
The night-light in a nursery for ever;
Also a bus-conductor's uniform –
He collapsed beside his carpet-slippers
Without a murmur, shot through the head
By a shivering boy who wandered in
Before they could turn the television down
Or tidy away the supper dishes.
To the children, to a bewildered wife,
I think 'Sorry Missus' was what he said.

MASTER OF CEREMONIES

My grandfather, a natural master of ceremonies
('Boys! Girls! Take your partners for the Military Two-step!')
Had thrown out his only son, my sad retarded uncle
Who, good for nothing except sleepwalking to the Great War,
Was not once entrusted with rifle or bayonet but instead
Went over the top slowly behind the stretcher parties
And, as park attendant where all hell had broken loose,
Collected littered limbs until his sack was heavy.
In old age my grandfather demoted his flesh and blood
And over the cribbage board ('Fifteen two, fifteen four,
One for his nob') would call me Lionel. 'Sorry. My mistake.
That was my nephew. His head got blown off in No Man's Land.'

SECOND SIGHT

My father's mother had the second sight.
Flanders began at the kitchen window –
The mangle rusting in No Man's Land, gas
Turning the antimacassars yellow
When it blew the wrong way from the salient.

In bandages, on crutches, reaching home
Before his letters, my father used to find
The front door on the latch, his bed airing.
'I watched my son going over the top.
He was carrying flowers out of the smoke.'

I have brought the *Pocket Guide to London*,
My *Map of the Underground*, an address –
A lover looking for somewhere to live,
A ghost among ghosts of aunts and uncles
Who crowd around me to give directions.

Where is my father's house, where my father?
If I could walk in on my grandmother
She'd see right through me and the hallway
And the miles of cloud and sky to Ireland.
'You have crossed the water to visit me.'

GHETTO

I

Because you will suffer soon and die, your choices
Are neither right nor wrong: a spoon will feed you,
A flannel keep you clean, a toothbrush bring you back
To your bathroom's view of chimney-pots and gardens.
With so little time for inventory or leavetaking,
You are packing now for the rest of your life
Photographs, medicines, a change of underwear, a book,
A candlestick, a loaf, sardines, needle and thread.
These are your heirlooms, perishables, worldly goods.
What you bring is the same as what you leave behind,
Your last belonging a list of your belongings.

II

As though it were against the law to sleep on pillows
They have filled a cathedral with confiscated feathers:
Silence irrefrangible, no room for angels' wings,
Tons of feathers suffocating cherubim and seraphim.

III

The little girl without a mother behaves like a mother
With her rag doll to whom she explains fear and anguish,
The meagreness of the bread ration, how to make it last,
How to get back to the doll's house and lift up the roof
And, before the flame-throwers and dynamiters destroy it,
How to rescue from their separate rooms love and sorrow,
Masterpieces the size of a postage stamp, small fortunes.

IV

From among the hundreds of thousands I can imagine one
Behind the barbed-wire fences as my train crosses Poland.
I see him for long enough to catch the sprinkle of snowflakes
On his hair and schoolbag, and then I am transported
Away from that world of broken hobby-horses and silent toys.
He turns into a little snowman and refuses to melt.

V

For street-singers in the marketplace, weavers, warp-makers,
Those who suffer in sewing-machine repair shops, excrement-
Removal workers, there are not enough root vegetables,
Beetroots, turnips, swedes, nor for the leather-stitchers
Who are boiling leather so that their children may eat;
Who are turning like a thick slice of potato-bread
This page, which is everything I know about potatoes,
My delivery of Irish Peace, Beauty of Hebron, Home
Guard, Arran Banners, Kerr's Pinks, resistant to eelworm,
Resignation, common scab, terror, frost, potato-blight.

VI

There will be performances in the waiting room, and time
To jump over a skipping rope, and time to adjust
As though for a dancing class the ribbons in your hair.
This string quartet is the most natural thing in the world.

VII

Fingers leave shadows on a violin, harmonics,
A blackbird fluttering between electrified fences.

VIII

Lessons were forbidden in that terrible school.
Punishable by death were reading and writing
And arithmetic, so that even the junior infants
Grew old and wise in lofts studying these subjects.
There were drawing lessons, and drawings of kitchens
And farms, farm animals, butterflies, mothers, fathers
Who survived in crayon until in pen and ink
They turned into guards at executions and funerals
Torturing and hanging even these stick figures.
There were drawings of barracks and latrines as well
And the only windows were the windows they drew.

IN MEMORY OF CHARLES DONNELLY

Killed in Spain, 27.2.37, aged 22

I

Minutes before a bullet hits you in the forehead
There is a lull in the machine-gun fire, time to pick
From the dust a bunch of olives, time to squeeze them,
To understand the groans and screams and big abstractions
By saying quietly: 'Even the olives are bleeding'.

II

Buried among the roots of that olive tree, you are
Wood and fruit and the skylight its branches make
Through which to read as they accumulate for ever
The poems you go on not writing in the tree's shadow
As it circles the fallen olives and the olive-stones.

CEASEFIRE

I

Put in mind of his own father and moved to tears
Achilles took him by the hand and pushed the old king
Gently away, but Priam curled up at his feet and
Wept with him until their sadness filled the building.

II

Taking Hector's corpse into his own hands Achilles
Made sure it was washed and, for the old king's sake,
Laid out in uniform, ready for Priam to carry
Wrapped like a present home to Troy at daybreak.

III

When they had eaten together, it pleased them both
To stare at each other's beauty as lovers might,
Achilles built like a god, Priam good-looking still
And full of conversation, who earlier had sighed:

IV

'I get down on my knees and do what must be done
And kiss Achilles' hand, the killer of my son.'

BUCHENWALD MUSEUM

Among the unforgettable exhibits one
Was an official apology for bias. Outside

Although a snowfall had covered everything
A wreath of poppies was just about visible.

No matter how heavily the snow may come down
We have to allow the snow to wear a poppy.

PARTISANS

He hacks at a snowdrift:
She skims the pine needles
That drop into their soup,
Scattering on the snowcrust
Ideograms of 'peace'
And 'love', suchlike ideals.

SEAMUS HEANEY
b. 1939

Heaney was born in rural County Derry, and educated at Queen's University. He was appointed Oxford Professor of Poetry in 1989 and won the Nobel Prize for Literature in 1995. He is the author of several poetry collections, volumes of essays and translations, including *Beowulf* (1999).

ENGLAND'S DIFFICULTY

I moved like a double agent among the big concepts.

The word 'enemy' had the toothed efficiency of a mowing machine. It was a mechanical and distant noise beyond that opaque security, that autonomous ignorance.

'When the Germans bombed Belfast it was the bitterest Orange parts were hit the worst.'

I was on somebody's shoulder, conveyed through the starlit yard to see the sky glowing over Anahorish. Grown-ups lowered their voices and resettled in the kitchen as if tired out after an excursion.

Behind the blackout, Germany called to lamplit kitchens through fretted baize, dry battery, wet battery, capillary wires, domed valves that squeaked and burbled as the dial-hand absolved Stuttgart and Leipzig.

'He's an artist, this Haw Haw. He can fairly leave it into them.'

I lodged with 'the enemies of Ulster', the scullions outside the walls. An adept at banter, I crossed the lines with carefully enunciated passwords, manned every speech with checkpoints and reported back to nobody.

TRIAL RUNS

WELCOME HOME YE LADS OF THE EIGHTH ARMY. There had to be some defiance in it because it was painted along the demesne wall, a banner headline over the old news of REMEMBER 1690 and NO SURRENDER, a great wingspan of lettering I hurried under with the messages.

In a khaki shirt and brass-buckled belt, a demobbed neighbour leaned against our jamb. My father jingled silver deep in both pockets and laughed when the big clicking rosary beads were produced.

'Did they make a Papish of you over there?'

'Oh damn the fear! I stole them for you, Paddy, off the Pope's dresser when his back was turned.'

'You could harness a donkey with them.'

Their laughter sailed above my head, a hoarse clamour, two big nervous birds dipping and lifting, making trial runs across a territory.

IN MEMORIAM FRANCIS LEDWIDGE

killed in France 31 July 1917

The bronze soldier hitches a bronze cape
That crumples stiffly in imagined wind
No matter how the real winds buff and sweep
His sudden hunkering run, forever craned

Over Flanders. Helmet and haversack,
The gun's firm slope from butt to bayonet,
The loyal, fallen names on the embossed plaque –
It all meant little to the worried pet

I was in nineteen forty-six or -seven,
Gripping my Aunt Mary by the hand
Along the Portstewart prom, then round the crescent
To thread the Castle Walk out to the strand.

The pilot from Coleraine sailed to the coal-boat.
Courting couples rose out of the dunes.
A farmer stripped to his studs and shiny waistcoat
Rolled the trousers down on his timid shins.

Francis Ledwidge, you courted at the seaside
Beyond Drogheda one Sunday afternoon.
Literary, sweet-talking, countrified,
You pedalled out the leafy road from Slane

Where you belonged, among the dolorous
And lovely: the May altar of wild flowers,
Easter water sprinkled in outhouses,
Mass-rocks and hill-top raths and raftered byres.

I think of you in your Tommy's uniform,
A haunted Catholic face, pallid and brave,
Ghosting the trenches like a bloom of hawthorn
Or silence cored from a Boyne passage-grave.

It's summer, nineteen-fifteen. I see the girl
My aunt was then, herding on the long acre.
Behind a low bush in the Dardanelles
You suck stones to make your dry mouth water.

It's nineteen-seventeen. She still herds cows
But a big strafe puts the candles out in Ypres:
'My soul is by the Boyne, cutting new meadows …
My country wears her confirmation dress.'

'To be called a British soldier while my country
Has no place among nations ...' You were rent
By shrapnel six weeks later. 'I am sorry
That party politics should divide our tents.'

In you, our dead enigma, all the strains
Criss-cross in useless equilibrium
And as the wind tunes through this vigilant bronze
1 hear again the sure confusing drum

You followed from Boyne water to the Balkans
But miss the twilit note your flute should sound.
You were not keyed or pitched like these true-blue ones
Though all of you consort now underground.

IN THE BEECH

I was a lookout posted and forgotten.

On one side under me, the concrete road.
On the other, the bullocks' covert,
the breath and plaster of a drinking place
where the school-leaver discovered peace
to touch himself in the reek of churned-up mud.

And the tree itself a strangeness and a comfort,
as much a column as a bole. The very ivy
puzzled its milk-tooth frills and tapers
over the grain: was it bark or masonry?

I watched the red-brick chimney rear
its stamen, course by course,
and the steeplejacks up there at their antics
like flies against the mountain.

I felt the tanks' advance beginning
at the cynosure of the growth rings,
then winced at their imperium refreshed
in each powdered bolt-mark on the concrete.
And the pilot with his goggles back came in
so low I could see the cockpit rivets.

My hidebound boundary tree. My tree of knowledge.
My thick-tapped, soft-fledged, airy listening post.

ANAHORISH 1944

'We were killing pigs when the Americans arrived.
A Tuesday morning, sunlight and gutter-blood
Outside the slaughterhouse. From the main road
They would have heard the squealing,
Then heard it stop and had a view of us
In our gloves and aprons coming down the hill.
Two lines of them, guns on their shoulders, marching.
Armoured cars and tanks and open jeeps.
Sunburnt hands and arms. Unknown, unnamed,
Hosting for Normandy.
                Not that we knew then
Where they were headed, standing there like youngsters
As they tossed us gum and tubes of coloured sweets.'

THE AERODROME

First it went back to grass, then after that
To warehouses and brickfields (designated
The Creagh Meadows Industrial Estate),
Its wartime grey control tower rebuilt and glazed

Into a hard-edged CEO-style villa:
Toome Aerodrome had turned to local history.
Hangars, runways, bomb stores, Nissen huts,
The perimeter barbed wire, forgotten and gone.

But not a smell of daisies and hot tar
On a newly-surfaced cart-road, Easter Monday,
1944. And not, two miles away that afternoon,
The annual bright booths of the fair at Toome,

All the brighter for having been denied.
No catchpenny stalls for us, no
Awnings, bonnets, or beribboned gauds:
Wherever the world was, we were somewhere else,

Had been and would be. Sparrows might fall,
B-26 Marauders not return, but the sky above
That land usurped by a compulsory order
Watched and waited – like me and her that day

Watching and waiting by the perimeter.
A fear crossed over then like the fly-by-night
And sun-repellent wing that flies by day
Invisibly above: would she rise and go

With the pilot calling from his Thunderbolt?
But for her part, in response, only the slightest
Back-stiffening and standing of her ground
As her hand reached down and tightened around mine.

If self is a location, so is love:
Bearings taken, markings, cardinal points,
Options, obstinacies, dug heels and distance,
Here and there and now and then, a stance.

SEAMUS DEANE
b. 1940

Deane was born in County Derry and educated at Queen's and Cambridge, teaching for many years at UCD. A poet, novelist and critic, he was General Editor of the *Field Day Anthology of Irish Writing* and was Professor of Irish Studies at the University of Notre Dame.

SHELTER

Two years after one war,
And some time before another,
In nineteen forty-seven,
Came a heavy fall of snow
That drifted over the slab
Of the air-raid shelter roof.

Before, there had been an infinite
Summer, full of the pock
And applause of the false spirit
Of cricket. As our reproof,

Came the savage winter
When the boiler burst
And the water in the lavatory bowl
Shook. To tell the truth,

I could see nothing wrong.
Winter was like Russia
At last and the war-games,
Ice-pointed, less uncouth.

Perhaps I heard my mother
Dreading the thaw and frost.
When I turned to look, though,
She was at the fire, face aloof

In concentration. Doing the sums
For food and clothes, the future
In endless hock. I went out
To the air-raid shelter roof

To throw snowballs. The whole summer's
Bowling went into my swing
And I flung them splat on the wall.
Damned winter. Her spirit, unsheltered,
Made me numerate at last
And, since forty-seven, weather-proof.

DEREK MAHON
b. 1941

Mahon was born in Belfast and educated at TCD and the Sorbonne. He worked for years as a freelance journalist. A poet and translator, his *Collected Poems* was published in 1999 and in 2007 he was honoured with the David Cohen Prize for Literature in recognition of lifetime achievement.

from AUTOBIOGRAPHIES
(for Maurice Leitch)

1
The Home Front

While the frozen armies trembled
At the gates of Leningrad
They took me home in a taxi
And laid me in my cot,
And there I slept again
With siren and black-out;

And slept under the stairs
Beside the light meter
When bombs fell on the city;
So I never saw the sky
Ablaze with a fiery glow,
Searchlights roaming the stars.

But I do remember one time
(I must have been four then)
Being held up to the window
For a victory parade –
Soldiers, sailors and airmen
Lining the Antrim Road;

And, later, hide-and-seek
Among the air-raid shelters,
The last ration coupons,
Oranges and bananas,
Forage caps and badges
And packets of Lucky Strike.

Gracie Fields on the radio!
Americans in the art-deco
Milk bars! The released Jews
Blinking in shocked sunlight ...
A male child in a garden
Clutching the *Empire News*.

A KENSINGTON NOTEBOOK

I

South Lodge is blue-
Plaqued where Ford set out
His toy soldiers on the
Razed table of art.

There was a great good place
Of clean-limbed young men
And high-minded virgins,
Cowslip and celandine;

Henry James to be visited,
Lawrence to be prized,
Conrad to be instructed,
Yeats to be lionized.

Sussex chirped in the sun.
A man could stand up
Then, and a woman too,
Before the thunderclap.

(Intrigue at German spas,
Bombast on golf-courses,
Perfidy in the ministries,
Generals in country houses ...)

What price the dewy-eyed
Pelagianism of home
To a lost generation
Dumbfounded on the Somme?

An old cod in a land
Unfit for heroes,
He consecrates his new life to
Mnemosyne and Eros.

'The last of England'
Crumbles in the rain
As he embarks for
Paris and Michigan.

II

The operantics of
Provence and Languedoc
Shook the Gaudier marbles
At No. 10 Church Walk

Where 'Ezra Pound, M.A.,
Author of *Personae*',
Sniffed out the image with
Whiskery antennae;

Rihaku, nursed Osiris'
Torn limbs; came to know
Holland St. stone by stone
As he knew San Zeno;

And watched in disbelief
An innocent abroad,
Dirigibles like buzzards
Above the Brompton Rd.

Meanwhile his Sunday mornings
Are scrambled by the din
Of bells from St. Mary
Abbots down the lane.

(Not Dowland, not Purcell
'The age demanded',
But the banalities
Of the *Evening Standard*.)

The Spirit of Romance
Flowered briefly there
Among jade animals;
And years later where,

Confucius of the dooryard,
Prophet of *to kalòn*
He drawls 'treason' into
A Roman microphone.

Asquith was not amused
When the editor of *Blast*,
Dining with the Prince of Wales
At Lady Drogheda's, placed

A pearl-handled revolver
On the white tablecloth –
Anarchy masquerading
As art, dangerous both.

Aesthetic bombardiering
Prefigured the real thing,
The *monstre gai* in a vortex
Of 'stone laughing' –

A moonscape, trees like gibbets,
Shrapnel, wire, the thud
Of howitzers, spike-helmeted
Skeletons in the mud.

War artist, he depicts
The death-throes of an era
While Orpen glorifies
Haig, Gough etc.;

Holed up in Holland Park,
Practises an implacable
Ordnance of the body
And casts out the soul.

Vitriol versus cocoa,
Adam versus the Broad
Church of received opinion,
He goads the Apes of God.

Nietzschean politics,
Urbane rejection, debt,
Six years of Canadian
Exile, psychic defeat.

IV

No more parades …
Ghostly bugles sound
The 'Last Post'; the last fox
Has gone to ground

Beneath the shadow of
A nuclear power plant,
Its whirling radar dishes
Anxious and vehement.

Empire is fugitive
And the creative thrust.
Only the chimps remain;
The rest is dust.

Tragic? No, 'available
Reality' was increased,
The sacred flame kept alive,
The Muse not displeased;

And if one or two
Were short on *agapè*,
What was that to the evil
Done in their day?

Ford dies abroad,
A marginal figure still;
And Lewis, self-condemned,
Eyeless in Notting Hill.

Pound, released, reads
To his grandchildren; 'helps'
With the garden; dozes off in a high
Silence of the Alps –

Un rameur, finally,
Sur le fleuve des morts,
Poling his profile toward
What farther shore?

ONE OF THESE NIGHTS

(for Fleur Fitzgerald)

A pregnant moon of August
Composes the roof-tops'
Unventilated slopes;
Dispenses to the dust
Its milky balm. A blue
Buzzard blinks in the zoo.

Cashel and Ank'hor Vat
Are not more ghostly than
London now, its squares
Bone-pale in the moonlight,
Its quiet thoroughfares
A map of desolation.

The grime of an ephemeral
Culture is swept clean
By that celestial hoover,
The refuse of an era
Consumed like polythene
In its impartial glare.

A train trembles deep
In the earth; vagrants sleep
Beside the revolving doors
Of vast department stores
Past whose alarm systems
The moonlight blandly streams.

A breeze-ruffled news-stand
Headlines the dole queues,
The bleak no-longer-news
Of racism and inflation –
Straws in the rising wind
That heralds the cyclone.

It all happened before –
The road to Wigan Pier,
The long road from Jarrow
To the tea room at the Ritz;
Munich, the Phony War,
The convoys and the Blitz.

One of these nights quiescent
Sirens will start to go
– A dog-howl reminiscent
Of forty years ago –
And sleepy people file
Down to the shelters while

Radiant warplanes come
Droning up the Thames from
Gravesend to Blackfriars,
Westminster and Mayfair,
Their incandescent flowers
Unfolding everywhere.

Enchanted foliage, bright
Water as in an old film
In sumptuous black and white
– This is the true realm,
The real earth before
Business and empire;
And life begins tonight.

AT THE SHELBOURNE

(Elizabeth Bowen, Nov. 1940)

Sunrise in the Irish Sea, dawn over Dublin Bay
after a stormy night, one shivering star;
and I picture the harsh waking everywhere,
the devastations of a world at war,
airfields, radio silence, a darkened convoy
strung out in moonlight on a glittering sea.
Harsh the wide windows of the hotel at daybreak
as I light up the first ciggie of the day,
stormy the lake like the one in Regent's Park,
glittering the first snow on the Wicklow hills.
Out back, a precipitous glimpse of silent walls,
courtyards, skylights of kitchen and heating plant,
seagulls in rising steam; while at the front
I stand at ease to hear the kettle sing
in an upper room of the Kildare St. wing,

admiring the frosty housetops of my birthplace
miraculously immune (almost) to bomb damage.
Sun through south-facing windows lights again
on the oval portrait and the polished surface
where, at an Empire writing-table, I set down
my situation reports for the Dominions Office,
pen-sketches of MacEntee, James Dillon and the rest,
letters to friends in Cork or in Gower St.,
– Virginia, Rosamond and the *Horizon* set –
bright novelistic stuff, a nation on the page:
'... *deep, rather futile talks. It is hard afterwards*
to remember the drift, though I remember words,
that smoke-screen use of words! Mostly I meet
the political people; they are very religious.'
There is nothing heroic or 'patriotic' about this;
for here in this rentier heaven of racing chaps,
journalists, cipher clerks, even Abwehr types
and talkative day-trippers down from Belfast,
the Mata Hari of the austerity age,
I feel like a traitor spying on my own past.
It was here the ill-fate of cities happened first –
a cruiser in the Liffey, field-guns trained on the GPO,
the kicking-in of doors, dances cancelled, revolvers
served with the morning tea on silver salvers,
a ghostly shipboard existence down below,
people asleep in corridors as now
in the London Underground, mysterious Kôr,
a change of uniforms in the cocktail bar
though the bronze slave-girls still stand where they were,
Nubian in aspect, in manner art-nouveau.
I must get the Austin out of the garage,
drive down this weekend to Bowen's Court
if I can find petrol, and back for the Sunday mail-boat –
though this is home really, a place of warmth and light,

a house of artifice neither here nor there
between the patrician past and the egalitarian future,
tempting one always to prolong one's visit:
in war, peace, rain or fog you couldn't miss it
however late the hour, however dark the night.

DURING THE WAR

There are those of us who say 'during the war'
as if the insane scramble for global power
doesn't continue much as it did before.
Red buses and black taxis then as now
in thundering London, even in sloppy Soho.
The light-bowl flickers and the lifts are slow
but I bounce on sneakers up a winding stair:
even at sixty I can still walk on air.

I'm reading Bowen again in mysterious Kôr
and picturing the black-out in Regent's Park,
fierce moonlight blazing down on rail and door,
lost lovers, changing lights, fugitive smiles,
one car, silence, ponds white in the dark,
the whole place clearly visible for miles –
now visible, a bright smudge, from outer space.
No serious myth since the first days of 'peace'.

… This morning in Wardour St., a skip, a tip,
a broken pipe, some unfinished repair work.
A basin of mud and junk has choked it up,
reflecting the blown sky and a baroque
cloud cinema beyond earthly intercourse:
a hole in the road where cloud-leaves gather,
each one framed for a moment in stagnant water
and trailing out of the picture in due course.

This is nothing, this is the triumph of time,
waste products mixing in the history bin,
rain ringing with a harsh, deliberate chime
on scrap iron, plastic and depleted tin,
its grim persistence from the rush-hour sky
a nuisance to the retail trade. Andrei
on his back, wounded, during his own war.
'I never really saw the clouds before ...'

No more shy whispers in a darkening square.
Strip lighting writes the dusk out everywhere
on corporate space and stadium, while slow
flashes go hacking up like tracer fire
and lasers fence among the clouds for show.
The spiteful rain, filmic, begins to freeze,
grown sentimental and considering snow:
to spin at leisure amid naked trees!

December night; night vision; a slash of hail.
An east wind gathering force on water streams
up here like shirts blown from the shining Thames
to *Ronnie Scott's* and *Mme. JoJo's, Soho Jazz & Soul.*
Time now to watch for the dawn of a new age.
Down there, gleaming amid the porn and veg.,
its rippling skin mutating by the minute,
a shivering dump with one faint star in it.

BARBARA

after Prévert

Barbara remember
It poured continuously on Brest that day
And you came smiling through the rain
Radiant rapturous dripping wet
Barbara remember
I saw you in the rue da Siam
You smiled and I smiled too
Even if you don't know who I am
Barbara remember
You whom I never knew
Nor you me even so
Remember don't forget
The young man in a doorway
Sheltering from the downpour
Who called your name Barbara
You ran to him in the rain
Rapturous radiant dripping wet
And flung yourself in his arms
Barbara remember that
And don't mind if I talk to you
Like this I always talk like this
To those I love even if I've only
Seen them once I always talk
Like this to those in love
Even if we've never met
Barbara never forget
The happy quiet rain
On your happy face
On the happy town
The rainfall on the sea
On the dockyard on the island boat
Oh Barbara damn the war
I wonder where you are

After the rain of iron
Of steel and blood and fire
And he who took you in his arms
So lovingly has he gone
Is he dead is he still alive
Oh Barbara it has poured all day
On ruined Brest as it did before
But it's not the same any more
In these dire desolate rains
And now the storm is past
Of steel and blood and iron
There are only clouds that burst
Like dead dogs in the drains
That drift away disperse
In a downpour from the west
And break up far from Brest
Nothing of which remains.

EILÉAN NÍ CHUILLEANÁIN
b. 1942

Ní Chuilleanáin was born in Cork and educated at University College Cork (UCC) and Oxford University. She became a lecturer at TCD in 1966. Ní Chuilleanáin's poetry collections include *Site of Ambush* (1975), *The Magdalene Sermons and Other Poems* (1991) and *Selected Poems* (2008). She has translated the poetry of the Romanian writer Ileana Mălăncioiu and was appointed editor of *Poetry Ireland Review* in 2007.

from SITE OF AMBUSH

2

NARRATION

At alarming bell daybreak, before
Scraping of cats or windows creaking over the street,
Eleven miles of road between them,
The enemy commanders synchronised their heartbeats:
Seven forty-five by the sun.
At ten the soldiers were climbing into lorries
Asthmatic engines drawing breath in even shifts.
The others were fretting over guns
Counting up ammunition and money.
At eleven they lay in wait at the cross
With over an hour to go.
The pine trees looked up stiff;
At the angle of the road, polished stones
Forming a stile, a knowing path
Twisting away; the rough grass
Gripped the fragments of the wall.
A small deep stream glassily descended:
Ten minutes to the hour.

The clouds grew grey, the road grey as iron,
The hills dark, the trees deep,
The fields faded; like white mushrooms
Sheep remote under the wind.
The stream ticked and throbbed
Nearer; a boy carried a can to the well
Nearer on the dark road.
The driver saw the child's back,
Nearer; the birds shoaled off the branches in fright.

Deafly rusting in the stream
The lorry now is soft as a last night's dream.
The soldiers and the deaf child
Landed gently in the water
They were light between long weeds
Settled and lay quiet, nobody
To listen to them now.
They all looked the same face down there:
Water too thick and deep to see.
They were separated for good.
It was cold, their teeth shrilling.
They slept like falling hay in waves.
Shells candied their skin; the water
Lay heavy and they could not rise but coiled
By scythefuls limply in ranks.
A long winter stacks their bodies
And words above their stillness hang from hooks
In skeins, like dark nets drying,
Flapping against the stream.
A watch vibrates alone in the filtering light;
Flitters of hair wave at the sun.

SITE OF AMBUSH

When the child comes back
Soaked from her drowning
Lay fast hold of her
And do not let go

Your arms will be burnt
As she turns to flame
Yellow on your dress
A slight flowering tree

A muscular snake
Spidery crawling
Becoming a bird
Then an empty space

Seawaves overwhelm
Your arms your hair and
Wind bites them until
Shivering naked
The child exhausted
Comes back from her sleep

      – troubling for a minute the patient republic
Of the spider and the fly
On the edge of the aspic stream
Above the frail shadows of wreckage
The white water-plant glinting upward
While the tall tree adds a rim to its age
And water focuses to a fish jumping
The rims of time breaking slowly on the pebbles like a bell
Eyes slacken under the weight
As the saint's arm began to sag
His hand spread under the warm nesting wren
But did not give way.

The spider swayed on the end of his thread
A pendulum. The child came back from the well.
Symmetrical breasts of hills criss-crossed.
The trees grew over the sun.

ON LACKING THE KILLER INSTINCT

One hare, absorbed, sitting still,
Right in the grassy middle of the track,
I saw when I fled up into the hills, that time
My father was dying in a hospital –
I see her suddenly again, borne back
By the morning paper's prize photograph:
Two greyhounds tumbling over, absurdly gross,
While the hare shoots off to the left, her bright eye
Full not only of speed and fear
But surely in the moment a glad power,

Like my father's, running from a lorry-load of soldiers
In nineteen twenty-one, nineteen years old, never
Such gladness, he said, cornering in the narrow road
Between high hedges, in summer dusk.
                                    The hare
Like him should never have been coursed, but clever
She'll fool the stupid dogs, double back
On her own scent, downhill, and choose her time
To spring away out of the frame, all while
The pack is labouring up.
                            The lorry was gaining
And he was clever, he saw a house
And risked an open kitchen door. The soldiers
Found six people in a family kitchen, one
Drying his face, dazed-looking, the towel
Half-covering his face. The lorry went off,
The people let him sleep that night, and he came out

Into a blissful dawn. Should he have gone there?
If the sheltering house had been burned down, what good
Could all his bright running have done
For those kind people?
                              And I should not
Have run away, but I went back to the city
Next morning, washed in brown bog water, and
I thought about the hare, in her hour of ease.

EAVAN BOLAND
b. 1944

Boland was born in Dublin and educated at TCD. A renowned critic, she is a professor of creative writing at Stanford University, California. Her *Collected Poems* was published in 1995 and subsequent collections include *Domestic Violence* (2007).

YEATS IN CIVIL WAR

Presently a strange thing happened:
I began to smell honey in places
where honey could not be.

In middle age you exchanged the sandals
Of a pilgrim for a Norman keep
In Galway. Civil war started, vandals
Sacked your country, made off with your sleep;

Somehow you arranged your escape
Aboard a spirit-ship which every day
Hoisted sail out of fire and rape,
And on that ship your mind was stowaway.

The sun mounted on a wasted place,
But the wind at every door and turn
Blew the smell of honey in your face
Where there was none. Whatever we may learn

You are its sum, struggling to survive –
A fantasy of honey your reprieve.

THE WAR HORSE

This dry night, nothing unusual
About the clip, clop, casual

Iron of his shoes as he stamps death
Like a mint on the innocent coinage of earth.

I lift the window, watch the ambling feather
Of hock and fetlock, loosed from its daily tether

In the tinker camp on the Enniskerry Road,
Pass, his breath hissing, his snuffling head

Down. He is gone. No great harm is done.
Only a leaf of our laurel hedge is torn –

Of distant interest like a maimed limb,
Only a rose which now will never climb

The stone of our house, expendable, a mere
Line of defence against him, a volunteer

You might say, only a crocus its bulbous head
Blown from growth, one of the screamless dead.

But we, we are safe, our unformed fear
Of fierce commitment gone; why should we care

If a rose, a hedge, a crocus are uprooted
Like corpses, remote, crushed, mutilated?

He stumbles on like a rumour of war, huge,
Threatening; neighbours use the subterfuge

Of curtains; he stumbles down our short street
Thankfully passing us. I pause, wait,

Then to breathe relief lean on the sill
And for a second only my blood is still

With atavism. That rose he smashed frays
Ribboned across our hedge, recalling days

Of burned countryside, illicit braid:
A cause ruined before, a world betrayed.

A SOLDIER'S SON

for Andrew

A young man's war it is, a young man's war,
Or so they say and so they go to wage
This struggle where, armoured only in nightmare,
Every warrior is under age –
A son seeing each night leave, as father,
A man who may become the ancestor

In a backstreet stabbing, at a ghetto corner
Of future wars and further fratricide.
Son of a soldier who saw war on the ground,
Now cross the peace lines I have made for you
To find on this side if not peace then honour,
Your heritage, knowing as I do

That in the cross-hairs of his gun he found
You his only son, and when he aimed
And when the bullet cracked, the only sound
Was of his son rifling his heart. You twist
That heart today; you are his killed, his maimed.
He is your war; you are his pacifist.

WE WERE NEUTRAL IN THE WAR

This warm, late summer there is so much
to get in. The ladder waits by the crab apple tree.
The greenhouse is rank with the best
Irish tomatoes. Pears are ripening.

Your husband frowns at dinner, has no time
for the baby who has learned to crease three
fingers and wave 'day-day'. This is serious,
he says. This could be what we all feared.

You pierce a sequin with a needle.
You slide it down single-knotted thread
until it lies with all the others in
a puzzle of brightness. Then another and another one.

Let the green and amber marrows rise up
and beat against it and the crab apples and
the damson-coloured pram by the back
wall: you will not sew them into it.

The wooden ledge of the conservatory
faces south. Row on row,
the pears are laid out there, are hard
and then yellow and then yellow with

a rosiness. You leave them out of it.
They will grow soft and bruised at the top
and rot, all in one afternoon. The light,
which made them startling, you will use.

On the breakfast table the headlines are
telling of a city under threat where
you mixed cheese with bitter fennel and
fell in love over demitasse. Afterwards,

you walked by the moonlit river and stopped
and looked down. A glamorous circumference is
spinning on your needle, is
that moon in satin water making

the same peremptory demands on
the waves of the Irish sea and as each
salt-window opens to reveal
a weather of agates, you will stitch that in

with the orchard colours of the first preserves
you make from the garden. You move the jars from
the pantry to the windowsill where
you can see them: winter jewels.

The night he comes to tell you this is war
you wait for him to put on his dinner jacket.
The party is tonight.
The streets are quiet. Dublin is at peace.

The talk is of death but you take
the hand of the first man who asks you.
You dance the fox-trot, the two-step,
the quick-step,

in time to the music. Exclusions
glitter at your hips and past and future are
the fended-off and far-fetched
in waltz time below your waist.

PAUL DURCAN
b. 1944

Durcan was born in Dublin and educated at UCD and UCC. His first poetry collection, *O Westport in the Light of Asia Minor*, was published in 1975, and his seminal work, *The Berlin Wall Cafe*, in 1985. He has also held the Ireland Chair of Poetry.

DEATH CAMP
After Frankl

It is crucial that never a day should pass
That I do not recollect my comportment in death camp:
Staring out through the barbed wire
I see on the tangled point of a barb
The smiling face of my wife in the burnt, sulphurous air;
In the slime of my shame I see her smiling face –
She who was turned into lampshades six months ago
On my say-so, when as Camp Commandant of Treblinka
I locked myself into a tiny white world of pure evil
Until I myself was arrested and deported to Birkenau.
Nothing now that the Camp Commandant can do
Can stop me from seeing my wife smiling on the barbed wire.
Day in, day out, such knowledge is the most precious secret
    of all:
I carry it with me all the days of my burning.

THE JEWISH BRIDE
After Rembrandt

At the black canvas of estrangement,
As the smoke empties from the ruins under a gold winter sky,
Death-trains clattering across the back gardens of Amsterdam –
Sheds, buckets, wire, concrete,
Manholes, pumps, pliers, scaffolding –
I see, as if for the first time,
The person you were, and are, and always will be
Despite the evil that men do:
The teenage girl on the brink of womanhood
Who, when I met you, was on the brink of everything –
Composing fairytales and making drawings
That used remind your friends of Anderson and Thurber –
Living your hidden life that promised everything
Despite all the maimed, unreliable men and women
Who were at that moment congregating all around you:
Including, of course, most of all, myself.
You made of your bedroom a flowing stream
Into which, daily, you threw proofs of your dreams;
Pinned to your bedroom wall with brass-studded drawing pins
Newspaper and magazine photographs of your heroes and
    heroines.
People who met you breathed the air of freedom,
And sensuality fragile as it was wild:
'Nessa's air makes free,' people used say,
Like in the dark ages, 'Town air makes free.'
The miracle is that you survived me.
You stroll about the malls and alleyways of Amsterdam,
About its islands and bridges, its archways and jetties,
With spring in your heels, although it is winter;
Privately, publicly, along the Grand Parade;
A Jewish Bride who has survived the death camp,
Free at last of my swastika eyes
Staring at you from across spiked dinner plates
Or from out of the bunker of a TV armchair;

Free of the glare off my jackboot silence;
Free of the hysteria of my gestapo voice;
Now your shyness replenished with all your old cheeky
    confidence –
That grassy well at which red horses used rear up and sip
With young men naked riding bareback calling your name.
Dog-muzzle of tension torn down from your face;
Black polythene of asphyxiation peeled away from your soul;
Your green eyes quivering with dark, sunny laughter
And – all spreadeagled and supple again – your loving, freckled
    hands.

FJORD

You were Abraham but you were also Jesus.
In your Jesus suit
You liked to teach for the sake of teaching.
You were a teacher before you were a judge.

You'd descend with a word like 'fjord',
By the light of the standard lamp
On a winter's night in firelight,
Savour it, bless it, deposit it on my tongue.

'*Fjord*' – you'd announce – 'is a Norwegian word.'
I'd gaze up at your icicle-compacted face
As if you'd invented Norway and the Norwegian language
Especially for me.

You'd confide that we had fjords of our own in Ireland
And the noblest of all our fjords was in County Mayo,
The Killary fjord in the safe waters of whose deep, dark thighs
German submarines had lain sheltering in the war.
Look into your Irish heart, you will find a German U-boat,

A periscope in the rain and a swastika in the sky.
You were no more neutral, Daddy, than Ireland was,
Proud and defiant to boast of the safe fjord.

ANTHONY GLAVIN
1945–2006

Glavin was born in Dublin and educated at UCD and TCD. He was Professor of Music at the Royal Irish Academy of Music and his poetry collection, *The Wrong Side of the Alps*, was published by Gallery Press in 1989.

from LIVING IN HIROSHIMA

> *Killing is one of the forms*
> *of our wandering mourning.*
>
> RILKE

OBLIVION'S THROE

Everybody Lives in Hiroshima – Time, *August 1985*
By now it's in the blood and nobody's immune –
T-cell amnesia, a kind of lightstain

Whiting-out memories and the memory of memories,
A video shimmering after the picture's gone.

To Thine Own Self
Ripeness? Don't ask. Read Jung. Remember Plato.
'The psyche cannot leap beyond itself ...'

'The atom's not substantive as an apple ...'
Such innocence! Such a dose of the need to know!

Sky High

B-san, lightened, screamed in a 60° dive
To clear the 'All-Clear' delta, to watch and wait.

The tail-gunner put on his special-issue glasses.
No one knew quite what to expect. No one.

8.16 a.m.

A fleeing Nazi skis across an Alpine glacier.
Pius XII bows low to intone the *Agnus Dei*.

Heartbeats. Lifetimes. Seconds ticking away.
The sky blurts open like a Morning Glory.

Ground Zero

Morbid incandescence. I snap awake.
A warhead, sky high? No, you're standing there,

Flashing your Instamatic, grinning. I freak.
How should I ever bring home to you the horror?

A White Shadow

Again I slip its leash and watch alone
Unerring hunger haunch itself and spring –

Bone-ash emblazon flashed on heat-split stone
Thrown clear where a bird had just been singing.

The Scream

A sudden scald of sun melts through the room.
Would Saul have recognised it? Or the heat?

You try to blink. No eyelids. You try to scream.
Fishtails of windowglass blither in your throat.

Now You See It

An eye-blink, violet, suddenly a blazing stadium
Two miles wide and maybe half a mile high –

Blinding whiteness annihilating space and time
In an instant, in silence, in the twinkling of an eye.

Flight-Log

'I can taste the brilliance.' 'What a relief it worked!'
'It's like the ring around some distant planet

Detached itself and coming straight up at us …'
'Pretty terrific!' 'Look at that son-of-a-bitch go!'

Newton to Oppenheimer

'A second, reflected, shock-wave will occur
If the fission is triggered at about 2,000 feet …'

It was. It did. A three-mile radius, flattened,
And a smell like rancid apples settled everywhere.

Magic!

Thunder like Mt. Fuji swallowing itself alive.
A bicycle sagged and melted in its own shadow.

Stones bled. Birds fell roasted out of the sky.
We just stood there, helpless. You can't hate magic.

Aioi Bridge

Slime-strips of skin that flapped like seaweed,
No mouths, no noses, eyeless, faceless, screaming,

They dived in hundreds off the twisted girders.
The river was warm and merciful. It killed quickly.

The Stare

Whole families drift like sewage in the river.
He wants to float there too, past thought, past caring.

'Die!' he prays, 'Die!' But can't. Not yet. Not here.
His radiant stare a thousand miles of nothing.

Handfuls

Somewhere in that wide field of ash and debris
Once a school, vaporized, her son and daughter ...

She grew empty. Her mind floated out on white air.
To choose a ceremony of handfuls. To sift. To weep.

Lovers

They crawl through charred bamboo to the river's edge.
The water is hot to touch, but they slither in

And stroke and hold. At each caress, the skin
Dries instantly, then glows, then splits like porcelain.

Fall Out

Black rain, thick blobs the size of soya beans.
A sense of infinite movement slowing to infinity

Where ions multiply like instant griefs
As though such griefs might now inherit the earth.

Sphinx

So it's grief, is it, honeycombs that gaze
Akhenaten saw through clearly, and Sophocles?

The TV crews head back to Cairo. She knows
Nothing but ion-riddles on the desert breeze.

At the Cavendish Laboratory c. 1933

The beast can't turn aside. Those jaws! That smile!
Fixed forward, insatiable, an eating machine. So,

Behind his back, Rutherford, whose need to know
Unleashed the atom, was nicknamed *The Crocodile*.

Hirohito Highway

Clear sky lay all before them, and clear sea.
Jubilant, watching the fist recede, they noticed

Cloud-wisps pointing and streaking their flightpath south.
Tibbets radioed ahead: 'Tail-winds. Home for tea.'

Airways

On Tinian, the groundcrews were already icing beer,
Oblivious of ion-dances in the atmosphere

Creating havoc with the codes to Washington:
'LITTLE BOY ...' – blort! crackle! – '... damage done'.

Yelling the Generals

Truman cradled the scrambler and made us wait.
And that's okay, I mean, it's protocol

Purifies motive, makes what you say seem adequate:
'Gentlemen,' he faced us, 'we have entered History!'

A Month Early

Even then I must have raged at being confined.
But to push for freedom *that* Bank Holiday weekend!

My father homing from Youghal in his chrome V8
To hold my mother, then me, then celebrate ...

Petals

In the shambled courtyard of Hijiyama Castle,
Petals and smokedrift brim the dried-up pond

As two American POWs are japanned
In a hail of masonry into the bloody ground.

Echo Shroud

An eerie numbness fallen everywhere,
A seamless dark weave stained with radiance:

Woven through it, laments and distant cries,
As though the earth itself could suffer pain.

Who?

'This isn't happening, it can't be, not to me ...'
Thrown there, drifting slowly beyond all pain,

A lost soul wondering who the lost soul was,
Observing his death as though it weren't his own.

Vertigo

Heat-buckled girders. Alive with bodies. No choice.
Fistfuls of skin and tissue slimed each palm,

A squelch of something yellow where stepped-on eyes ...
She sickened, steadied herself, continued to climb.

Snow

He dug through a frenzied rubble of slate and bricks.
No mother, no father, no food. And not a sound.

But there, untouched, his beloved *History Primer*!
He tore it page by page to snowflakes.

A Fire Child

She knelt to cover her suppurating nakedness
As the men raced past with water, not noticing.

Flame licked her thighs, then climbed and immolated.
Her arms unfolded in a gesture of beseeching.

Standstill

They tell of a stallion – blind-eyed, head bowed low,
One flank bleached white and seared with trellis-shadow,

Brooding like a funerary marble among the ruins –
One move and it might stumble on the dead and dying.

Surviving

It seemed that life and death were out of phase.
By day, white ion-haze in place of sunlight,

By night, blue soul-fire dancing above the bodies ...
You had to be patient. It wasn't over yet.

Haemorrhage

'If we are punished it is because we have been guilty.'
The words half-whispered, eyes averted in disgrace.

But thought itself can haemorrhage and mutate.
'If we are guilty it is because we have been punished.'

Perish the Thought

And the thought of having been experimented on!
A dull aching rage without surcease.

The most important thing to do
Was sleep, not think. Not think. Sleep.

Debriefing

'It's all on film – ion-flash, shock-waves, brain-cloud.'
'Visible for a hundred miles, seething, umbilical,

Sizzling like a burned-out sun into the sea.'
'A burst mandala, the end of the world – beautiful.'

Not There

Haunted, haunting, those eyes that stare and stare,
Their freeze-frame half-lives shimmering on the air –

They are searching for their loved ones in the streets,
But the once familiar streets are no longer there.

Burial Detail

Row on accusing row, their eyes wide open.
You see yourself, as in a mirror, ashamed forever

Of all you've seen and done, not seen, not done.
Walk in silence, therefore, walk looking down.

Immortality

A fire-ball of the planet and the species?
Absurd! Of course it could never happen –

Alone among the bye-blows of creation,
We know an ideal sentience that never dies.

Nostalgia

What once so bright now starts to fade and blur
As we are closed-out by our memories –

But oh! such lightfall, such idyllic skies
That summer before ... before it all ... before ...

Grief

An ion-burst of rage that haunts me always
Like an all too elegiac word or phrase

That sighs a million sighs like ricochets
And dies away and leaves an empty space.

HALF-LIVES

Refugee

All he thinks of exile's a kind of haemorrhage,
An ion-blitz where homelife used to be –

Nothing to call his own but memory
And the need to know and grief disguised as rage.

Arriving at Auschwitz

'I have many names. I come from anywhere.'
Enraged, they flung him in a half-filled hip-bath,

Chose an electrode, dipped it, chose another –
Ask no reliving of such a Witches' Sabbath.

The Cherryblossom Theatre Company

Her turn to make breakfast. She hums in the kitchen.
Next thing, she's on a stretcher at the Railway Station.

Dante would sing of her with love and pity,
Not slough her features off in the first half-second.

Samurai

He thought a meteor had struck the earth
Until he heard the Emperor's 'We have surrendered,'

And raged, then, on his knees, and dared the earth
No meteor had defeated, and plunged his sword.

Buchenwald 1939

'I will not sign.' Steel-whipped. 'You'll sign tomorrow!'
He's strong – a week like this, he'll seem a hero –

'Go! Case closed!' The grain of morphine we got him
He wouldn't – 'No use; by dawn – ' By then, they'd shot him.

Black Market

Whenever the metal-seekers found 'a white shadow,'
Bleached outlines of a head, a leaf, a hand,

They'd barter with the stone-collector –
'Ngoya Street, third tree-stump, a copper kettle.'

With Eisenhower at Nordhausen

A pile of leathery corpses stacked like cordwood.
Deep in, an eye, still blinking. I turned, sickened,

Jostled a captured guard, backed off, and giggled.
'Having trouble hating them?' asked Eisenhower.

The Shriek

For what do we grieve? Their lives or our own?
How can we need to know an agony

Not theirs or ours or Earth's or anyone's,
But a shrieking lesion, a rage in the nature of being?

Metempsychosis

A myth, according to my analyst –
'Projective identification. An ego mechanism.'

But all these voices shrieking in my ear –
If I write as I hear them, I'm their ghost.

A Failed Torpedo

He'd have died at sea but that war's over now
And life's a quiet tea-room listening to Mozart

Before line-call rehearsals for this year's *Ghosts*
In the waiting-room at the re-built Railway Station.

Ill Fares the Land

All that freedom they could buy for nothing,
If they signed in place of the unaccounted dead –

The clerks in the Savings Bank were happy, their laughter
Trilled at lunchtime across the sunlit square.

Surgeon

'Suction!' he snapped, 'this isn't an abattoir!'
And rage flashed back along his scalpel blade –

His own grief-stricken eyes, and the weeping cheloid
He knew no art could cauterize or cure.

The Domei News Agency

HQ reacted swiftly to reports
That rumours of 'Atom Sickness' had reached the West –

The Domei Agency was ordered closed.
Such is the use of silence. Silence aborts.

Vigil

The mirror has been taken down, the window opened.
A nurse pours brandy. The chaplain frowns and hurries.

Something that once had laughed and sang lies ebbing,
Its white-corpuscle count a sea of zeroes.

An Image from Breugel

Imagine Breugel's *Triumph*, his frame of mind
As the work melts down, unfinished, to an ion-glow

All bare of truth or beauty, a glair-white canvas,
Gene-pools rampant on contaminated ground.

What Truman Knew

'When will the Russians be able to build the Bomb?'
'Dunno,' said Oppy. Truman grinned. 'I know!'

Oppy was puzzled. 'When?' 'Never!' said Truman,
And went on believing it to the day he died.

Museum Time

Fused *sake* cups, blent watches, melt-lumped coins –
And nothing we can ever learn from them

But rage and outrage fixed in a half-life aftersilence
Where the time is always 8.16 a.m.

Kapitza to Rutherford

'Remember, we're only particles of floating matter
Eddying briefly on a stream called Fate –

Governed by the stream, at most we can hope
To deflect our path a little, and stay afloat.'

Earthrise

'One small step … a giant leap …' And there,
Blue-white, a sea-pearl, eyeing us from empty space …

My headset's gone – repeat, *You quite asleep, girl?*
Ghost-zone. Interference. Wish you were here.

In Plato's Cave

'Our present historical velocity …' Godspeed!
Can there be sunlight now without contamination?

My analyst sighs – no comment, he can wait …
The ceiling flickers like a video screen.

VAN MORRISON
b. 1945

Morrison was born in Belfast, the son of a shipyard worker. He joined his first band at the age of twelve and played with *The Monarchs* and *Them* in the 1960s. Inducted into the Rock and Roll Hall of Fame in 1993 and the Songwriters Hall of Fame in 2003, Morrison has released over thirty albums including *Astral Weeks* (1968), *Moondance* (1970) and *Hard Nose the Highway* (1973).

WILD CHILDREN

We were the War Children
Born 1945
When all the soldiers came marching home
Love looks in their eye, in their eye

Tennessee, Tennessee Williams
Let your inspiration flow
Let it be around when we hear the sound
When the spring time rivers flow, rivers flow

Rod Steiger and Marlon Brando
Standing with their heads bowed on the side
Crying like a baby thinking about the time
James Dean took that fatal ride, took that ride

Tennessee Williams
Let your inspiration go
Will you be around to hear the sound
When the spring time rivers flow, rivers flow

And Steiger and Marlon Brando
With their heads bowed on the side
Crying like a baby thinking about the time
James Dean took that fatal ride, took that ride

And we were the Wild Children, 1945
When all the soldiers came marching home
Love looks love looks in their eyes, in their eyes

POSTSCRIPT

THE CAPITAL OF THE RUINS

SAMUEL BECKETT

On what a year ago was a grass slope, lying in the angle that the Vire and Bayeux roads make as they unite at the entrance of the town, opposite what remains of the second most important stud-farm in France, a general hospital now stands. It is the Hospital of the Irish Red Cross in Saint-Lô, or, as the Laudiniens themselves say, the Irish Hospital. The buildings consist of some prefabricated wooden huts. They are superior, generally speaking, to those so scantily available for the wealthier, the better-connected, the astuter or the more fragrantly deserving of the bombed-out. Their finish, as well without as within, is the best that their priority can command. They are lined with glass-wool and panelled in isorel, a strange substance of which there are only very limited supplies available. There is real glass in the windows. The consequent atmosphere is that of brightness and airiness so comforting to sick people, and to weary staffs. The floors, there where the exigencies of hygiene are greatest, are covered with linoleum. There was not enough linoleum left in France to do more than this. The walls and ceiling of the operating theatre are sheeted in aluminium of aeronautic origin, a decorative and practical solution to an old problem and a pleasant variation on the sword and ploughshare metamorphosis. A system of covered ways connects the kitchen with refectories and wards. The supply of electric current, for purposes both of heat and of power, leaves nothing to be desired, though painstakingly anonymous attempts were made, in this country, as recently I think as last winter, to prove the contrary. The hospital is centrally heated throughout, by means of coke. The medical, scientific, nursing and secretarial staffs are Irish, the instruments and furniture (including of course beds and bedding), the drugs and food, are supplied by the Society. I think I am right in saying that the number of in-patients (mixed) is in the neighbourhood of ninety. As for the others, it is a regular thing, according to recent reports, for as many as two hundred to be seen in the out-patients department in a day. Among such ambulant cases a large number are suffering from scabies and other diseases of the skin, the result no doubt of malnutrition or an ill-advised diet. Accident cases are frequent. Masonry falls when least expected, children play with detonators and demining continues. The laboratory, magnificently equipped, bids well to become the official laboratory for the department, if not of an even wider area. Considerable work has already been done in the analysis of local waters.

These few facts, chosen not quite at random, are no doubt familiar already to those at all interested in the subject, and perhaps even to those of you listening to me now. They may not appear the most immediately instructive. That the operating-theatre should be sheeted with an expensive metal, or the floor of the labour room covered with linoleum, can hardly be expected to interest those accustomed to such conditions as the *sine qua non* of reputable obstetrical and surgical statistics. These are the sensible people who would rather have news of the Normans' semi-circular canals or resistance to sulphur than of his attitude to the Irish bringing gifts, who would prefer the history of our difficulties with an unfamiliar pharmacopia and system of mensuration to the story of our dealings with the rare and famous ways of spirit that are the French ways. And yet the whole enterprise turned from the beginning on the establishing of a relation in the light of which the therapeutic relation faded to the merest of pretexts.

What was important was not our having penicillin when they had none, nor the unregarding munificence of the French Ministry of Reconstruction (as it was then called), but the occasional glimpse obtained, by us in them and, who knows, by them in us (for they are an imaginative people), of that smile at the human conditions as little to be extinguished by bombs as to be broadened by the elixirs of Burroughs and Welcome, – the smile deriding, among other things, the having and the not having, the giving and the taking, sickness and health.

It would not be seemly, in a retiring and indeed retired storekeeper, to describe the obstacles encountered in this connection, and the forms, often grotesque, devised for them by the combined energies of the home and visiting temperaments. It must be supposed that they were not insurmountable, since they have long ceased to be of much account. When I reflect now on the recurrent problems of what, with all proper modesty, might be called the heroic period, on one in particular so arduous and elusive that it literally ceased to be formulable, I suspect that our pains were those inherent in the simple and necessary and yet so unattainable proposition that their way of being we, was not our way and that our way of being they, was not their way. It is only fair to say that many of us had never been abroad before.

Saint-Lô was bombed out of existence in one night. German prisoners of war, and casual labourers attracted by the relative food-plenty, but soon discouraged by housing conditions, continue, two years after the liberation, to clear away the debris, literally by hand. Their spirit has yet to learn the blessings of Gallup and their flesh the benefits of the bulldozer. One may thus be excused if one questions the opinion generally received, that ten years will be sufficient for the total reconstruction of Saint-Lô. But no matter what period of time must still be endured, before the town begins to resemble the pleasant and prosperous administrative and agricultural centre that it was, the hospital of wooden huts in its gardens between the Vire and Bayeux roads will continue to discharge its function, and its cures. 'Provisional' is not the term it was, in this universe become provisional. It will continue to discharge its function long after the Irish are gone and their names forgotten. But I think that to the end of its hospital days it will be called the Irish Hospital, and after that the huts, when they have been turned into dwellings, the Irish huts. I mention this possibility, in the hope that it will give general satisfaction. And having done so I may perhaps venture to mention another, more remote but perhaps of greater import in certain quarters, I mean the possibility that some of those who were in Saint-Lô will come home realising that they got at least as good as they gave, that they got indeed what they could hardly give, a vision and sense of a time-honoured conception of humanity in ruins, and perhaps even an inkling of the terms in which our condition is to be thought again. These will have been in France.

SUGGESTED READING

Arnold, Bruce. *Orpen: Mirror to an Age* (1981)

Barry, Sebastian. *A Long Long Way* (2005)

Bartlett, Tom and Keith Jeffery (eds). *A Military History of Ireland* (1996)

Bowen, Elizabeth. *The Last September* (1929)

Boyce, George. *'The Sure Confusing Drum': Ireland and the First World War* (1993)

Brearton, Fran. *The Great War in Irish Poetry: W.B. Yeats to Michael Longley* (2000)

Brown, Terence. *Ireland: A Social and Cultural History 1922–2001* (2004)

———. 'Who Dares to Speak? Ireland and the Great War' in *English Studies in Transition*, ed. Robert Clark and Piero Boitani (1993)

Curtayne, Alice. *Francis Ledwidge: A Life of the Poet* (1998)

D'Arcy, Fergus A. *Remembering the War Dead: British Commonwealth and International War Graves in Ireland since 1914* (2007)

Denman, Terence. *Ireland's Unknown Soldiers: The 16th (Irish) Division in the Great War 1914–1918* (1992)

Devine, Kathleen (ed.). *Modern Irish Writers and the Wars* (1999)

Dolan, Anne. *Commemorating the Irish Civil War, History and Memory, 1923–2000* (2003)

Dungan, Myles. *They Shall Not Grow Old: Irish Soldiers and the Great War* (1997)

Dunsany, Lord. *My Ireland* (1937)

English, Richard. *Irish Freedom: The History of Nationalism in Ireland* (2006)

Farrell, J.G. *Troubles* (1970)

Fisk, Robert. *In Time of War: Ireland, Ulster and the Price of Neutrality 1939–1945* (1983)

Fitzpatrick, David (ed.). *Ireland and the First World War* (1988)

———. *The Two Irelands: 1912–1939* (1998)

Fussell, Paul. *The Great War and Modern Memory* (1975)

Gibbon, Monk. *Inglorious Soldier* (1968)

Girvan, Brian. *The Emergency: Neutral Ireland 1939–1945* (2006)

Girvan, Brian and Geoffrey Roberts. *Ireland and the Second World War: Politics, Society and Remembrance* (2000)

Gregory, Adrian and Seina Paseta (eds). *Ireland and the Great War: 'A War to Unite Us All?'* (2002)

Haughey, Jim. *The First World War in Irish Poetry* (2002)

Hopkinson, Michael. *The Irish War of Independence* (2002)

Jeffery, Keith. *Ireland and the Great War* (2000)

Johnson, N.C. *Ireland, the Great War and the Geography of Remembrance* (2003)

Johnston, Jennifer. *How Many Miles to Babylon?* (1974)

Kiberd, Declan. *Inventing Ireland: The Literature of the Modern Nation* (1995)

Leitch, Maurice. *The Smoke King* (1999)

Loftus, Richard J. *Nationalism in Modern Anglo-Irish Poetry* (1964)

Longley, Edna. *Poetry in the Wars* (1986)

——. *The Living Stream: Literature and Revisionism in Ireland* (1994)

MacGill, Patrick. *The Great Push: An Episode of the Great War* (1916)

McBride, Ian (ed.). *History and Memory in Modern Ireland* (2001)

McBride, Lawrence W. *Images, Icons and the Irish Nationalist Imagination* (1999)

McGarry, Fearghal. *Irish Politics and the Spanish Civil War* (1999)

McGuinness, Frank. *Observe the Sons of Ulster Marching Towards the Somme* (1985)

Montague, John. 'The War Years in Ulster' in *The Figure in the Cave* (1989)

Morrison, George. *Mise Éire* (1959), film

Myers, Kevin. 'The Irish and the Great War: A Case of Amnesia' in *Ideas Matter: Essays in Honour of Conor Cruise O Brien*, ed. Richard English and Joseph Morrison Skelly (1998)

O'Casey, Sean. *The Silver Tassie* (1928)

O'Flaherty, Liam. *Insurrection* (1950)

O'Malley, Ernie. *On Another Man's Wound* (1936)

O'Meara, Liam. *Lantern on the Wave: A Study of the Life of the Poet Francis Ledwidge* (1999)

Ormsby, Frank. *A Northern Spring* (1986)

Orpen, William. *An Onlooker in France* (1921)

Paulin, Tom. *The Invasion Handbook* (2002)

Plunkett, James. *Strumpet City* (1969)

Stallworthy, Jon. *Anthem for Doomed Youth: Twelve Soldier Poets of the First World War* (2002)

Stradling, Robert A. *The Irish and the Spanish Civil War 1936–1939* (1999)

Stuart, Francis. *Black List Section H* (1971)

Thompson, William Irwin. *The Imagination of an Insurrection: Dublin, Easter 1916* (1967)

Townsend, C. *Easter 1916: The Irish Rebellion* (2005)

Wills, Clair. *That Neutral Island: A Cultural History of Ireland During the Second World War* (2007)

Winter, Jan. *Sites of Memory, Sites of Mourning: The Great War in European Cultural History* (1990)

Winter, Jay and Emmanuel Sivan. *War and Remembrance in the Twentieth Century* (1999)

ACKNOWLEDGEMENTS

The editor would like to thank the following for their help in responding to queries and/or their advice during the compilation of this book:

Dorothea Melvin, Caroline Walsh, Derek Mahon, Margaret Farrington, Terence Brown, Patrick Nowlan, Lilian Foley, Eunan O'Halpin, Bruce Arnold, Jonathan Williams, Thomas Kilroy, Maureen McDonnell, Gerard Smyth, Robert Greacen, Eoin O'Brien, Brendan Kennelly, Maeve Calthorpe, Victor Hamilton, Olive Scott, David Webster, Pádraig Ó Snodaigh, Hylda J. Beckett, Padraig O'Cuanachain, Nicholas Grene, Norma Richardson, Gerald Morgan, Aodán Mac Póilin, Cormac Kinsella, Anne Haverty, Manus O'Riordain, Edna and Michael Longley, Mark O'Brien, Phyllis Gaffney, Bridget O'Toole, Jane Leonard, Helen Cooney, Patrick Crotty, Rita Kelly, Robert Thompson, Philip Lecane;

The School of English, Trinity College Dublin, The Military Heritage of Ireland Trust Ltd, Edward King and John Mc Hugh, The Achill Heinrich Böll Committee for a residency at the Heinrich Böll Cottage at Dugort, Achill, County Mayo;

Patsy Horton, Janice Smith, Michelle Griffin, Cormac Austin, and all the crew at Blackstaff Press for their energy and commitment;

The librarian and staff at Old Printed Books; Berkeley and Ussher Libraries, Trinity College Dublin; The Linen Hall Library, Belfast; Irene Stevenson, The Library, the *Irish Times*, Dublin; The Arts Council of Northern Ireland; The Burns Library, Boston College, Boston, in particular Robert K. O'Neill and John Attebury; David Horn, Beth Sweeney and Shelley Barber; the Faculty at Connolly House, Boston College, including Rob Savage, Majorie Howes, Thomas Hachey, Kevin Kenny, Joseph Nugent and Elizabeth Sullivan;

And special thanks and acknowledgement to Maria Johnston for compiling the biographical notes.

The editor and publisher gratefully acknowledge permission to include the following copyright material:

BAX, ARNOLD (DERMOT O'BYRNE) 'Dublin Ballad', 'Martial Law in Dublin', 'Shells at Oranmore' and 'The Irish Mail' from *Ideala: Early Love Letters and Poems* (Fand Music, 2001), by kind permission of Lewis Foreman.
BECKETT, SAMUEL, 'Saint-Lô' from *Collected Poems in English and French* by Samuel Beckett. Copyright © 1977 by Samuel Beckett. Used by permission of Grove/Atlantic, Inc. and Faber and
Faber Ltd; 'The Capital of the Ruins' from *The Complete Short Prose 1929–1989* by Samuel Beckett. Copyright © 1995 by the Estate of Samuel Beckett. Used by permission of Grove/Atlantic, Inc. and Faber and Faber Ltd.
BOLAND, EAVAN, 'Yeats in Civil War', copyright © 2005, 1962 by Eavan Boland; 'The War Horse', copyright © 2005, 1975 by Eavan Boland; 'A Soldier's Son', copyright © 2005, 1975 by Eavan Boland; 'We were Neutral in the War', copyright © 2005, 1990 by Eavan Boland; from Eavan Boland, *New Collected*

Poems (Carcanet Press Limited, 2005; W.W. Norton, 2008). Used by permission of Carcanet Press Limited and W.W. Norton & Company, Inc.

BRADY, GEORGE M., 'Have You Walked', 'The Conquerors' and 'The Hosts' from Leslie Daiken (ed.), *They Go, The Irish: A Miscellany of War-time Writing* (Nicholson & Watson, 1944), copyright holder not traced.

BUCHANAN, GEORGE, 'Kilwaughter', 'On Film', 'On the Dead Killed in Two World Wars', 'Poets of the Next Century' and 'War Pilot', reproduced by kind permission of Dr Sandra Buchanan.

CARNDUFF, THOMAS, 'Graves of Gallipoli', 'Messines, 17 June, 1917', 'My Land', 'The Graves of the Unknown' and 'Ypres, September, 1917', from *Poverty Street and Other Poems* (Lapwing Press, 1993), published with the kind permission of Sarah Ferris. The Carnduff Manuscript Collection (MS 21) is held in Special Collections at the Main Library, QUB.

CLARKE, AUSTIN, 'At the House of Commons', extract from 'Mnemosyne Lay in Dust', extract from 'Rightful Rhymes', 'Six Sentences', 'The Last Republicans' and 'The Subjection of Women' from *Selected Poems* (Lilliput Press, 1991), reproduced by kind permission of R. Dardis Clarke, 17 Oscar Square, Dublin 8.

COFFEY, BRIAN, extract from 'Death of Hektor' from *Poems and Versions 1929–1990* (Dedalus Press, 1991), reproduced by permission of Dedalus Press, www.dedaluspress.com.

CRAIG, MAURICE, 'Spring 1943' from Robert Greacen (ed.) *Northern Harvest: An Anthology of Irish Writing* (Derrick Maccord, 1944); 'Kilcarty to Dublin' (unpublished), both reproduced by kind permission of the author.

CRONIN, ANTHONY, 'Encounter', extract from 'The End of the Modern World' and 'War Poem' from *Collected Poems* (New Island Books, 2004), reproduced by permission of New Island Books.

DAIKEN, LESLIE, 'Nightfall in Galway' from *They Go, The Irish: A Miscellany of War-time Writing* (Nicholson & Watson, 1944), copyright holder not traced.

DAY LEWIS, C., 'Bombers', 'In the Shelter', 'Newsreel', 'Remembering Con Markievicz', 'The Dead', 'Watching Post', 'Where are the War Poets?' and 'Will it be so Again?' from *The Complete Poems of C. Day Lewis* published by Sinclair-Stevenson (1992). Copyright © 1992 in this edition The Estate of C. Day Lewis. Reprinted by permission of The Random House Group Ltd.

DEANE, SEAMUS, 'Shelter' from *Rumours* (Dolmen Press, 1977), reproduced by kind permission of the author.

DEVLIN, DENIS, 'Annapolis', 'Concentration Camps', 'Little Elegy' and 'The Tomb of Michael Collins' from *Denis Devlin: Collected Poems* (Dedalus Press, 1999), reproduced by permission of Dedalus Press, www.dedaluspress.com.

DUNSANY, LORD, 'A Dirge of Victory', 'Songs from an Evil Wood', 'To the Fallen Irish Soldiers' and 'The Memorial' from *War Poems* (Hutchinson, 1900). Reproduced with permission of Curtis Brown Group Ltd, London on behalf of the Estate of Lord Dunsany. Copyright © Lord Dunsany 1941.

DURCAN, PAUL, 'Death Camp' and 'The Jewish Bride' from *The Berlin Wall Café* (Harvill Press, 1995); 'Fjord' from *Daddy, Daddy* (Blackstaff Press, 1990), all reproduced by kind permission of the author.

(Gallery Press, 2002); 'The Defeated' from *Done into English* (Gallery Press, 2003), all by kind permission of the author and The Gallery Press, Loughcrew, Oldcastle, County Meath, Ireland.

IREMONGER, VALENTIN, 'Soldier from the Wars' from *Horan's Field and Other Reservations* (Dolmen Press 1972), copyright holder not traced.

JENNETT, SEÁN, extracts from 'Always Adam' from *Always Adam* (Faber, 1943); 'For Thomas Flanagan', 'The Letter', 'Morning' and 'Explosion' from *The Cloth of Flesh* (Faber, 1945), copyright holder not traced.

KAVANAGH, PATRICK, 'Beyond the Headlines', 'Epic', 'I Had a Future', extract from 'Lough Derg' and extract from 'The Great Hunger' reprinted from *Collected Poems* edited by Antoinette Quinn (Allen Lane, 2004), by kind permission of the Trustees of the Estate of the late Katherine B. Kavanagh, through the Jonathan Williams Literary Agency.

KELLEHER, D.L., 'An Upper Room' from Mary Devenport O'Neill (ed.) *Prometheus and Other Poems* (Cape, 1929), copyright holder not traced.

KENNEDY, JIMMY, 'We're Going to Hang out the Washing on the Seigfried Line', reproduced by permission of EMI Music Publishing.

KENNELLY, BRENDAN, 'Bomb', 'Old Soldier' and 'Wall' from *Familiar Strangers: New & Selected Poems 1960–2004* (Bloodaxe Books, 2004) by permission of Bloodaxe Books.

KINSELLA, THOMAS, 'Downstream', 'The Laundress' and '38 Phoenix Street' from *Collected Poems* (Carcanet Press Limited, 2001), reproduced by kind permission of the author and Carcanet Press Limited.

LAUGHTON, FREDA, 'The Bombed House' from Geoffrey Taylor (ed.) *Irish Poems of Today* (Irish People's Publications, 1944), copyright holder not traced.

LETTS, WINIFRED M., 'Casualty', 'Dead', 'Hallow-e'en, 1914', 'Screens', 'The Call to Arms in Our Street' and 'The Deserter' from *Hallow-e'en and Poems of the War* (Smith, Elder, 1916), reproduced by kind permission of Chloe Alexander and Oriana Conner, great-nieces of Winifred M. Letts.

LEWIS, C.S., 'Apology', 'Death in Battle', 'French Nocturne' and 'Victory' from *The Collected Poems of C.S. Lewis* (Fount Paperbacks, 1994). Poems by C.S. Lewis copyright © C.S. Lewis Pte. Ltd. 1994. Reprinted by permission.

LONGLEY, MICHAEL, 'Buchenwald Museum', 'Ceasefire', 'Ghetto', 'In Memoriam', 'In Memory of Charles Donnelly', 'Master of Ceremonies', 'Partisans', 'Second Sight' and 'Wounds' from *Collected Poems* (Cape 2006), © Michael Longley 2006, reprinted by kind permission of Lucas Alexander Whitley Ltd.

MacDONAGH, DONAGH, 'He is Dead and Gone Lady . . .' and 'Just an Old Sweet Song' from *A Warning to Conquerors* (Dolmen Press, 1968) by kind permission of Iseult and Kevin McGuinness.

MacDONOGH, PATRICK, 'Over the Water' and 'War Widow' from *Poems* (Gallery Press, 2001). By kind permission of the Estate of Patrick MacDonogh and The Gallery Press, Loughcrew, Oldcastle, County Meath, Ireland.

MacGABHANN, LIAM, 'Connolly' and 'The Roads of Kerry' from Leslie Daiken (ed.) *Good-Bye, Twilight: Songs of the Struggle in Ireland* (Lawrence & Wishart, 1936), copyright holder not traced.

MacGILL, PATRICK, 'A Soldier's Prayer', 'Before the Charge', 'I Oft Go Out at Night-time', 'It's a Far, Far Cry', 'The Dug-out' and 'The London Lads' from *The Navvy Poet: The Collected Poetry of Patrick MacGill* (Caliban Books, 1984), copyright holder not traced.

MacGREEVY, THOMAS, 'De Civitate Hominum', 'Nocturne' and 'The Six Who Were Hanged' from Susan Schriebman (ed.) *Collected Poems of Thomas MacGreevy* (Anna Livia Press, 1991), reproduced by kind permission of Margaret Farrington and Robert Ryan.

MacMAHON, BRYAN, 'Corner Boys' from Leslie Daiken (ed.) *Good-Bye, Twilight: Songs of the Struggle in Ireland* (Lawrence & Wishart, 1936), reproduced by kind permission of Maurice McMahon, copyright holder.

MacNEICE, LOUIS, 'Aubade', 'Bottleneck', 'Carrickfergus', 'Convoy', extract from 'Entered in the Minutes', 'Neutrality', 'The Atlantic Tunnel' and extract from 'The Closing Album' from *Collected Poems* (Faber, 2007), by permission of David Higham Associates.

MAHON, DEREK, 'A Kensington Notebook', 'At the Shelbourne', 'Autobiographies' and 'One of these Nights' from *Collected Poems*, (Gallery Press, 1999) and 'During the War' from *Harbour Lights* (Gallery Press, 2005), all reproduced by kind permission of the author and The Gallery Press, Loughcrew, Oldcastle, County Meath, Ireland; 'Barbara' (unpublished), reproduced by kind permission of the author c/o The Gallery Press, Loughcrew, Oldcastle, County Meath, Ireland.

MCFADDEN, ROY, 'A Song for Victory Night', 'Armistice Day 1938', 'Dublin to Belfast: Wartime', 'Portrush', 'Post-war' and '2 September 1939' from *Collected Poems 1943–1995* (Lagan Press, 1996), reproduced by kind permission of Grania McFadden.

MILLAR, RUDDICK, 'The Somme' from Leslie Daiken (ed.) *Good-Bye, Twilight: Songs of the Struggle in Ireland* (Lawrence & Wishart, 1936), copyright holder not traced.

MILNE, EWART, 'Sierran Vigil', 'Speech on Behalf of Inishfail', 'The Wind of Bombers Moon' and 'Thinking of Artolas' from Leslie Daiken (ed.), *They Go, The Irish: A Miscellany of War-time Writing* (Nicholson & Watson, 1944), copyright holder not traced.

MONTAGUE, JOHN, 'A Bomber's Moon', 'A Welcoming Party', 'This Neutral Realm' and 'Waiting' from *Collected Poems* (Gallery Press, 1995; Wake Forest University Press, 1995); 'A Fertile Balance' and an extract from 'Wreaths' from *Drunken Sailor* (Gallery, 2004; Wake Forest University Press, 2005), all reproduced by kind permission of the author, The Gallery Press, Loughcrew, Oldcastle, County Meath, Ireland, and Wake Forest University Press; 'Speech Lesson' (unpublished) reproduced by kind permission of the author c/o The Gallery Press, Loughcrew, Oldcastle, County Meath, Ireland.

MORRISON, VAN, 'Wild Children', words & music by Van Morrison © WB Music Corp & Caledonia Soul Music. All rights administered by Warner/Chappell Music Ltd, London W6 8BS. Reproduced by permission.

MURPHY, RICHARD, 'Carlyon Bay Hotel', 'Oxford Staircase', 'Suntrap' and

'Wellington College' from *Collected Poems* (Gallery Press, 2000; Wake Forest University Press, 2001), reproduced by kind permission of the author, The Gallery Press, Loughcrew, Oldcastle, County Meath, Ireland, and Wake Forest University Press.

NÍ CHUILLEANÁIN, EILÉAN, extracts from 'Site of Ambush' from *The Second Voyage* (Gallery Press, 1986), reproduced by kind permission of the author and The Gallery Press, Loughcrew, Oldcastle, County Meath, Ireland; 'On Lacking the Killer Instinct' (unpublished), reproduced by kind permission of the author.

Ó TUAIRISC, EOGHAN, extracts from 'Aifreann na Marbh' from *Lux Aeterna* (Cois Life, 2000), reproduced by kind permission of Rita Kelly; English translation, 'The Mass of the Dead', reproduced by kind permission of Aidan Hayes and Anna Ní Dhomhnaill.

O'BRIEN, THOMAS, 'Always Battling', 'Beauty We Have Heard Your Voice', 'Connolly', 'International Brigade Dead', 'Marching Feet' and 'Terror'. Poems by Thomas O'Brien originally published in *Strong Words, Brave Deeds* edited by H. Gustav Klaus, by The O'Brien Press, 1994. © Copyright the Estate of Thomas O'Brien.

O'NEILL, MARY DEVENPORT, 'Dead in Wars and in Revolutions' from *Prometheus and Other Poems* (Cape, 1929), copyright holder not traced.

REAVEY, GEORGE, 'Hiroshima and After', 'The Rape of Europe' and 'The Sinking of SS *Jutland*' from *The Colours of Memory* (Grove Press, 1955), reproduced by kind permission of the Reavey Estate.

RODGERS, W.R., 'Escape', 'The Interned Refugee' and 'War-time' from *Poems* (Gallery Press, 1993), reproduced by kind permission of the Estate of W.R. Rodgers and The Gallery Press, Loughcrew, Oldcastle, County Meath, Ireland.

SALKELD, BLANAID, 'Casualties' from Valentine Cunningham (ed.) *The Penguin Book of Spanish Civil War Verse* (Penguin Books Ltd, 1980), copyright holder not traced.

SHANAHAN, EILEEN, 'Pastorale, 1946' from *Irish Times* (Saturday 11 January 1947); 'Free State' (unpublished), reproduced by kind permission of Mr J.S. Webster.

SIMMONS, JAMES, 'A Man's a Soldier', 'Death of a Poet in Battle-dress' and 'The Use of History' from *In the Wilderness* (Bodley Head Ltd, 1969) and 'Remembrance Day' (unpublished), all reproduced by kind permission of Janice Fitzpatrick Simmons; 'In the Desert War' and 'Uncle Jack' from *Poems 1956–1986* (Gallery Press, 1986), reproduced by kind permission of the Estate of James Simmons and The Gallery Press, Loughcrew, Oldcastle, County Meath, Ireland.

STUART, FRANCIS, 'Berlin, 1944', 'Coogan's Wood', 'In Time of War', 'Ireland', 'Morning in a Town under Bombardment', 'Out of the Swim' and 'The Trees in the Square' from *We Have Kept the Faith: Poems 1918–1992* (Raven Arts Press, 1992), © Finola Graham Stuart.

WILLIAMSON, BRUCE, 'Homage of War' from Donagh MacDonagh (ed.) *Poems from Ireland* (Irish Times, 1944), copyright holder not traced.

INDEX OF POETS

Æ 18–29

Bax, Arnold 64–8
Beckett, Samuel 152, 394–7
Boland, Eavan 370–4
Brady, George M. 234–6
Buchanan, George 128–31

Carnduff, Thomas 70–4
Clarke, Austin 95–104
Coffey, Brian 148–51
Craig, Maurice J. 241–2
Cronin, Anthony 293–300

Daiken, Leslie 218–19
Day Lewis, C. 132–40
Deane, Seamus 349–50
Devlin, Denis 191–8
Donnelly, Charles 222–5
Dunsany, Lord Edward 34–8
Durcan, Paul 375–8

Fallon, Pádraic 146–7
Fennessy, L.J. 239–40
Fiacc, Padraic 269–74

Galvin, Patrick 275–83
Gibbon, Monk 105–8
Glavin, Anthony 379–91
Gore-Booth, Eva 30–3
Greacen, Robert 254–61
Gwynn, Stephen 3–7

Hayes, Aidan 245–53 *trans.*
Heaney, Seamus 342–8
Hetherington, George 232–3
Hewitt, John 178–90
Hutchinson, Pearse 284–9

Iremonger, Valentin 237–8

Jennett, Seán 206–17

Kavanagh, Patrick 141–5
Kelleher, D.L. 69
Kennedy, Jimmy 114
Kennelly, Brendan 326–31
Kettle, Thomas 55

Kinsella, Thomas 301–8
Laughton, Freda 162
Ledwidge, Francis 79–84
Letts, Winifred M. 58–63
Lewis, C.S. 109–12
Longley, Michael 332–41

MacDonagh, Donagh 220–1
MacDonagh, Thomas 39–45
MacDonogh, Patrick 115–17
MacGabhann, Liam 199–201
MacGill, Patrick 85–9
MacGreevy, Thomas 90–4
MacMahon, Bryan 204–5
MacNeice, Louis 163–9
Mahon, Derek 351–64
McFadden, Roy 262–6
Millar, Ruddick 170
Milne, Ewart 122–7
Montague, John 309–20
Morrison, Van 392–3
Murphy, Richard 290–2

Ní Chuilleanáin, Eiléan 365–9
Ní Dhomhnaill, Anna 245–53 *trans.*

O'Byrne, Dermot. *See* Arnold Bax
Ó Tuairisc, Eoghan 243–53
O'Brien, Thomas 226–31
O'Neill, Mary Devenport 53–4
Orpen, William 46

Pearse, Pádraic H. 47–52
Plunkett, Joseph Mary 75–8

Reavey, George 171–7
Rodgers, W.R. 202–3

Salkeld, Blanaid 56–7
Shanahan, Eileen 113
Simmons, James 321–5
Stuart, Francis 118–21

Tynan, Katharine 1–2

Williamson, Bruce 267–8
Wingfield, Sheila 153–61

Yeats, W.B. 8–17

INDEX OF TITLES

A Bomber's Moon 313
A Day of Rebellion 277
A Dirge of Victory 34
A Dream of Hell 42
A Dublin Ballad – 1916 67
A Fertile Balance 314
A Kensington Notebook 352
A Man's a Soldier 325
A Soldier's Grave 82
A Soldier's Prayer 89
A Soldier's Son 372
A Song for Victory Night 264
A Song of Victory 3
A Welcoming Party 311
After a Year 40
After Court Martial 81
Aifreann na Marbh (extract) 244
Always Adam (extract) 206
Always Battling 227
An Irish Airman Foresees His Death 8
An Upper Room 69
Anahorish 1944 346
Annapolis 191
Apocalyptic 26
Apology 111
Armistice Day 1938 264
At the House of Commons 104
At the Shelbourne 359
Aubade 163
August 1939 185
Autobiographies (extract) 351

Barbara 363
Battle Ardour 25
Beauty We Have Heard Your Voice 227
Before the Charge 87
Before the Glory of Your Love 77
Belfast 254
Berlin, 1944 120
Beyond the Headlines 143
Bomb 329
Bombers 132
Bottleneck 167
Brown's Bay, Islandmagee, Spring 1917 179
Buchenwald Museum 341

Camaradas y Compañeros 183
Carlyon Bay Hotel 291
Carrickfergus 163
Casualties 56
Casualty 60
Ceasefire 340
Chivalry 22
Christmas 1915 51
Christmas Eve in Prison 30
Comrades 31
Concentration Camps 197
Connolly (MacGabhann) 200
Connolly (O'Brien) 226
Continuity 21
Convoy 166
Coogan's Wood 121
Corner Boys 204

Dardanelles 1916 147
De Civitate Hominum 90
Dead 63
Dead in Wars and in Revolutions 53
Death Camp 375
Death in Battle 112
Death of a Poet in Battle-dress 324
Death of Hektor (extract) 148
Der Bomben Poet 269
Downstream 302
Dublin to Belfast: Wartime 265
During the War 361

Easter 1916 9
Easter Week 30
Encounter 300
Encounter Nineteen Twenty 181
England's Difficulty 342
Entered in the Minutes (extract) 166
Epic 144
Epitaph for a Conscript, 1940 185
Escape 202
Explosion 217

Fjord 377
Flower of Youth 1
For Thomas Flanagan 215
For Victory 45
Francis Sheehy-Skeffington 32

Free State   113
French Nocturne   109

Ghetto   336
Gods of War   23
Graves of Gallipoli   70

Hallow-e'en, 1914   58
Have You Walked   236
He is Dead and Gone, Lady …   220
Heroes 1916   146
Heroic Heart   224
Hiroshima and After   177
Homage of War   267
Home   84

I Had a Future   144
I Oft Go Out at Night-time   86
I.M. Leslie Owen Baxter 1919–1995   261
Ici   106
In Absence   39
In Memoriam   332
In Memoriam Francis Ledwidge   343
In Memory of Charles Donnelly   339
In the Beech   345
In the Desert War   321
In the Mediterranean – Going to
   the War   80
In the Shelter   138
In Time of War   118
Inscription for a Fountain   7
International Brigade Dead   230
Ireland   119
It's a Far, Far Cry   85

Judengasse   288
Just an Old Sweet Song   221

Kilcarty to Dublin   242
Kilwaughter   129

Lament for France   258
Las Raices   233
Little Elegy   195
Living in Hiroshima   379
Lost Hopes   106
Lough Derg (extract)   142

Marching Feet   228
Martial Law in Dublin   64
Master of Ceremonies   335
Meditations in Time of Civil War
   (extract)   14
Men in War (extract)   153
Messines, 17th June, 1917   72
Minor Poet's Dilemma, 1940   185
Mnemosyne Lay in Dust (extract)   101
Morning   216
Morning in a Town under
   Bombardment   118
My Father Spoke with Swans   275
My Land   71

Neutrality   168
New Love   76
Newsreel   133
Nightfall in Galway   218
Nineteen Sixteen, or the Terrible
   Beauty   180
Nocturne   90

O'Connell Street   83
Of a Poet Patriot   44
Old Soldier   326
On a Political Prisoner   12
On Behalf of Some Irishmen Not
   Followers of Tradition   18
On Being Asked for a War Poem   9
On Film   128
On Lacking the Killer Instinct   368
On the Dead Killed in Two World
   Wars   128
One of these Nights   357
Ostfriesland   285
Out of the Swim   120
Over the Water   115
Oxford Staircase   290

Partisans   341
Pastorale, 1946   113
Pinehurst   33
Poem   223
Poem to K.D.   256
Poem Written in September   255
Poets of the Next Century   131
Politics   17
Portrush   266

Portstewart, July 1914   178
Post-war   262

Remembering Con Markievicz   139
Remembrance Day   323
Remembrance Sonnet, 1941
Reprisals   13
Rightful Rhymes (extract)   100

Saint-Lô   152
Salutation   19
Screens   61
Second Front: Double Summertime,
   July 1943   186
2 September 1939   262
Second Sight   335
See the Crocus' Golden Cup   78
Shells at Oranmore   64
Shelter   349
Sierran Vigil   126
Site of Ambush (extract)   365
Six Sentences   98
Sixteen Dead Men   11
Soldier from the Wars   237
Soldiering   105
Soldiers   271
Son of a Gun   270
Songs from an Evil Wood   35
Sonnet   232
Speech Lesson   318
Speech on Behalf of Inishfail   122
Spring 1943 (Greacen)   254
Spring, 1943 (Craig)   241
Statesmen   28
Strangers and Neighbours   186
Sunday in County Monaghan, 1935   260
Suntrap   292

Terror   231
The Aerodrome   347
The Atlantic Tunnel   169
The Bombed House   162
The British Connection   273
The Call to Arms in our Street   59
The Call to Ireland   79
The Capital of the Ruins   394
The Church, Zillebeke   46
The Claim that has the Canker on the
   Rose   75

The Closing Album (extract)   165
The Conquerors   235
The Dead   136
The Defeated   284
The Deserter   61
The Dug-out   88
The End of the Modern World
   (extract)   296
The Flowering Bars   222
The Fool   48
The Glorious Twelfth   257
The Graves of the Unknown   73
The Great Hunger (extract)   141
The Hosts   234
The Interned Refugee   203
The Irish in Gallipoli   83
The Irish Mail   65
The Jewish Bride   376
The Last Republicans   99
The Laundress   301
The Letter   215
The London Lads   87
The Mass of the Dead (extract;
   trans.)   245
The Memorial   34
The Mother   47
The Other Man's Wound   270
The Poet Captain   41
The Prisoners on the Roof   183
The Rape of Europe   176
The Rebel   49
The Roads of Kerry   199
The Sinking of the SS Jutland   171
The Six Who Were Hanged   92
The Somme   170
The Subjection of Women   95
The Tolerance of Crows   223
The Tomb of Michael Collins   193
The Trees in the Square   119
The Troubles, 1922   182
The Use of History   324
The Volunteer   180
The War Horse   371
The Wayfarer   52
The Wind of Bombers Moon   125
The YCVs and the Ulster Division   179
Thinking of Artolas   123
38 Phoenix Street   306
This Neutral Realm   309
Thomas MacDonagh   80

411

Three Songs to the One Burden
  (extract) 16
To C.M. on Her Prison Birthday 31
To Grace 77
To Mrs Joseph Plunkett 82
To my Daughter, Betty, the Gift
  of God 55
To the Fallen Irish Soldiers 38
To the Memory of James Connolly 181
To the People of Dresden 190
Tragedy 28
Trial Runs 343
Twenty-Four 239

Ulster Winter (1942) 189
Uncle Jack 322
Victory 110

Waiting 312
Wall 327

War 81
War Pilot 131
War Poem 293
War Widow 116
War-time 202
Waste 25
Watching Post 134
We Were Neutral in the War 373
We're Going to Hang Out the Washing
  on the Siegfried Line 114
Wellington College 291
When I am Dead 75
Where are the War Poets? 135
Wild Children 392
Will it be so Again? 137
Wounds 334
Wreaths (extract) 317

Yeats in Civil War 370
Ypres, September, 1917 72